My lord after my most humble recommendacions this shall be to gyue vnto yo grace

as J am most bownd my humble thankes for the gret payn and trauell that yo

grace doth take in stertdyeng by yo wysdome and gret dylygens howe to bryng

to pas honurably the gretyst welth that is possible to cum to any creatur lyuyng

and in especyall remembryng howe . . . . and bultzthy J ondur tayneng

to his hyghnes / and for you J do knowe . . . . bestwyd by my desyr b

that you shuld take this gret payn . . . . nes J do pray te

by all my ffrendes and though that J ha . . . . them the dayly

proffe of yo dede doth declare yo wordes and wrytyng toward me to be

trewe no the good my lord yo dyscressyon may consider as yet howe lytell it

is in my power to recompens you but all onely w my good wyl the whiche

J assewr you that after this matter is brought to pas you shall fynd me

as J am bownd in the meane tym to owe you my slyse and then looke

what thyng in this worelde J can in magen to do you pleasur in you

shall fynd me the gladdyst woman in the worelde to do yt and next

vnto the kynges grace of one thyng J make you full promes to be assewryd

to haue yt and that is my harty loue vnfaynydly duryng my lyf

and beyng ffully determynd w goddes grace neuer to change thys

porpos J make ansud of thys my rude and trewe mxdnyd letter

praynng other lord to send you muche increse of honor w long lyfe

wrytten w the hand of her that besechyb yo grace to acept this letter

as predydyng from one that is most bownde to be

From Mrs Anne Bullen befor hir mariady to the kinge.

yo humble and
obedient seruant

Anne Boleyn

ANNE BOLEYN

ANNE BOLEYN

FATAL ATTRACTIONS

G.W. BERNARD

YALE UNIVERSITY PRESS

NEW HAVEN AND LONDON

Published with assistance from the foundation established in memory of
Oliver Baty Cunningham of the Class of 1917, Yale College.

For information about this and other Yale University Press publications, please
contact:
U.S. Office: sales.press@yale.edu   www.yalebooks.com
Europe Office: sales@yaleup.co.uk   www.yaleup.co.uk

Set in Sabon by IDSUK (DataConnection) Ltd
Printed in Great Britain by TJ International Ltd, Padstow, Cornwall

Library of Congress Cataloging-in-Publication Data

Bernard, G.W.
   Anne Boleyn/George Bernard.
      p. cm.
   Includes bibliographical references.
   ISBN 978–0–300–16245–5 (cloth: alk. paper)
   1.   Anne Boleyn, Queen, consort of Henry VIII, King of England, 1501?–1536.
2.   Queens—England—Biography. 3.   Great Britain—History—Henry VIII,
1509–1547—Biography. 4.   Great Britain—Kings and rulers—Biography. 5.   Henry
VIII, King of England, 1491–1547—Marriage. I. Title.
   DA333.B6B45 2010
   942.05'2092—dc22
   [B]   2009039203

A catalogue record is available for this book from the British Library

10 9 8 7 6 5 4 3 2 1

CONTENTS

ILLUSTRATIONS

Endpapers: Letter from Anne Boleyn to Thomas, Cardinal Wolsey, *c*.1528 (British Library, Cotton MS, Vespasian F xiii fo. 141 © British Library Board. All Rights Reserved).

Frontispiece: Hans Holbein the Younger, *Anna Bollein Queen* (The Royal Collection © 2010 Her Majesty Queen Elizabeth II).

1. Letter from Anne Boleyn to her father, Sir Thomas Boleyn, written at La Vure (Terveuren), near Brussels, *c*.1513–14 (Corpus Christi College, Cambridge, MS 119 fo. 21 © Corpus Christi College, Cambridge).

2. *Catherine of Aragon*, artist unknown, *c*.1530 (© National Portrait Gallery, London).

3. Miniature attributed to Lucas Horenbout, thought to be Anne Boleyn, inscribed ANO XXV (© Royal Ontario Museum, Toronto).

4. The Boleyn pub, Upton Park, London (Jonathan Bailey © English Heritage (NMR)).

5. Hans Holbein the Younger, *Apollo and the Muses on Parnassus*, design for a coronation pageant (© Staatliche Museum, Berlin, Kupferstichkabinett (1662.165.81)).

6. *Thomas Wolsey*, artist unknown (© National Portrait Gallery, London).

7. Hans Holbein the Younger, sketch of a table fountain (© Offentliche Kunstsammlung, Basel, Kupferstichkabinett (26.08.04)).

8. Portrait medal, inscribed A.R. [Anna Regina] and the motto 'The Moost Happi 1534' (© The Trustees of the British Museum).

9. *Anne Boleyn, wife of Henry VIII* (inscribed), artist unknown (© National Portrait Gallery, London).

10. *Anne Boleyn, queen of England* (inscribed), artist unknown (Hever Castle, Kent © The Bridgeman Art Library).

11. Hans Holbein the Younger, *Anna Bullen Regina* (© The Trustees of the British Museum).

12. Interrogation of John Skip, Anne Boleyn's almoner, April 1536 (The National Archives, Public Record Office, SP6/1 fos 7–10).

13. The tomb effigy of Elizabeth Browne, countess of Worcester, Chepstow parish church (by permission of the vicar and churchwardens; photo © Ruth Sharville).

14. Book of Hours, Paris, *c.*1528 (© Hever Castle).

15. Hans Holbein the Younger, portrait of Henry VIII. (© Museo Thyssen-Bornemisza, Madrid).

16. Attributed to Jean and François Clouet, *Francis I, c.*1535 (Musée du Louvre, Paris. RMN © Hervé Lewandowski).

PREFACE

Most of us acquire our first historical impressions at an early age from some vivid story or image. We learn about Alfred burning the cakes, for example, about the bloodthirsty and feuding medieval nobility, about the ignorance and immorality of the monks and clergy of the later Middle Ages—and about Bluff King Hal, about Henry VIII's lustful pursuit of a dazzling succession of court ladies. Such images are powerful, leaving a lasting impact. Many of us go on to read historical novels or watch historical films and plays, and acquire what seem clear and utterly persuasive views of the past. Many have come across Anne Boleyn in novels and films and have greatly enjoyed the ways in which their writers and directors have told her story.

But a professional historian—someone who studies and teaches history at university—will want to warn you that matters are not quite so straightforward. My interest in Anne Boleyn began in much the same way as anyone else's: I was intrigued by the remarkable and dramatic events that led to Henry VIII's break with Rome, by Anne's part in them, and then by her extraordinary downfall. But as a professional historian I wanted to test what I had been told. Those powerful images of Anne that we have seen in films or read in novels may well not be the whole story. On what are they based? How can we know that they are true?

Prompted by such curiosity, I set off on a voyage of discovery shared with you here. It may well be that the destination turns out to be rather different from that which you expect. Not the least of the challenges is that there is rather less evidence surviving from the early sixteenth century than one would wish. I should emphasise that much must unavoidably remain uncertain. In Green Road, East Ham, just along from West Ham football stadium, the Boleyn ground, are the Boleyn pub, built in 1898, and the Boleyn cinema, built in 1938. They are called after Anne Boleyn because there was once (as illustrations show) a Tudor brick house with typical chimneys here. It was owned by Richard Breame, a minor servant of Henry VIII. And, so the story goes, this was one of the places which Henry visited when courting Anne. There is no surviving evidence to that effect; it is not impossible; but we lack anything like proof.

The greatest shortcoming of the surviving sources is that we are short of information about what people thought and why they did what they did. Consequently a good deal must be inferred from actions: a reasonable proceeding, but one to be undertaken carefully and openly. Historical playwrights, historical novelists and film directors are perfectly free to use their imaginations to fill in the enormous gaps in our knowledge, and if they do so to dramatic effect, that undoubtedly makes for good reading and viewing. But precisely because such representations can be powerful and make a deep impact, they risk embedding images that are at best fanciful and at worst downright false. My approach is rather to ask questions at every turn, always to show where our information comes from, whether from a letter written by Anne herself (though there are very few of those) or from a despatch by one of the foreign ambassadors in England (notably Eustace Chapuys, the imperial ambassador from 1529), or from a near-contemporary narrative history (such as those of George Cavendish, sometime servant and then biographer of Thomas Wolsey, or of the martyrologist John Foxe) and to share with you my reasoning, and indeed my speculation, albeit I hope informed speculation, on matters on which the evidence alone is tantalisingly inconclusive or frustratingly absent.

ACKNOWLEDGEMENTS

It was in the middle of a class on the politics of Henry VIII's reign that it first occurred to me that Anne Boleyn might not have been entirely innocent of the adulteries of which she was accused. And many generations of students have since discussed and argued with me about Anne Boleyn's fate: I am greatly indebted to them. My late colleague T.B. Pugh supplied me with references and first encouraged me to go further. As I did so, in writing the articles in which I first sketched my claims (for permission to draw on which I thank Oxford Journals and Cambridge University Press) and more recently in preparing this biography, I benefited from the advice and the questioning of many friends, including Cliff Davies, the late Jennifer Loach, Penry Williams, Peter Gwyn, Jenny Wormald, Steve Gunn, Greg Walker, David Katz, the late Geoff Dickens, Rhys Robinson, Henry James, Wendy Toulson, Edward Wilson, Mark Stoyle, Janet Dickinson, Anne Curry and John Painter. Both Peter Gwyn and Mark Stoyle are due special thanks for undertaking the labour of reading and commenting on successive drafts. At Yale University Press, I specially wish to thank Robert Baldock, Tom Buhler and Beth Humphries. The British Academy and the University of Southampton financed research in the Haus-, Hof- und Staatsarchiv, Vienna: I am very grateful to the staff there for their most helpful assistance. An award by the Arts and Humanities Research Council doubled the study leave given me by my own university and so enabled me to complete this study.

'These bloody days have broken my heart'
THE FALL OF ANNE BOLEYN

On 30 April 1536 Mark Smeaton, a musician at Henry VIII's court, was arrested and interrogated. Maybe he was tortured. George Constantyne, himself suspected of treason when testifying three years later, declared that 'the saying was that he was first grievously racked', but immediately added the qualification, 'which I could never know of a truth'.[1] Tortured or not, Mark confessed that he had on three occasions made love to Anne Boleyn, Henry VIII's queen. That, quite understandably, was enough to send him to the Tower. The arrests did not end there. Henry Norris, chief gentleman of Henry's privy chamber, the closest of the king's personal servants, was sent to join Smeaton in the Tower, after Henry VIII had personally interrogated him the following day. Anne Boleyn followed, after she had been interrogated by the king's council, together with her brother, George, Viscount Rochford. Several courtiers were sent there too: William Brereton and Sir Francis Weston, both gentlemen of the privy chamber, the poet Sir Thomas Wyatt, and Sir Richard Page, another courtier. Wyatt and Page were shortly set free. But Anne, her brother, Smeaton, Norris, Brereton and Weston were all indicted.

What had they done to deserve this treatment? Anne had allegedly seduced them by her conversation, gifts and kisses. For three years and more, Anne, 'despising her marriage' and 'entertaining malice against the king', had been 'following daily her frail and carnal lust'. 'By base conversations and kisses, touchings, gifts, and other infamous incitations',

Anne had led several of the king's close servants to be her 'adulterers and concubines'.

The indictment specified the charges. On 6 October 1533 and several days before and after, Anne, 'by sweet words, kisses, touches and otherwise', seduced Henry Norris to 'violate' her on 12 October 1533. They had illicit intercourse at various other times, both before and after, sometimes at his instigation, sometimes hers. On 2 November 1535, and several times before and after, Anne had incited her own brother, George, to have sex with her, 'alluring him with her tongue in his mouth and his in hers' and also by kisses, presents and jewels. George on 5 November 1535, and on several other days before and after, made love to his sister at Westminster, sometimes at his, sometimes at her, instigation, 'despising the commands of God and all human laws'. The indictments against William Brereton, Sir Francis Weston and Mark Smeaton were then set out in identical ways. On named dates, and on several days before and after, Anne had seduced them, and on specified dates between five days to a fortnight later, they had had sex, sometimes at Anne's instigation, sometimes at theirs: William Brereton in December 1533, Mark Smeaton in April 1534 and Sir Francis Weston in May 1534. In a parallel indictment the charges against these men were identical—but the dates given were somewhat different, in four cases a month later, in that of Brereton a month earlier.

In other words, having married Henry VIII in early 1533, Anne Boleyn had then allegedly had sexual relationships with Henry Norris in October or November 1533, with William Brereton in November or December 1533; with Mark Smeaton in April or May 1534; with Sir Francis Weston in May or June 1534; and with her brother in November and December 1535. Not surprisingly, the five men, 'inflamed with carnal love of the queen', became very jealous of each other, and gave her secret gifts and pledges. In turn the queen could not bear it when any of them talked to another woman, and encouraged them by giving them great gifts. On 31 October 1535 (or on 8 January 1536) the queen and the five men allegedly 'conspired the death and destruction of the king', Anne often saying that she would marry one of them as soon as the king died, and declaring that she would never love the king in her heart.[2] Such acts were regarded as treason, the greatest of crimes, for which the penalty was death. Accordingly, first the commoners Norris, Smeaton, Weston and Brereton, and then on Monday 15 May Anne and her brother, were convicted and executed.

All of this was unprecedented. Not surprisingly it has given rise to heated debate. Many contemporaries were astonished. Thomas Cranmer, archbishop of Canterbury, was 'clean amazed'.[3] And many, indeed most, modern historians believe that all this is too preposterous for words. Following the martyrologist John Foxe, who thought the charges, not least that of incest with her brother, 'so contrary to nature that no natural man will believe it',[4] they assert that Anne and her alleged lovers could not possibly have behaved like this.[5] The only plausible explanation, such historians believe, is that they were framed, and so they elaborate complex theories about why and how that was done. But maybe that is too hasty a response. Was there rather more substance to the charges for which Anne and her friends paid with their lives?

Who was Anne Boleyn?

Anne Boleyn is often presented as a 'self-made' woman, rising from lowly origins to the top before her dramatic fall. But that is nonsense. Anne was not 'a poor knight's daughter' as one Nicholas Delanoy allegedly said to a skinner of St Omer Calais.[1] Such talk was and is highly misleading. Anne was born into the English social and political elite. Her father was Thomas Boleyn, who as Anne was growing up was an increasingly prominent courtier-administrator at the court and in the government of Henry VIII.

He was not the type of courtier who springs up from obscurity thanks solely to royal favour. He came from a landed and wealthy background. His father was Sir William Boleyn, a Norfolk landowner. It had been Sir William's father, Geoffrey Boleyn, who, migrating from provincial obscurity, had been a remarkably successful merchant in London, making his fortune, serving as alderman and in 1457–58 as Lord Mayor, buying lands in the country, notably building Hever Castle in Kent. He married into the peerage: his wife was Anne, daughter and co-heiress of Thomas Hoo, Lord Hoo. It was, then, the fortune that he had built up that allowed his son, William, knighted in 1483, and as a JP clearly one of the leading men in the county, to live the life of a landed gentleman in Norfolk. Sir William followed his father's example by marrying into the nobility: his wife was Margaret, daughter and co-heiress of Thomas Butler, earl of Ormond. Their son Thomas, Anne Boleyn's father, continued what was becoming a family tradition by marrying Elizabeth

Howard, daughter of Thomas Howard, second duke of Norfolk, by his second wife. Anne Boleyn was thus born into privilege. When Henry VIII later referred to her descent of 'right noble and high parentage',[2] he was not exaggerating.

We do not know for certain when Anne Boleyn was born. Like so much of Anne's life, this has been the stuff of lively debate. The scholar and antiquarian William Camden, writing towards the end of Elizabeth's reign, said she was born in 1507, and something like that date is implied by Henry Clifford in his 'Life of Jane Dormer', duchess of Feria, when he said that at her execution Anne was not twenty-nine years of age, though it is possible that Clifford had taken his information from Camden.[3]

But the most telling evidence for Anne's age is the handwriting in a letter that she wrote to her father in French in 1513–14 from La Vure (Terveuren) near Brussels, in the Low Countries, one of the residences used by the Archduchess Margaret of Austria.[4] It is written in a neat and regular hand. It is most improbable that anyone younger than say ten or eleven could write as clearly and as firmly as this. It would have been unusual, to say the least, if Anne had been sent abroad to serve as a maid of honour in a foreign court if she were not at least twelve or thirteen. A telling parallel is to be found in a letter from Emperor Maximilian to Don Diego de Guevarre, in charge of the emperor's son Charles, in which Maximilian confirmed his earlier promise that Don Diego's niece should join the imperial household at Malines now she had reached the appropriate age: she was just over thirteen. So it is very likely that Anne was born in the early 1500s—most likely in 1501.[5]

Where was she born? Tradition suggests Hever Castle; but Matthew Parker, Queen Elizabeth's archbishop, who in Henry's reign had been close to Anne as one of her chaplains, said that she came from Norfolk, so Blickling in Norfolk, the principal residence of her father's father Sir William, is the most probable location.[6]

Anne Boleyn had a sister, Mary, and a brother, George, who will feature prominently in this account of her life. No more than for Anne do we know when they were born; or whether they were older or younger than Anne. There is, nonetheless, a good deal of circumstantial or later evidence which suggests that Mary came first. In 1597, George,

Lord Hunsdon—who had the previous year succeeded his father, Henry Carey, Lord Hunsdon, Mary Boleyn's son—explored the possibility of the revival of the earldom of Ormond in his favour. It had become extinct because his great-grandfather, Thomas Boleyn, Anne's father, had no surviving male heirs (his son George had no children). If the earldom were allowed to descend through the female line, then George, Lord Hunsdon, had a plausible claim—but only, obviously, if his grandmother Mary had been Thomas Boleyn's *elder* daughter. It is implausible that Hunsdon should have lied, not least since Queen Elizabeth, as Anne's daughter, would have known the truth very well. And the circumstances of Mary's life fit much better if she had been born in, say, 1499 or 1500 rather than some years later. Like Anne she was sent to the French court in 1514–15 but while Anne remained in France, Mary returned to serve at the English court, which would have been much more likely if she was then in her mid-teens than if she were only ten. She was married on 4 February 1520 (we know the date because a payment of 6s. 8d. by the king is recorded in his book of payments).[7] As it would have been unusual for a younger daughter to be married before an older daughter, this reinforces the case that Mary was indeed older than Anne.

George Boleyn's date of birth is also uncertain. A remark in verses by George Cavendish, Cardinal Wolsey's gentleman-usher, suggests that he served in the privy chamber before 'years thrice nine' had gone, in other words before he was twenty-seven; since we know that he was removed from the privy chamber in 1526, this implies that he was born no later than 1499 and probably earlier. But George was reappointed to the privy chamber in 1529: and if it was that date that Cavendish intended, then George could have been born in 1503 or 1504, after his sister Anne.

Of Anne's early years, as of the childhood of all in her position, we know next to nothing. In these years her father Thomas Boleyn was rising in importance and favour. In May 1512 he was sent by Henry VIII as his ambassador to the court in the Low Countries of the Archduchess Margaret of Austria. On returning to England in summer 1513 he sent Anne to serve there, where she stayed mainly at Malines. Margaret found Anne 'so bright and pleasant for her young age'[8] that she was more beholden, she said, to him for sending her than he was to her. Anne evidently studied under a tutor called Symonnet.

It was then that she wrote the letter to her father that we have already discussed. Anne assured her father that she had written the letter herself. Her handwriting is more impressive than her French. The letter is a mixture of an emphatic willingness to obey her father's wishes, together with hints, not least in the wayward orthography, that she might be falling short. She acknowledged her father's wish that she should be 'touss onnette fame'—a wholly honest, that is chaste, woman—once she came to court. She noted that her father told her that 'la Rene' (the queen) would take the trouble to talk with her: Anne assured her father that she rejoiced to think that she would be talking with such a wise and honest person. And that would make her want even more to continue to speak French well 'et oussy especy ale man'—and also especially German.[9] It is unlikely that the queen intended was Henry VIII's queen, Catherine of Aragon: it would have been Spanish, not French, that would have been the language to learn if Anne were seeking to impress her. And it is unlikely that Catherine, whose knowledge of French was poor, would have been taken by the idea of improving her French by bringing into her service and then talking with a young lady who had just come from a sojourn in a court in which French was spoken.[10] So it is implausible that Thomas Boleyn's intention in sending Anne to Margaret was that she should acquire sufficient French to be employable in Catherine's household. It is much more likely that Anne was using the words 'la Rene' slightly inaccurately to mean the Archduchess Margaret.

In Margaret's court it is very likely that Anne was much influenced by the paintings and music that Margaret commissioned. Moreover Margaret's nephew Charles, the future Emperor Charles V, and her nieces, Eleonore, Isabeau and Marie, all future queens, were in her household in these years.[11] Anne was one of eighteen ladies and maids of honour.[12] We do not know exactly what Anne did but ladies and maids in such households were both companions and servants, keeping their mistress company and running errands. That could mean playing musical instruments, singing and dancing; it might mean assisting with embroidery or the preparation of clothing. Such ladies and maids would also be involved in festivities. While Anne was resident at Archduchess Margaret's court, Henry VIII had, with his ally the Emperor Maximilian, invaded France and captured first Thérouanne and then Tournai. After each successful siege, the Archduchess Margaret had joined in the triumphs— and presumably the young Anne Boleyn attended them as well.

Anne stayed just over a year. On 14 August 1514 her father wrote to the archduchess asking for Anne to return home. He explained that Henry VIII had decided to marry his sister Mary to Louis XII, king of France, and that Mary would need attendants who could speak French. 'Which request', he wrote, 'I neither could nor knew how to refuse'.[13]

And so Anne was summoned away. Whether she actually went to France at this point is not entirely clear. A list (itself a copy of a lost original) in the Bibliothèque Nationale in Paris of those attending the wedding celebrations includes Anne's sister Mary but not Anne. A 'Madamoyselle Boleyne' was then included on another list. Did Anne go too? Lancelot de Carles, whose life of Anne we shall consider later, wrote that she did. Maybe she arrived only just in time for the marriage celebrations and coronation in November, her departure from the Low Countries possibly delayed by an archduchess by no means delighted by the Anglo-French *rapprochement* symbolised by the marriage between Louis XII and Mary Tudor.[14]

But the marriage was short-lived: Louis died on 1 January 1515. Then Mary secretly married Charles Brandon, who had been sent to negotiate her return. Mary Boleyn probably returned to England with them. But Anne did not. Astonishingly, she joined the household of Queen Claude, wife of the new young king of France, Francis I.

We do not know how or why all of this happened. This is where the historian sighs enviously, thinking of how an historical novelist might paint the scene. Later gossip, of no evidential weight, had it that Francis I, a serial womaniser, included Anne among his sexual conquests. A novelist might imagine that in the few weeks that Anne was at the French court in the autumn of 1514, she caught the eye of the young Francis; and that when he succeeded as king, he asked her to stay. But for such a romantic story there is absolutely no evidence. We can do no more than speculate, knowing only that Anne did indeed remain in France.

Most probable as an explanation is that Queen Claude, much the same age as Anne, had struck up a friendship with her during the short weeks that Mary Tudor had been Louis XII's queen, and wanted Anne to stay: Anne's biographer, Lancelot de Carles, states that Anne 'was detained by Claude'.[15] If, during her year in the archduchess's household, Anne had mastered French and become fluent in the language, that might well have endeared her to her French hosts once she was at the French court. Very likely Anne had also, as de Carles emphasised, learned to play the lute and to dance and sing so well that she would have been an asset to any court.

Whatever the reason, and however it came about, from 1514 until 1521 Anne served as a member of Queen Claude's household. Of what she did in those years we have, frustratingly, next to no detailed knowledge. We know that Queen Claude travelled to Lyons and Marseilles to welcome Francis home after his shattering victory at Marignano in autumn 1515: quite probably Anne went with her. Queen Claude was crowned in Saint-Denis in May 1516: surely Anne was present there. In June 1519 Anne's father Thomas Boleyn attended the christening of Henri, the future Henri II, Queen Claude's second child: it would have been inconceivable for Anne not to have been present too. When Henry VIII met Francis I at the Field of Cloth of Gold near Calais in June 1520, we know that Thomas Boleyn was present. Queen Claude was certainly there. Very likely Anne attended as one of her ladies.

Judging from later correspondence, Anne also made the acquaintance of Francis's sister, Marguerite of Angoulême. In September 1535 one of the French ambassadors in England would write to tell Marguerite how Anne had said that her greatest wish, next to having a son, was to see her again.[16] Discounting for diplomatic flattery, we are left in little doubt that Anne had known Marguerite well. In the instructions Henry gave Anne's brother when he was sent to Francis in 1534, he stated that there was nothing that Anne regretted more than that she had not had an interview with Marguerite. Of course, at that point Henry was anxious that Francis might snub him, and ordered Anne's brother to temper his communication with Francis 'so that he smelt not that the king was overmuch desirous of it, but all in the queen's name'—to make it seem as if it was Anne, rather than the king, who was eager for a meeting with Marguerite. But once more making allowances for the imperatives of diplomacy, Anne's wish for an interview with Marguerite would have carried far less weight if they had not already been well acquainted.[17]

Anne spent the most formative years of her adolescence at the French court. However shaky the French of her earlier letter to her father, she must surely have thoroughly mastered the language. When we come to consider Henry VIII's love letters to Anne, we shall see that most of them were written in French. Was Henry trying to impress Anne by his own command of the language?

Francis, his wife Claude, his sister Marguerite, and his mother Louise of Savoy were all committed patrons of the arts, and Anne very likely absorbed some of their tastes. Anne and her brother George would later build up a significant collection of books in French, printed in Paris, and it was surely during her years in France that she acquired that interest. Later we shall consider how far Anne might have been influenced by Marguerite of Angoulême's interest in church reform in these years.

Again we can do no more than speculate about whether Anne remained chaste or whether she enjoyed flings with courtiers: once more, that must be left to the imagination of historical novelists. As the younger daughter of an English gentleman, albeit one who was rising in royal service, Anne would probably not have been regarded as an especially good match for any eligible young French courtier; and her father would have strained to afford an appropriate dowry. At all events, no marriage proposals appear to have been made. De Carles insisted that Queen Claude offered her an example of virtuous living.[18]

At the end of 1521 Anne was recalled to England. Diplomatic reasons largely explain her return. While she had been in Queen Claude's household, Henry VIII and Francis had been at peace, and had, indeed, in the Treaty of London in 1518 and the Field of Cloth of Gold in 1520 spectacularly celebrated their entente cordiale. But in 1521 the tide turned and Henry was on a path that was to take him to war against France in 1522, intensifying in 1523. It would not have been appropriate for Anne to have remained at the French court, not least given the prominence of her father as one of Henry's leading counsellors. So she returned to England. At the end of January 1522 Francis noted her departure, along with that of the English scholars in Paris, suspecting that all of this meant that Henry intended to make war on him.[19]

Henry VIII's great minister, Cardinal Wolsey, the imperial ambassadors
reported, had told the French ambassadors that he himself was responsible for Anne's recall and that he intended, by arranging her marriage,
to pacify certain quarrels and litigation between her father and other
English noblemen, but obviously Wolsey would not have told them that
Henry was preparing an offensive alliance against France, so what he
said must be treated cautiously.[20]

Wolsey's remarks alluded to Anne's father's wish to see her well
married as she entered her twenties. Here a significant development
had been the death of Thomas Boleyn's maternal grandfather, the
Irish nobleman Thomas Butler, earl of Ormond, in 1515. Who should
succeed him as earl? He had no surviving sons, only two daughters, one
of whom, Margaret, had married Thomas Boleyn's father William. Did
that give Thomas Boleyn a plausible claim? Or was it more proper to go
back further along the Butler line and was Piers Butler a more fitting
claimant? Best of all, what about a marriage between Piers Butler's son
James and Anne Boleyn? That was what Thomas Howard, earl of Surrey,
whose sister Elizabeth had by 1500 been married to Thomas Boleyn, was
asked by the king to explore in September 1520, while serving as Lord
Deputy in Ireland.[21] Surrey indeed thought that such a marriage would
be advantageous.[22] Such a marriage alliance, strengthening the position
of Butler, who had shown himself zealous in the king's service as Surrey
noted, appeared to offer significant political advantages as it would link
Butler more closely to the English ruling elite.[23]

Nothing happened at once, but a year later, in autumn 1521, Henry
and Wolsey were prepared to entrust Butler with significant powers, if
warily. It would be as well to wait, Wolsey wrote, to see how Sir Piers
Butler acquitted himself; 'no doubt', Wolsey added, 'his son James being
in England, he do all the better in order to get him home the sooner'.
And Wolsey, once back from diplomatic negotiations in Calais, planned
to discuss with Henry how to bring about the marriage between James
and Thomas Boleyn's daughter, a good pretext for keeping him at court
in England.[24] It was soon after this letter was written that Anne was
recalled, but in the event nothing happened. Later events suggest that
Sir Thomas Boleyn had greater ambitions and aimed at securing the
earldom of Ormond for himself, rather than less directly through the

children that Anne might have if she married James Butler. In 1528–29, in a complex set of transactions, the Butlers abandoned their claim to the earldom of Ormond in exchange for the title of earl of Ossory; they kept their lands, but as long-term and low-rent paying tenants. And in autumn 1529 Sir Thomas Boleyn became earl of Ormond, though that title was overshadowed by the English titles he also received. In short, Sir Thomas aimed at, and succeeded in, gaining his ends without having to marry Anne with a substantial dowry to James Butler. How long all this remained unresolved is hard to say: when did it become clear that Anne's future did not lie with the Butlers?

In these years Anne's father was rising in prominence and his daughter was evidently a lady at court, though as always we cannot be very specific. We know she took part in a pageant at Cardinal Wolsey's residence York Place in March 1522, at Shrovetide, playing the part of Perseverance, as she is mentioned in the accounts. Beauty, Honour, Perseverance, Kindness, Constance, Bounty, Mercy and Pity kept a castle; beneath the castle were eight ladies: Danger, Disdain, Jealousy, Unkindness, Scorn, Malbouche and Strangeness. Then eight lords entered—Amorous, Nobleness, Youth, Attendance, Loyalty, Pleasure, Gentleness and Liberty—led by the king, who ran against the castle with dates and oranges while the ladies defended it with rose water and comfits. Ultimately the lords took the ladies of honour as prisoners by the hands, and danced 'very pleasantly'.[25] Whether Henry especially noticed Anne, whether anything like a relationship then began, is unknowable; but given what we do know of the force of Henry's passion in 1527 and 1528, it seems unlikely that it began as early as 1522. And that detail apart, almost all that we know of Anne's life until the king fell in love with her is derived from much later accounts, the writers of which were well aware of her later fame, indeed notoriety, and may well have interpreted her actions through the distortions of hindsight. Maybe, by her father's means, she became one of the ladies of Queen Catherine's household, as Cavendish, Wolsey's biographer, says, echoed by George Wyatt in his later notes, but we cannot be sure.[26]

At some point there was evidently talk of marrying Anne to Henry Percy, heir of the fifth earl of Northumberland. For Anne's father, that would undoubtedly have been something of a coup, settling his daughter in the family of one of the leading noblemen of early Tudor England. As a further twist, it may be that the young Percy fell in love with Anne, transforming negotiations for a typical dynastic marriage alliance into something rather different.

As ever, our sources are meagre. Much depends on the truth of what George Cavendish, Cardinal Wolsey's gentleman-usher, writing much later, tells us. Henry Percy was serving in the cardinal's household. When Wolsey went to court, Percy would 'resort for his pastime' to the queen's chamber, where he 'would fall in dalliance among the queen's maidens', among whom was Anne Boleyn. 'There grew such a secret love between them', Cavendish continued, 'that at length they were ensured together intending to marry.' When the king heard of it, he was 'much offended' because he too had been smitten by Anne. And so he got Wolsey to 'enfrynge'—to break—the pre-contract between them.

Wolsey accordingly called Percy to the gallery of his palace at Westminster and berated him for his 'peevish folly' in not consulting his father and asking the king's permission. Wolsey moreover told Percy that the king had been working on an alternative marriage for Anne. Percy wept as he explained that he was able to find a wife 'where as my fancy served me best'. Disarming objections that he would be marrying below his rank, he declared that although Anne was only a knight's daughter, she came from right noble parentage. And Percy asked for Wolsey's favour and for him to intercede with the king on his behalf. Wolsey was angry and ordered Percy in the king's name not to see Anne. Percy's father, the fifth earl, was then sent for, and duly berated his son as 'a proud, presumptuous, disdainful and a very unthrifty waster' for having 'so unadvisedly ensured thy self' to Anne at the price of the king's 'displeasure intolerable for any subject to sustain'. After 'long debating and consultation' on his agreement with Anne, a way was found for it to be 'infringed and dissolved'. And it was then agreed that Percy should marry Mary Talbot, daughter of George, fourth earl of Shrewsbury. At all this, Anne Boleyn was 'greatly offended', blaming Cardinal Wolsey and saying that if it ever lay in her power she would do him 'as much displeasure', though, as Cavendish stressed, none of this was Wolsey's fault, but rather of the king's devising. Anne was sent away to stay with her father 'where at she smoked for all this', before returning to court where she 'flourished after in great estimation and favour'.[27]

There are unfortunately many problems with this much later account. Too much is just too convenient and almost certainly coloured by hind-sight: the fifth earl of Northumberland accusing his son of being a waster when the young Percy had yet to come into the inheritance which he was to squander, while Anne Boleyn's harbouring a long-running grudge against Wolsey is hard, as we shall see, to reconcile with the letters she wrote in 1528. That, however, Percy and Anne were entangled at some time in the 1520s seems clear. Chapuys, the imperial ambas-sador, would in May 1536 report gossip that a contract had been made and consummated 'charnellement' (carnally) more than nine years earlier between Percy and Anne, which invalidated Henry's marriage to her.[28] Charles Wriothesley, the chronicler, noted that it was on the grounds of her pre-contract with Percy that Cranmer would in 1536 declare Henry's marriage to her invalid.[29] It is intriguing that when Henry sought permission from the pope to marry in 1527, he asked for permission to marry a woman even though she had 'already contracted marriage with another, provided that it had not been consummated'.[30] That might be thought to fit Anne's situation rather well.

Why, then, did Anne not marry Percy? Was it because Henry had already fallen in love with her and employed Wolsey to block her marriage, as Cavendish suggests? Or were Henry and Wolsey still keen on Anne's marrying James Butler, and annoyed that Percy's passion had pre-empted their Irish policy-making (in which case much of Cavendish's tale could stand, with diplomacy rather than royal infatua-tion as the motive)? Or was it Percy's father who thought his son's marriage to a mere knight's daughter less fitting than marriage to the daughter of an earl? In Cavendish's account, it was after breaking up the relationship between Percy and Anne that Percy was married to Mary Talbot. But that was not correct: such a marriage was already being considered as early as 1516, with the fifth earl saying that he had concluded with Mary's father, the earl of Shrewsbury. In September 1523 the marriage was evidently thought to be imminent: Thomas Howard, earl of Surrey, wrote that a marriage between Percy and the earl of Shrewsbury's daughter would reinforce the defence of the border against the Scots.[31] Why, given the negotiations in 1516, had no marriage taken place? Had Percy jibbed? It was not till 1522, after her return from France, that he could have come to know Anne Boleyn, so that cannot be a full explanation of the delay. But if Percy then fell in love with her, it might indeed have been the earlier arrangements between the Percies and the Talbots that proved to be the obstacle to any marriage between Percy and Anne Boleyn. We can do no more than speculate. But there must have been something between Percy and Anne in these years, and the breaking off of the relationship, and Percy's subsequent marriage to Mary Talbot, cannot have been very joyful for Anne.

When exactly Percy married Mary—and so definitively blocked any marriage between himself and Anne—is not known for certain, and has been the subject of some speculation, though we do know incontrovertibly that it was after March 1525 and before 28 September 1526. An indenture dated 21 March 1525 makes various provisions in the event that Henry Percy took a wife, implying that he was not yet married; while a letter to one of his father's servants dated 28 September 1526 refers to 'my young lord and mistress', implying that he now was.[32]

Historians have taken trouble over the date of Percy's marriage because they suppose it might point to the beginning of Henry's infatuation with Anne. If we believe Cavendish's tale of how Wolsey blocked Percy's relationship with Anne, then it would be reasonable to date that to a short time before Percy's enforced marriage to Mary Talbot; and if Wolsey, as Cavendish says, intervened because Henry had already fallen for Anne, we should then be able to date Henry's passion. If Percy and Mary were married no later than September 1526 but no earlier than March 1525, this could offer some clues as to when Henry fell in love with Anne—if we take Cavendish at face value. But given that Percy's father, the fifth earl, did indeed come to court in June 1523, an unusual visit that has often been seen as the moment at which the alliance between Percy and Anne was barred, this complicates Cavendish's tale still more, since there is no evidence for Henry's interest in Anne as early as that.

Anne was also pursued by Thomas Wyatt in these years. The son of Sir Henry Wyatt of Allington Castle near Maidstone, Kent, treasurer of the chamber, Thomas had married Elizabeth Brooke, daughter of Thomas, Lord Cobham, around 1520, and a son, Thomas, had been born in 1521, followed by a daughter. It looked like a typical elite marriage uniting two prominent landed families in Kent. But about 1526 Wyatt separated from his wife, accusing her of adultery. His career as a courtier was developing in these years. In 1524 he became clerk of the king's jewels, in 1526–27 he served as a diplomat, and between October 1529 and November 1530 he was high marshal of Calais.

Wyatt was also a poet: and his poems, not printed in his lifetime, offer much scope for speculation. Many are studies in unrequited love; 'short poems purporting to record isolated moments of personal emotional experience'.[33] Was he projecting himself imaginatively and expressing what a thwarted lover might be thought to feel; or do these poems tell us about Wyatt's personal emotional experiences? Unfortunately he does not identify the woman or women whom he is addressing. There is little that is definite about Anne Boleyn in Wyatt's poems. When the poet asks 'what word is that, that changeth not/though it be turned and made in vain', he evidently means 'Anna', a word that may be read from left to right and right to left.[34] 'There is written her fair neck round about/Noli me tangere [do not touch me], for Caesar's I am/And wild for to hold though I seem tame' could readily be thought to capture the hauteur of a newly elevated queen, warning off a lover or a suitor from her past.[35] 'Whoso list to hunt: I know where is an hind/But for me, helas, I may no more' clearly refers to a passion which is no longer permitted—which could be Wyatt's now impossible love for Anne.[36] There are several poignant but vague references to unrequited love: 'sometime I fled the fire that me brent'; 'alas poor man, what hap have I/that must forbear that I love best'; 'pain of all pain, the most grievous pain/is to love heartily and cannot be loved again, though some scholars question whether these words were written by Wyatt).[37]

Manifestly, once Anne had become the king's mistress, let alone his queen, it would have been suicidal folly for Wyatt to have written about Anne Boleyn more directly; the frustratingly tantalising opacity of Wyatt's verse may well reflect a shrewdly prudential self-censorship, with Wyatt consoling himself for the lost dream of a relationship with Anne by pouring out his woes in private verses. None of this offers the certainty that we might wish for, yet it seems very plausible on the evidence of his poems that Wyatt had fallen in love with Anne, though whether Anne ever reciprocated his feelings is far from clear. Wyatt, as a married man, would not have been available to her as a husband, and Anne might have hesitated to compromise her standing by engaging in an affair with him, which carried all the risks of illegitimate children. Nor can Wyatt's infatuation be dated, though it is not impossible that it happened some time in the mid-1520s. And there is certainly nothing in the poems to suggest that any relationship continued once Anne had submitted to Henry.

There are two further tales about Wyatt and Anne. Wyatt's grandson, George, told a story of how Wyatt fell in love with Anne who, however, rejected him since he had been married ten years. Annoyed, Wyatt seized a jewel hanging from her pocket and refused to return it. When later Henry boasted to Wyatt that he had won Anne's love, and proved it by showing him Anne's ring, Wyatt countered by showing him the jewel he had taken from her.[38] It seems hardly credible that a courtier should act with such flagrant provocation. Only if women were never believed would Wyatt have survived Anne's likely vehement denial of any impropriety. But that Wyatt fell in love with her does seem plausible.

The *Chronicle of King Henry VIII of England*, written in Spanish and usually known as the *Spanish Chronicle*, was evidently put together by catholics hostile to Queen Elizabeth much later than the events it describes. It tells how, before marrying Anne, Henry asked Wyatt what he thought of her. Wyatt told the king not to marry her because she was a bad woman; when years later Wyatt was arrested after Anne was accused of adultery, he reminded the king of what he had said, adding that he knew what Anne was like, since she had been willing, many years ago, to kiss him, until they had been disturbed by the sound of stamping overhead—and, presumably, if they had not been disturbed they would not have stopped at kissing. The *Spanish Chronicle* is hardly an unimpeachable or even (when details can be checked against other evidence) a factually accurate source. If there is anything in it, what it suggests is that before Henry pursued Anne she had been wooed by Wyatt and had, perhaps, briefly been prepared to accept him.[39]

There is one further suggestive detail. In February 1533 Anne was reported by Chapuys, the imperial ambassador, to have told 'someone whom she had loved well and whom the king, from jealousy, had earlier sent away from court' that she thought she was pregnant. We do not know the identity of this person: could it have been Wyatt, did Anne have other admirers, or was this all empty gossip? We cannot say.[40]

In the early and mid-1520s, then, Anne Boleyn, daughter of an influential courtier-administrator, was at court, had been talked of as a wife for James Butler, and had very likely been pursued by Henry Percy and Thomas Wyatt, but had not yet made a marriage. Once again the historian might envy the historical novelist who can present Anne as unperturbed and liberated or as desperate and unhappy. No surviving sources can help us.

'Whose pretty dukkys I trust shortly to kiss'
HENRY VIII'S INFATUATION WITH ANNE

The historian can more reasonably postulate that Anne was an attractive young woman, but answering the question, 'What did Anne look like?' is not at all straightforward. De Carles, who wrote a history of Anne Boleyn to which we shall return, emphasised Anne's seductive eyes 'which she knew well how to exploit, sometimes holding them in reserve, sometimes sending them on message, carrying the secret witness of the heart'. And certainly their power was such that 'many surrendered to her obedience'.[1] There are few other detailed contemporary descriptions. The Venetian diarist Sanuto noted that 'Madam Anne is not one of the handsomest women in the world; she is of middling stature, swarthy complexion, long neck, wide mouth, bosom not much raised'; but he too remarked on her eyes, 'black and beautiful'.[2] William Barlow, dean of Westbury, on a diplomatic mission, was pressed by the imperial councillor Loys de Helwighen to compare Anne with Elizabeth Blount, Henry's earlier mistress: he conceded that Blount was 'prettier' but insisted that Anne was 'more eloquent and graceful, more really handsome'.[3] An overtly hostile description of Anne's coronation, in many respects palpably misinformed, would claim that 'a wart disfigured her very much' and that a swelling resembling a goitre was visible.[4] And then there was the Jesuit Nicholas Sander, writing in the second half of the reign of Queen Elizabeth, who stated that Anne[5] was rather tall of stature, with black hair, and an oval face of a sallow complexion, as if troubled with jaundice. She had a projecting tooth under the lower lip, and on her right hand six fingers. There was a large wen under her chin, and therefore to hide its ugliness she wore a high dress covering her throat. . . . She was handsome to look at, with a pretty mouth, amusing in her ways, playing well on the lute and was a good dancer.

George Wyatt, the poet's grandson, defended Anne against Sander but conceded that[6]

here was found indeed upon the side of her nail, some little show of a nail, which yet was so small by the report of those that have seen her, as the workmaster seemed to leave it an occasion of greater grace to her hand, which with the tip of one of her fingers might be and was usually by her hidden without any least blemish to it. Likewise there were said to be upon certain parts of her body certain small moles incident to the clearest complexions.

None of these descriptions is in the end especially credible. Much more important is that Henry Percy and Thomas Wyatt had found her attractive—and so would Henry VIII.

What might at first seem a more constructive way of determining what Anne looked like—examining the surviving portraits of her—turns out to disturb a hornet's nest, such are the confusions and uncertainties. The difficulty is that, except for a not very revealing damaged medal, the identities of the sitters in all the portraits claimed to be of Anne have been challenged by one scholar or another. Is the woman depicted in the best known of these portraits, those in the National Portrait Gallery and at Hever Castle, really Anne Boleyn? If she is, then Anne was of a fair complexion with red lips, bold eyes, striking hair. But it would be dangerous to build too much on such uncertain ground. I have set out the problems in an appendix.

Among the young ladies at court, Anne was unusual in having spent so long abroad, first in the court of Margaret of Austria, and then much longer in France in the court of Queen Claude. Moreover the years she spent there were the years of her adolescence, formative for everyone. Not only was she fluent in French but she had no doubt absorbed much of French ways during her stay. 'No doubt'—but the historian cannot offer any direct proof for such a claim. 'No one would ever have taken her to be English by her manners, but a native-born Frenchwoman' was de Carles's comment.[7]

We should allow that her earlier stay in the Low Countries influenced her strongly as well: that, of course, was her first experience abroad, and it is where the motto she would adopt, 'Ainsi sera, groigne qui groigne' [So it will be, grumble who may], comes from. Margaret of Austria was a significant patron, as reflected in the brilliance of the arts at her court.[8] It is thus highly plausible that Anne's experiences added to her attractions—and that they help to explain the depth of Henry's infatuation. It was Anne's 'excellent gesture and behaviour' that for Cavendish kindled Henry's love for her.[9]

Henry, of course, was already married. Immediately on coming to the throne as a young man of eighteen, he had taken Catherine of Aragon as his wife. Catherine, daughter of Ferdinand of Aragon and Isabella of Castile, had previously been married, as part of Henry VII's diplomatic and dynastic alliances, to Arthur, Henry VII's first-born son. But within a few months, Arthur had died, leaving Catherine a widow. The imperatives of diplomacy impelled Henry VII to keep Catherine in England and to envisage a marriage between Catherine and his younger son Henry. Various arrangements and permissions were sought so that Henry could marry his brother's widow but while Henry VII lived, no marriage took place. On his father's death Henry VIII acted decisively and made Catherine his queen. It seems to have been a conventionally satisfactory royal marriage. Catherine was frequently pregnant, although only Mary, born in 1516, survived. As early as 1510 an ambassador remarked on Henry's interest in another woman, and by the late 1510s Henry was clearly enjoying a relationship with Elizabeth Blount, by whom he had a son, Henry Fitzroy, born in 1519.

After that Mary Boleyn, Anne's sister, was for a time Henry's mistress. 'For a time' is a deceptively precise phrase. Unfortunately we cannot date their relationship. We do know that Mary was married to the courtier William Carey on 4 February 1520. Was it before this marriage that she had had an affair with the king? It is intriguing (it is seemingly the only such payment in the three years 1519–21) that (as we have seen) Henry gave them the sum of 6s. 8d. on their wedding day.[10] Or was it in the early 1520s that she was his mistress, with the complaisant connivance of her father, ennobled in 1525 as Viscount Rochford, and her husband who was given lavish grants? Two children, Henry, in 1525, and Catherine most likely in 1526, were born to Mary in these years: were they the offspring not of William Carey but of the king?[11] John Hale, vicar of Isleworth, would depose in the early 1530s that 'Moreover, Mr Skidmore [Thomas Scudamore, one of the priests at the Brigittine nunnery of Syon] did show to me young Master Carew saying that he was our sovereign lord the king's son by our sovereign lady the queen's sister.'[12] No more than gossip, of course, but not without plausibility. That Henry did sleep with Mary is undoubted: there were many later references, and, intriguingly, when Henry sought a papal dispensation to marry again, he explicitly asked for permission to marry a woman with whose sister he had previously had sexual relations,[13] exactly the situation in which he would have found himself when seeking to marry Anne if he had earlier slept with Mary. It is a great pity that we cannot date Henry's relationship with Mary, since that would in turn allow more precise dating of Henry's infatuation with Anne, especially if we accept the arguments for seeing Henry and Catherine as Henry's offspring.

We must briefly note what seems to be a red herring. There was later gossip that Henry had also slept with Mary and Anne's mother, Sir Thomas Boleyn's wife. Thomas Jackson, chantry priest of Chepax, Yorkshire, would get into trouble in 1535 for saying not only that Henry's marriage to Anne was adulterous but also that Henry 'should first keep the mother'.[14] By 'keep' Jackson evidently meant 'keep as his mistress'. Mistress Amadas—wife of Robert Amadas, master of the king's jewel house—had allegedly declared that the king had kept both the mother and the daughter.[15] William Peto, the leader of the Observant Franciscans at Greenwich, would tell the Warwickshire gentleman and MP Sir George Throckmorton, so Sir George claimed in his later statement to the king, that 'he did show your grace that ye could never marry Queen Anne for that it was said that ye had meddled with the mother and the daughter'. Sir George later boastfully, but falsely, claimed that he too had spoken these words to Henry VIII.[16] It would also be alleged (though the wording is somewhat opaque) that John Hale had told some of the priests at Syon Abbey that the king's grace had meddled with the queen's mother.[17] All of this was later gossip by those who were strongly opposed to Anne Boleyn. That does not, of course, make it impossible, but it does seem rather implausible, and by making Henry VIII's behaviour appear grossly scandalous, it would have an obvious political purpose.

Of Henry's infatuation with Anne, there is no doubt. Alas, we lack compelling evidence of when it arose. Precise dates elude us. No foreign ambassadors, no noblemen's factotums at court wrote anything about the burgeoning of their relationship. What we do know, of course, is that this relationship turned out to be different from Henry's relationships with previous mistresses. Nor do we know precisely when Henry became convinced that his marriage to Catherine of Aragon had been invalid from the start—invalid because it broke a divine prohibition against a man's marrying his brother's widow. If he had never been validly married, then he was free to marry as for the first time. And it was Anne Boleyn whom he now resolved to marry. Henry began by seeking an annulment of his marriage in the conventional way, asking the church courts to pronounce on the matter. But when that quest failed, Henry would eventually break with Rome, repudiating all papal authority and declaring himself supreme head under Christ of the Church of England. Much then turns on our appreciation of Henry's sincerity. Had he, through deep study of the Bible, and through shrewd assessment of the political risks that would confront his realm in the future should he die without leaving a male heir, come to the view that his marriage had been so wrong that he had been punished by God, who had denied him any surviving sons by Catherine? Or had he simply fallen in love with Anne Boleyn, and was all that reasoning from the Bible no more than a rationalisation of his passion? When Henry's efforts to secure an annulment of his marriage ran into difficulties, whose idea was it to resolve the problem by breaking with Rome and acting independently? What was Anne's role: did she refuse to become Henry's mistress and insist on becoming his queen?

Several love letters, most in French, a few in English, sent by Henry to Anne survive—they are now in the Vatican Library, itself an inexplicable fact—but none is dated, and some are most plausibly assigned to a rather later period, the time of the sweating sickness of summer 1528, when Henry and Anne were apart.[18] Carefully read, these love letters reveal much, and allow us to trace the evolution of their relationship. That so many were written by the king, who disliked writing, is eloquent testimony to the depth of his passion. He calls Anne his mistress, his darling, his sweetheart; he longs to hold her in his arms and kiss her breasts.

One of the letters must come from an early stage in their relationship, since its contents make it plain that Anne had not yet committed herself to Henry fully. Henry acknowledged receiving letters from Anne, but had been brooding over their contents, 'in great pain', not knowing how to take them: whether to his disdavantage, as some parts suggested, or in his favour, as he understood other parts. He begged Anne to let him know explicitly 'your whole intention touching the love between us'. Necessity compelled him to pursue an answer. For more than a year, he said, he had been 'struck by the dart of love', but unsure whether he should fail—or whether he would find a place in her heart and her affection. That uncertainty, he added, had recently prevented him from naming her 'his mistress', for if she loved him only with ordinary love, that title would not be appropriate for her, because it denoted 'a singularity', that is to say a unique position, 'far removed from the norm'. But if it pleased Anne 'to do the office of a true, loyal mistress and friend, and give yourself body and heart to me', Henry, her very loyal 'serviteur'—literally translated as 'servant' although the sense is more that of 'suitor'—promised her that he would then not only give her the name of mistress, but take her as his sole mistress, banishing all others from his thoughts and affection, and 'serve you only'. Henry implored her for a full answer. And if she did not want to reply in writing, she should tell him where he 'could have by it by mouth' and he would gladly go there. For fear of annoying her, he wrote no more.[19]

From this remarkable letter we can safely infer that Henry's passion had already lasted over a year. Anne had evidently not yielded to him as he wished. Clearly there had been some sort of flirtation between them but Anne had not committed herself to the exclusive relationship that he wanted. Henry now offered to make her what he called 'his mistress' in name, and to be totally loyal to her: if she committed herself wholly, he would do the same. It is vital to note that what was in question was the title of royal mistress: there was no question here of Henry offering to marry Anne and make her his queen.[20] Henry seems to be alluding to a courtly world in which a king would conventionally 'serve' several ladies—emphasising the force of his desire for Anne by offering by contrast to make her his sole mistress.

Should these sentences be read as showing that 'the king was resolved upon a divorce at all hazards: his letter to Anne Boleyn admits of no other meaning'?[21] That is not compelling. After all, this would not be the first occasion on which Henry had been unfaithful to Catherine of Aragon. Given the double standard by which married men, and especially married kings who were even less likely to be publicly criticised, were in practice allowed to take lovers with impunity while women were not, that Henry should have made effusive promises to Anne did not definitively imply that he was on the point of seeking to divorce Catherine. Henry offered to cast aside other mistresses; he did not say that he would make Anne his queen. Nor does this letter in any way suggest that Anne had been laying down any such condition as the price of her submission to Henry.

If Henry had been pursuing Anne for above a year, that would, if we could date this letter, enable us to date the beginning of his infatuation, but, alas, nothing in this letter offers a secure point of reference. We know that Henry first publicly explored the possibility of an annulment in May 1527. That was when Thomas Wolsey, Henry's leading minister for over a decade, but more relevantly here, cardinal and papal legate, formally opened an inquiry into the legitimacy of Henry's marriage to Catherine.[22] In August Henry drafted a dispensation he asked the pope to grant that would have enabled him to marry someone to whom he was already linked by reason of a relationship with her sister—presumably alluding to his affair with Mary Boleyn, Anne's sister.[23] So, on the most cautious and sceptical reading, the very latest that Henry could have been committed to Anne—and she to him—was August 1527. This love letter must therefore date from some time before then, which implies that Henry first fell for Anne no later than early 1526. Could we go earlier? An imaginative reading of the chronicler Edward Hall's description of the jousts in late 1524 suggests that Henry then played the part of a tortured lover. But the wording is somewhat convoluted, and while such a reading is plausible, it is not compelling, and, above all, offers no independent evidence for the beginning of Henry's infatuation.[24]

There is another letter that from its contents also appears to date from the period in which Anne had yet to commit herself. Henry thanked her very cordially 'that you are still pleased to have some memory of me'. In an obscurely worded sentence, he willingly acceded to her wishes even though it was not the part of a gentleman 'to take his lady instead of a servant', if that meant that he would find her 'less ungrateful' ('mains ingrate') 'in the place she chose than in that given by him'. What was she asking for and what was Henry offering? Bafflingly, he ended his letter with a series of letters—B.N.A.I.de.A.O.Na.V.e.r— which no one has yet convincingly decoded.[25]

In a longer letter Henry wrote 'to my mistress'—wording which hints at a deeper relationship—that it seemed to him rather a long time since he had heard about her good health and about herself. His 'grande affec- tion' for her prompted him to send to her in order to be better informed about her health and her wishes. He had heard that the mood in which he had left her had totally changed and that she did not want to come to court, either with her mother or otherwise. If that news was true, Henry would wonder at it, given that he was sure he had never committed any offence against her. And it struck him as a very small return for the 'great love' he bore her to keep him away from the word and the person of the woman in the world whom he most esteemed. If Anne loved him with as much affection as he hoped she did, he was sure that their separ- ation would be 'somewhat annoying' for her, though that did not affect the mistress as much as it did the suitor. 'Consider well, my mistress,' Henry urged, 'that your absence greatly grieved me, hoping that it was not your will that this was so. But if I heard for sure that you willingly desired it, then I could do no more than lament my ill fortune in abating little by little my great folly.'[26]

Clearly there had been some sort of relationship before their parting. Henry signed off as Anne's 'serviteur' and addressed her as 'mon mestres'. But since then Anne had evidently not been in touch; indeed, Henry feared that she was no longer intending to come to court. He esteemed her more than any woman in the world, he insisted. If she did not want to commit herself to him, if her absence was deliberate, Henry would reluctantly have to accept such ill fortune and allow his passion to subside. But he still feared that, even though she had obviously gone some way, Anne was now rejecting his advances altogether; he was resigned to giving up, but manifestly that was the last thing he wanted to do. In so far as this letter throws any light on what was in Anne's mind, it lies in Henry's insistence that he had committed no offence against her; meaning, presumably, that he had not been sleeping with other women. Anne sought an exclusive relationship with Henry, but her demand for exclusivity was not directed at Catherine of Aragon. That would have been implausible, if only because for some years Henry's heart had not been devoted to Catherine, if it had ever been. Her demand was directed at Henry, intended to make him decide between her and other ladies of the court.

To surmise that this letter shows that what Anne wanted was for Henry to divorce Catherine and make Anne his queen is again to run way ahead of what is to be found in it. And it would have been a very risky strategy for Anne. After all, for Henry to divorce his wife would not be an easy matter; and since Henry's wife was not one of his native-born subjects but the aunt of the Holy Roman Emperor Charles V, any divorce would have substantial dynastic and diplomatic consequences. If Anne had indeed put such demands to Henry she would certainly have been acting in an unusual way. So unconventional, however, would her demands have been that she could not have entertained realistic hopes of success. There is in fact no compelling evidence that she did make any such demands, though it remains a theoretical possibility. But we should be wary of later sources on this point. When the scholar and divine Reginald Pole, who had gone abroad to study rather than become implicated in the king's divorce, attacked Henry in print hammer and tongs in 1536, he berated him for having done so many terrible things just for love of a woman. And Pole claimed that it was Anne who sent to Henry her chaplains, grave theologians, to tell him that it was not only lawful for Henry to put Catherine away but that he was in mortal sin by keeping her, in defiance of God's law, as his wife.[27] But we must be aware of Pole's polemical tactics here. In *De unitate* he was calling on Henry to repent, to return to

the fold of the church. By invoking Anne Boleyn as the *femme fatale* who
had seduced him and even given him the theological justification for the
divorce, Pole was offering Henry a way out, an excuse for what he had
done, should he now repent and agree to end his schism, as Pole vehe-
mently urged.

Something less than complete submission to Henry is also implicit in
another letter in which Henry addressed Anne as 'ma mestres'. Although
it had not pleased her to remember the promise she made when he was
last with her, namely to send him good news and to reply to his last letter,
nonetheless it seemed to him that it was part of a true servant (suitor) to
send to know the well-being of his mistress; he pressed her to let him
know her 'prosperity' which he prayed God would last as long as his own.
In order to make her think even more often of him, he sent her a buck he
had killed by his own hand late the previous night, hoping that when she
ate it, it would remind her of the hunter. This letter was, he concluded,
'written by the hand of her servant who very often wished that she was
in the place of her brother', presumably with the king at court.[28] Securely
dating this letter is extremely difficult: it may belong rather later in the
sequence, though it does make sense in the context of a developing but
by no means firmly based relationship.

At some point, Anne yielded; that is to say, Anne agreed to a full and
continuing relationship with Henry, though just what that meant in
detail we will consider later. One of the letters could well be from the
moment that Anne did so. Henry thanked her very cordially for 'so beautiful a present' that nothing could be more beautiful: a splendid diamond
with a ship in which a woman, on her own, was tossed about. But he
thanked Anne principally for her 'too humble submission'. It would have
been difficult for him to have deserved this had her great humanity and
favour not come to his assistance. He had sought, was seeking, and
would continue to seek her favour by every kindness that he could. In that
favour 'my hope has put its unchanging purpose: either here or nowhere',
he went on in another convoluted sentence. Anne had evidently written
Henry a letter including, as he put it, expressions of her affection in beautiful words 'so cordially expressed' that they bound him, he insisted, to
honour, love and serve her for ever. In a still more convoluted and
ungrammatical sentence, he begged her to go on showing him such

expressions of affection, and assured her that for his part he would do more than simply reciprocate 'if loyalty of heart and the desire to please you can advance it'. He prayed her that if he had in any way offended her up till then, she should give him the same absolution that she had asked from him. He assured her, 'henceforth my heart will be devoted to you only, greatly wanting that my body also could be', as God could arrange it if it pleased him. Once a day he begged God to do so, hoping that at length his prayer would be heard. He wished that the time would be short—thinking it was long—until they saw each other again. His letter was written 'by the hand of the secretary who in heart, body and intention is your loyal and most assured servant'. And between the two words of his usual subscription 'Henry Rex' he added a somewhat feebly drawn heart containing the initials AB, and on either side the words 'aultre' and 'ne cherse': Henry was not looking for another.[29]

By the time this letter was written, indeed perhaps when it was being written, Anne had accepted Henry's overtures. No longer did she stay away from court, no longer did Henry write about abating his great folly. On what terms had Anne agreed to so intimate a relationship as later letters reveal? Anne had made cordial demonstrations of affection; Henry had promised that henceforth his heart would be devoted to her only. Anne had submitted affectionately, asking to be forgiven any offences; Henry devoted himself entirely to her. And it was that exclusive devotion to her that, as we saw earlier, was what Henry evidently believed Anne had been seeking before she would commit herself to him. Nothing here shows that Anne had demanded that Henry seek a divorce from Catherine of Aragon as the price of her submission. What Anne more plausibly feared was the fate of royal mistresses, to be used and discarded at the king's pleasure. The experience of her sister Mary may have influenced her strongly here. What she accordingly sought was some reassurance—a binding commitment from Henry that his heart would be devoted to her only. Of course, no argument from the silence of the sources can be completely convincing. But if Anne had been insisting on becoming Henry's queen, then his letters might have been expected to refer directly and explicitly to that: what he offered and promised Anne would have in some measure reflected and responded to her demands. If Anne had demanded that, then for Henry to promise to make Anne his only mistress and to devote his heart only to her—which we have seen that he did—would have fallen so far short of what Anne was supposedly demanding that it is hard to see why he would have made such promises to her or why Anne would have found them sufficient to accept them. What seems more reasonable, and what the wording of the letter amply supports, is that Anne was demanding total commitment from Henry.

It may just be that what overcame Anne's reservations and won her compliance was an unsolicited and unexpected promise by Henry to make her his queen. None of the letters offer any specific support for such a suggestion, but we do of course know that by August 1527 at the very latest Henry was set on just that, as exemplified by the 'torrent of gifts' he gave her that month.[30] But there is nothing to show that the plan to make Anne his queen had come from Anne, rather than, as is much more likely, from Henry's own ruminations on the circumstances in which he found himself. And he must have told Anne what he was intending to do, namely divorce Catherine and marry her. It is thinkable that he had offered Anne such a deal to overcome her hesitations; it is just as likely, and indeed more likely, that it occurred to Henry after Anne had yielded and once their relationship had been consolidated.

Interesting here are Henry's assurance that from then on his heart would be devoted to her alone and his fervent wish that his body could also be. Is that best read as Anne continuing to refuse a full commitment to Henry? Although she had now accepted Henry's love, 'as for her body, he would have to wait. Only when—if—they were married would she give him that.'[31] But there is a more plausible way of interpreting Henry's words. Henry's reference to God—'God could do it if it pleased him. He begged God once a day to do it, hoping that at length his prayer would be heard'—should be read not as an appeal by Henry to God to soften Anne's heart, but as prayers to God that he should see to the annulment of Henry's marriage to Catherine. It is hard to think of what Henry could have had in mind other than that annulment, swiftly followed by marriage to Anne. Then, as he put it, his body could be devoted to Anne only, as his heart already was. Thus when Henry wished that his body could be devoted to Anne, he was not berating Anne for holding him back, for refusing to sleep with him until he had made her his queen: it was Henry who refrained, and what he regretted was not reluctance or resistance on the part of Anne but the complexities and delays imposed by the laws and procedures of the church.

The early love letters offer no support for the conventional view that Anne refused Henry's advances until he had actually made her his lawful wife and queen. What is abundantly clear from the succeeding letters is that any notion that it was Anne who held Henry's advances back for six years is nonsense. Indeed it may well be that once Anne had responded favourably to his advances, Henry and Anne slept together for a time. Why else should Henry in the draft dispensation he sent the pope in autumn 1527 have asked for permission to marry someone with whom he had already had intercourse?[32] It was manifestly Henry, once he set off on his campaign for a divorce, not Anne, who then deliberately refrained from full sexual relations.

Why should Henry have refrained? Because if it became obvious that his reason for seeking annulment of his marriage was his passion for Anne, not scruples of conscience over the validity of his marriage to Catherine, then his moral case for that annulment would be undermined. The risks were most vividly expressed by the French ambassador Jean du Bellay in June 1529. 'I very much fear that for some time past this king has come very near Mme Anne.' It would not be surprising, he said, if the king and his advisers wanted to hasten the resolution of the matter 'because if the belly grows, all will be spoilt'.[33] If Anne were to become pregnant, everything would be ruined. So Henry had every rational reason to refrain, however hard that might be. And Henry was also determined that any child that might come from his relationship with Anne would indisputably be legitimate, not the controversial offspring from a relationship not yet validated. Hall was surely right when he wrote in his chronicle of these years that 'there was a gentle woman in the court, called Anne Boleyn, daughter to Thomas Boleyn, viscount Rochford, whom the king much favoured in all honesty, and surely none otherwise'—'honesty' being a synonym for chastity.[34]

The degree of intimacy revealed in these letters casts further doubt on Anne's ability to hold Henry back. If they spent evenings in each other's arms and if Henry was used to kissing Anne's pretty breasts, it is hard to think that she could have held him back if he had been determined to go further.[35] Anne would have been no match physically for a king who could all but murder his fool (in 1535, for calling Catherine queen—when in the king's eyes she was queen no longer—and Anne 'ribald').[36]

Many letters are hard to reconcile with the claim that Anne was holding Henry back until she became his wife. The bearer of one of the letters and his fellow, Henry informed 'darling' Anne, were being sent with 'as many things to compass our matter and to bring it to pass as our wits could imagine or devise'. Once brought to pass, as he trusted by their diligence it would be shortly, 'you and I shall have our desired end, which should be more to my heart's ease and more quietness to my mind than any other thing in this world'. With God's grace it would be done shortly—but not as soon as he wished. Yet he assured Anne that 'there shall be no time lost that may be won'. 'Further cannot be done,' he continued, quoting the Latin proverb *Ultra posse non est esse* ('further it is impossible to be'). Henry urged Anne not to detain the bearer of the letter too long: 'the sooner we shall have word from him the sooner shall our matter come to pass'. Henry's subscription—'written with the hand of him which desireth as much to be yours as you do to have him'—once again hints that it was Henry who was holding back: why else would he assure her that he wanted her to be his as much as she wanted him to be hers? If Anne was refusing his advances, such a remark would make no sense, indeed it would be counter-productive. It suggests, rather, that it was Anne who was urging Henry on to make love to her but that it was Henry who was holding back until all had been settled.[37]

On another occasion Henry wrote to inform Anne 'what joy it is to me to understand of your conformableness to reason and of the suppressing of your inutile and vain thoughts and fantasies with the bridle of reason.' All the good in the world could not have given him greater satisfaction. Continue 'my sweetheart' the same, he urged, 'for thereby shall come, both to you and me the greatest quietness that may be in this world'. It is hard to read this except as urging patience—'conformableness to reason'—on Anne until the church found in his favour. Once more, this is not Anne holding Henry back, but rather Henry determined that his marriage to Anne should be fully legal and his offspring legitimate.[38]

Above all it reinforces the impression that it was Henry who displayed self-restraint. That is in no way to minimise the depth of Henry's passion, vividly revealed in many of the letters. In one, Henry informed Anne—'mine own sweetheart'—of his 'great loneliness' since her departure. He thought the time longer since her departing than he used to find a whole fortnight. 'I think your kindness and my fervence of love cause it. For otherwise I would not have thought it possible that for so little a while it should have grieved me.' But now that he was coming to her, his pains had been half released. It was then that he described himself as 'wishing myself specially an evening in my sweetheart's arms whose pretty dukkys [breasts] I trust shortly to kiss', in a letter 'written with the hand of him that was, is and shall be yours'.[39]

In another letter Henry wrote that he was greatly cheered that what had taken so long was now approaching. All the same, 'the full accomplishment' would not happen until 'the two people assembled'—which assembly he wanted more than any other worldly thing. 'For what joy can be greater in this world than to have the company of she who is my dearest friend, knowing that she feels the same, a thought that gives me great pleasure.' Her absence caused him more heartbreak than spoken words or writing could express. When he saw her he would tell her about the rest of his sufferings in her absence. He wished himself privately with her, signing himself as 'he who is and for ever will be your loyal and most assured servant'. Once again he added her initials in a heart between the words Henry and Rex, and added the words 'aultre' (another) and 'ne cherse' (I am not seeking) on either side.[40] When he excused himself in another letter for not writing more to 'mine own darling' for lack of time, he added 'but that I would you were in mine arms or I in yours for I think it long since I kissed you'. 'By the hand of him which I trust shortly shall be yours.'[41]

A sequence of letters most plausibly dating from the spring and summer of 1528 during an outbreak of sweating sickness when Henry and Anne were apart vividly illustrates the king's love for Anne. It was on 18 June that du Bellay reported that one of the ladies of the chamber of Madame de Boulan was found infected with the sweat: Henry in great haste dislodged and went twelve miles hence, Anne was sent to her brother in Kent.[42] On 23 June Thomas Hennage reported how that morning he had heard that both Anne and her father had had the sweat—but were out of danger.[43] She was still in Kent on 30 June,[44] was reported to have returned to court by 20 August,[45] but was with her mother in Kent in early October.[46]

We might think that Henry should have joined Anne, come what may; but the sweating sickness was too lethal for that. Several courtiers had been victims: and both Sir William Compton, who for nearly twenty years had been Henry's groom of the stool, and William Carey, who was married to Anne's sister Mary, had died. Many of the king's household, du Bellay noted, had succumbed within three or four hours.[47] If one of Anne's ladies had been affected, then there was a high probability that Anne would be too, as indeed she was; it would have been thought irresponsible for Henry, as king, to have joined Anne and risked exposing himself to infection. During their separation, Henry wrote several letters: they eloquently testify to his passion.

'Ma mastres et amye' (my mistress and friend), he began one letter. He and his heart put themselves in Anne's hands; he begged her that absence would not diminish her affection. Her absence caused him more pain than he could ever have thought possible, reminding him of a point of astronomy (not an accurate one): 'the longer the days, the further off the sun is—yet the sun is then hotter'. So it was with his love, which 'retained its fervour' despite their separation, at least on his side. Henry hoped that was true of her as well. The 'pain' of absence was already too great: any longer would be intolerable without his firm hope of Anne's indissoluble affection for him. And to remind her of it now and again, and since he could not be with her, he sent the closest thing possible, his picture set in bracelets—a miniature portrait encased in jewels—together with a 'device' or motto, wishing he could be there in their place. He signed himself 'vostre loyall serviteur et amy'.[48]

Henry was much troubled by fears over Anne's health, and only knowing the truth would give him peace of mind. But since she had so far not been unwell, he hoped and was reassured that it would be with her as it was with him. When he was at Waltham, two ushers, two *valets de chambre*, Anne's brother and master treasurer (Sir William Fitzwilliam) had fallen sick but were at the time of writing again quite well. And since he had come to Hunsdon, not a single person had been ill, God be praised.

To encourage Anne further, Henry noted that few or no women had been ill; and none at court, and few outside, had died of it. So Henry urged Anne not to be afraid, nor should she be distressed by Henry's absence, 'for he who struggles against fortune all too often ends up further away'. She should therefore take comfort and be brave and keep away from the evil (i.e. the disease) as best she could. He wished her in his arms to relieve her a little of her unreasonable thoughts. Henry signed himself HR with the word 'immuable' (unchanging) split 'im' and 'muable' by those initials.[49]

In a letter dated by the editors of *Letters and Papers of Henry VIII* to 16 June 1528, Henry told Anne that he had suddenly received the most unpleasant news possible. He had heard of the illness of 'my mistress whom I value more than all the world' and whose health he wanted as much as his own. He would gladly bear half if that would cure her. He feared that he would be even longer pressed by his enemy Absence who until now had done him all the annoyance possible and who as far as he could judge was determined to do worse. Henry prayed God that he would rid him of so importunate a rebel. Henry's most trusted physician was away at a time when he might have done him the greatest pleasure, for he hoped through him and by his means to obtain one of his greatest joys in this world: to have his mistress cured. In default, Henry sent her his second doctor, praying God that he would soon make her well. Henry urged Anne to follow his advice about her illness, and hoped to see her again soon, 'which would be a greater tonic for me than all the precious stones in the world'. Henry signed himself Anne's loyal and most assured servant, and again set her initials AB in a heart between his own initials HR.[50]

Regret at their separation, concern over her health and news of who was afflicted are found in several more letters. 'Good sweetheart', Henry wrote in one, asking to know of Anne's good health and prosperity. He prayed God that it were his pleasure to send them together shortly. 'For I promise you I long for it', he assured 'my darling'. He sent her some meat 'representing his name, which is hart flesh for Henry'. 'I would we were together an evening,' he lamented.[51] In another letter Henry informed Anne—'my own darling'—that several courtiers—Walter Walsh, Master Brown, John Carr, Urion Brereton and John Coke, the apothecary—had fallen ill of the sweat in the king's house but had all recovered, thank God. As touching Anne's abode at Hever, 'do therin as best should like you, for you know best what air doth best with you'. But Henry hoped that it would not come to that. He longed to hear tidings from her as he supposed she did from him.[52] What joy could be greater in this world, Henry lamented in another letter, than 'to have the company of she who is my dearest friend, knowing that she feels the same, a thought that gives me great pleasure'? Her absence sickened him more than spoken words or writing could express. He begged her, his mistress, to tell her father from him that he asked him to come to court two days earlier than planned, failing which he would not 'serve the lovers' turn'. When Henry saw her he would tell her about the rest of his sufferings in her absence. He wished himself privately with her, signing himself as 'he who is and for ever will be your loyal and most assured servant'. Once again he added her initials in a heart between Henry and Rex and added the words 'aultre' and 'ne cherse' on either side.[53] The message was unmistakable.

'The King's Great Matter'
HENRY'S DIVORCE AND ANNE

What made Henry's passion unusual was that instead of simply luring Anne into his bed, Henry wanted to make her his wife and queen. As we have seen, we do not know for certain exactly how and when Henry came to his conviction that his marriage to Catherine had been null and void from the start. In May 1527 Cardinal Wolsey—presumably prompted by the king—had held a formal inquiry into the validity of Henry's marriage to Catherine; in August 1527 Henry sent his secretary William Knight to the pope in the vain hope of quickly obtaining permission to marry as for the first time; in the following December and January Knight persuaded the pope to approve a draft bull prepared by the king, conditionally allowing Henry to marry if his first marriage were annulled.[1]

Delays complicated matters. At first Henry kept his infatuation secret, but Knight's mission and the terms of the draft bull made the king's keenness to remarry all too clear. Before long ambassadors were reporting gossip about it, and as early as February 1528 Wolsey was forced to correct the misapprehension under which the pope had been labouring, namely that the king had set on foot this cause not from fear of his succession but out of a vain affection or undue love for a gentlewoman 'of not so excellent qualities as she is here esteemed'. After asserting that 'the king's desire was grounded upon justice, and not from any grudge or displeasure to the queen', and that 'as this matrimony is contrary to God's law, the king's conscience is grievously offended', Wolsey emphasised 'the approved, excellent virtuous qualities of the said gentlewoman, the purity of her life, her constant chastity, her maidenly and womanly pudicity, her soberness, chasteness, meekness, humility, wisdom, descent of right noble and high thorough regal blood, education in all good and laudable qualities and manners, apparent aptness to procreation of children, with her other infinite good qualities, more to be regarded and esteemed than the other progeny'.[2] That wording would be taken up again in diplomatic correspondence in 1534.[3]

It has already been suggested that it was Henry who held back from full sexual relations with Anne, not Anne who held Henry back. What is also abundantly clear is that Anne did not, as is so often thought, play a leading role in Henry's campaign for his divorce: if we concentrate on the contemporary sources that reveal Henry's campaign for his divorce in these years, a rather different impression of Anne's role in all this emerges. It is Henry, not Anne, who is in command. Several of his love letters refer directly or indirectly to his efforts, offering his latest assessment of their likely outcome. In one letter Henry wrote that he was 'right well comforted' inasmuch as his 'book makes substantially for my matter'. He had spent four hours on it that day, and for that reason and because of 'some pain in my head' he wrote a shorter letter to her. The book that Henry was compiling comprised biblical and patristic examples that justified his stand. It is worth noting that he made no attempt to involve Anne in the collection and elaboration of these materials. Anne's was the conventional role of the woman who waited, and received less attention and a shorter letter than usual, while her husband-to-be pressed on with the hard work that would make their marriage possible.[4] Most probably just a little later, Henry informed Anne, his 'darling', that though he had 'scant leisure', he remembered his promises to inform her 'in what case our affairs stood'. He had secured her a lodging by Wolsey's means. As far as their other affairs went, 'there can be no more done nor more diligence used, nor all manner of dangers better both foreseen and provided for, so that I trust it shall be hereafter to both our comforts'. There were details too long to write and not fit to be trusted to a messenger. Here again Henry is offering Anne genuine but general words of encouragement while avoiding going into any detail.[5]

That Henry was the dominant figure in the campaign for a divorce emerges clearly in the account that Edward Foxe wrote to Stephen Gardiner in Rome on 11 May 1528. The two men had been in Rome on the king's business; Foxe had now returned to England and was reporting his reception by Henry to Gardiner who remained in Rome. Foxe described how, on his arrival, Henry commanded him to go 'unto mistress Anne's chamber': Anne at that time lay in the gallery in the tiltyard as Princess Mary and others of the queen's maidens were ill with smallpox. To Anne, Foxe declared Gardiner's singular fidelity, diligence and dexterity in hastening the coming of the legate—the despatch of Cardinal Campeggio who was expected to come to pronounce the king's marriage to Catherine of Aragon invalid—'which she most thankfully received and seemed to take the same marvellously to heart rejoice and comfort, often times in communication calling *me* Master Stevens with promise of large recompence for your good acquittal in the premises'. Then the king came into the chamber and Anne departed. It is revealing, if understandable, that Anne should have confused Foxe with Gardiner, calling Edward Foxe 'Master Stevens': she would not have done so if she had been taking part in the consultations and discussions that had preceded the despatch of the two men to Rome. And it was after Anne left that the king asked Foxe to present the letters that he brought from the pope and from Bishop Staffileo, dean of the Rota, the principal court of appeal at Rome, as well as from Gardiner. At this point the news was good: it looked as if the pope would indeed be sending Cardinal Campeggio with the authority in effect to make a final and binding decision on the king's marriage. As Foxe reported to Gardiner: 'all which things his highness seemed to take marvellously thankfully and made marvellous demonstrations of joy and gladness calling in mistress Anne and causing me to repeat the same thing again before her'.[6] Once again, Henry was putting Anne in the picture; but it is very much Henry who takes the initiative, and Anne who is the subordinate recipient of what seemed like good tidings.

Henry continued to share with Anne his assessment of how things would develop. On 23 June, when Anne and her father were still stricken by sweating sickness, Henry told Brian Tuke, treasurer of the chamber, that he would send copies of letters from John Clerk, bishop of Bath and Wells, and from Francis I to the pope and to his ambassador in Rome, to mistress Anne for her consolation.[7] Later, in response to Anne's 'reasonable request', Henry sent her news that we can date to September 1528. Cardinal Campeggio—'the legate we most desire'—had reached Paris; he was soon expected in Calais, and then Henry trusted 'within a while after to enjoy that which I have so long longed for to God's pleasure and our both comfort'.[8] Once Campeggio had arrived, Henry excused his delay in seeing Anne (his sickness, Henry wrote, was 'unfeigned'). And he trusted verily that when God sent him health he would 'with diligence recompense his demowre [the cost of entertaining him]'. Henry was confident, despite the rumours, that Campeggio was not 'imperial' in this matter, in other words that he would side not with Catherine and her uncle the Emperor Charles V but with Henry and Anne.[9]

Anne, then, was not playing a leading and detailed role in the campaign for the divorce. Was she in these years, as so many have claimed, intriguing against Cardinal Wolsey, and did she ultimately bring him down? Wolsey had since the early 1510s been Henry's leading minister, Lord Chancellor since 1515, archbishop of York, cardinal and papal legate. In autumn 1529 he fell from power, resigning as Lord Chancellor. His fall, as we shall see, was indeed connected to Henry's desire for a divorce. But that Anne was opposed to Wolsey, or that she was leading a group of rivals anxious to bring him down, is much less plausible. Why should Anne have wanted to destroy Wolsey? If he had earlier blocked her marriage to Henry Percy, as Cavendish told, then Anne might well have had grounds for anger against Wolsey; but that story is, as we have seen, very speculative. But suppose it was true, if Anne had now fallen in love with Henry, or at least found Henry's approaches to her acceptable, she might by then have felt less annoyed with Wolsey for intervening to stop her marriage with Percy, but rather welcomed the slings and arrows of fortune that had made her the king's sweetheart. And it is hard to see why Anne should have seen herself as securing any benefit from Wolsey's downfall.

It is quite likely that Wolsey was not overjoyed by Henry's infatuation with Anne. He might well have preferred Henry, if he were to discard Queen Catherine, to look for a foreign princess: certainly that would strengthen England's diplomatic bargaining position. Conversely, for Henry to repudiate Catherine, Charles V's aunt, risked greatly complicating English foreign policy. So it is just possible that, as Cavendish says, Wolsey on his knees vainly tried to dissuade Henry from pursuing his divorce.[10] In July 1527 Henry sent a message to Wolsey: from Wolsey's response, it is clear that Henry suspected that Wolsey was unenthusiastic about his 'great matter'. Wolsey protested that on the contrary there was 'nothing earthly that I covet so much'. And it was in this letter that Wolsey developed technical objections to the king's marriage based on the impediment of public honesty, not expressly referred to in the papal bull allowing the marriage. He went into some detail as to how the king might, just possibly, secure his divorce on technical grounds. All that was immensely helpful, detailed and practical advice; it shows that Wolsey had been giving the matter a good deal of careful thought. And Wolsey concluded by praying God to give Henry 'the accomplishment of your desires', to the attaining of which Wolsey 'shall stick with your highness usque ad mortem'—to the death.[11]

The most likely explanation is not that Anne was already poisoning the king's mind against Wolsey, inducing Henry to doubt Wolsey's loyalty with the ultimate aim of bringing him down as punishment for blocking her marriage to Henry Percy. It is rather that Wolsey had indeed at some point in these months, though perhaps not as dramatically as in the too-perfect-to-be-true account by Cavendish, drawn to the king's attention the difficulties in the course of action on which he had embarked. Wolsey, his mind not clouded by love as Henry's was, could see the risks and dangers. A principled quarrel with the papacy could lead to schism; repudiation of Catherine would jeopardise relations with Charles V and offer Francis, king of France, easy diplomatic gains in return for insincere promises of support. But it is also clear that Wolsey quickly accepted Henry's desires as an unalterable fact to which everything else would have to be accommodated.

What we do not precisely know is when Wolsey realised that not only did Henry wish to have his marriage to Catherine annulled but that he also wished to marry Anne Boleyn. Did Wolsey already know this when holding the trial of Henry's marriage under his legatine powers in May 1527? When Wolsey suggested that the captivity of the pope—who

had fled from the Vatican to the Castel Sant' Angelo following the sack
of Rome by mutinous imperial troops that month and remained there as
a prisoner—might offer an opportunity to resolve the matter—if
Wolsey became pope or acting pope he could pronounce in the king's
favour—in summer 1527, did he do so ignorant of Henry's intention to
marry Anne?

Most likely he did know, at an early stage, that Anne Boleyn was at
the heart of the matter. Peter Gwyn has persuasively argued that a letter
from Richard Sampson, then with the king, to Wolsey in July 1527
shows that Wolsey was well aware of the 'great matter' from the start.
The wording is allusive but suggestive. The 'great matter' was 'in very
good train, good countenance, much better than was', in his opinion.
'The merry visage is returned, not less than was wont', referred to
Catherine; 'the other party, as your Grace knoweth, lacketh no wit, and
so sheweth highly in this matter' referred to Anne.[12] If this reasoning is
correct, at the very latest before he set off abroad Wolsey must have
known about Anne.

That summer Henry clearly did not consult Wolsey, who by then was
abroad, latterly at the French king's court at Amiens and Compiègne,
about his decision to send his secretary William Knight to the pope to
secure permission to remarry. Maybe Henry was unsure that Wolsey
would offer wholehearted support; more likely he was just embarrassed
about what he was doing.

What upset Wolsey about Knight's mission was not just that the king
had gone behind his back but that Henry's request for a dispensation to
remarry before securing an annulment of his first marriage risked undermining his moral standing: Henry's objections to his first marriage now
appeared merely a cover for his passion for Anne. Henry would no
longer be able convincingly to pose as a conscience-stricken unlawful
husband. When Wolsey found out about Knight's mission, he was
troubled—not because he feared some factional coup against him from
Anne, but because Henry had severely damaged his chances of success.[13]
Wolsey's objections itemised in a letter of 5 September were cogent and
telling: he thought that Knight would be less suitable as a negotiator for
the king with the pope than Girolamo Ghinucci, bishop of Worcester,
who was privy to the king's secret matter, more experienced, and would

have easier access to the pope.[14] When Knight, on his way to Rome, met Wolsey at Compiègne, Wolsey told him that he had expected that Henry would have accepted Wolsey's reasoning and refrained from sending him;[15] but on receiving Henry's letters, Wolsey sent Knight on to Rome. Wolsey was somewhat defensive, insisting that Henry would always find him a true and obedient servant, 'delighting in none earthly thing so much as to set forth, advance, and accomplish all your commandments and pleasures, without contradiction or sparing of my body, life or goods'.[16] Henry's anxiety to secure his divorce had clearly complicated his relationship with Wolsey, but there is no need to invoke rivalry between Wolsey and Anne to explain this.

In late 1527 and 1528 Henry and Wolsey bent their energies to obtaining from Pope Clement a decretal commission, that is to say a legal instrument that would allow two cardinals—Wolsey, and Lorenzo Campeggio who was to be despatched by the pope—to pronounce finally and irrevocably on the facts of Henry's marriage, finding it invalid. That done, Henry would be free to marry as for the first time. As we shall see, the strategy failed. Pope Clement did issue the appropriate decretal commission—but as the international situation changed and he became increasingly fearful of doing anything that might provoke Charles V, Catherine of Aragon's nephew, he ordered Campeggio to delay and then to refuse to pronounce on the case. And when Catherine of Aragon appealed to the pope, he would agree that the case should be tried in Rome. Hindsight makes all of this appear as inevitable. It seems implausible that the pope would ever have allowed the matter to be settled in England. But in early/mid-1528 it did not seem impossible. The pope was issuing the necessary commissions: Campeggio was on his way to England. Everything was happening in what even then seemed slow motion; but happening it was. And against that background there was no reason for Anne Boleyn to nurse any grudge whatsoever against Wolsey.

Moreover the early glimpses that our sources offer suggest that Anne was very much subordinate to Wolsey. In March 1528 Thomas Hennage reported how Henry had sent him down with a dish for Mistress Anne—and how Anne was bold enough to ask Wolsey for good meat—'she wished that she had some of your good meat as carps, shrimps or other.

I beseech your grace pardon me that I am so bold to write unto your grace it is the conceit and mind of a woman'—but nervous that Wolsey had forgotten her since he had not sent her a token:[17]

> And this day as the king was going to dinner Mistress Anne spoke to me and said she was afraid your grace had forgotten her because you sent her no token with Forest [a servant]; and she said she thought that was the matter that he came not to her. And I showed her that he came from your grace very timely and also your grace had such mind upon those letters sent by him that your grace did not remember to send any token at that time.

This illustrates the strength and the weakness of her position. And shortly afterwards Hennage reported that Mistress Anne 'thanketh your grace for your kind and favourable writing unto her and saith she is much bounden unto your grace and is your most bounden beadswoman'.[18] In June 1528 Hennage could inform Wolsey that Mistress Anne 'commendeth her humbly unto your grace and thinketh long till she speak with you'.[19]

Anne wrote Wolsey remarkable letters of thanks at this time. 'I do know the great pains and troubles that you have taken for me both day and night is never like to be recompensed on my part, but only in loving you next unto the king's grace above all creatures living. And I do not doubt that the daily proofs of my deeds shall manifestly declare and affirm my writings to be true.' Allowing for the exaggerations of Tudor flattery, this is still extravagantly generous praise. Anne's lines were followed by several in the king's hand: 'The writer of this letter', Henry explained, 'would not cease till she had caused me likewise to set to my hand.' And Henry added how much they wanted to see him and how joyous they were to hear that he had escaped 'this plague'. Here, then, we can document Anne's influence over Henry: when writing to thank Wolsey warmly for his efforts on her behalf, she cajoled Henry into adding some lines of his own. Interestingly, though, for any assessment of the making of policy, Anne simply assured Wolsey that 'I do long to hear from you news of the legate; for I do hope . . . they shall be very good'. She was eager to know that Cardinal Campeggio was on his way.

Henry, however, was more realistically cautious—'the not hearing of the legate's arrival in France causeth us somewhat to muse'—but nonetheless trusted 'by your diligence and vigilancy (and the assistance of almighty God) shortly to be eased out of that trouble'.[20]

Anne wrote Wolsey a very similar letter of profuse thanks, probably just a little later.

In my most humblest wise that my poor heart can think I do thank [your grace] for your kind letter and for your rich and goodly present the which I shall never be able to deserve without your great help of the which I have hitherto had so great plenty that all the days of my life I am most bound [of all] creatures next the king's grace to love and preserve your grace of the which I beseech you [never] to doubt that ever I shall vary from this thought as long as [breath] is in my body.

She had prayed for him during the outbreak of sweating sickness as she had prayed for the king, 'not doubting but that god [has preserved] you both for great causes known only of his [high wisdom]'. As for Campeggio's coming, she much desired it: 'and that if it be God's pleasure I pray him to send this matter shortly to a good end, and then I trust my lord to recompense part of your graces [great pains]'. She besought God to send Wolsey 'long life with continuance in honour'.[21] Once more that was fulsome praise.

Shortly afterwards she thanked Wolsey for giving a benefice to William Barlow, one of her chaplains, though pointing out an error in the grant. More generally 'for all these that hath taken pain in the king's matter it shall be my daily study to imagine all the ways that I can devise to do them service and pleasure . . . thanking your grace most humbly for the pains that you take for to write to me, assuring you that next the king's letters there is nothing that can rejoice me so much'. There followed the subscription 'with the hand of her that is most bound to be your most humble and obedient servant Anne Boleyn'.[22]

In another letter Anne gave Wolsey her 'humble thanks for the great pain and travail' that he was taking 'in studying by your wisdom and great diligence how to bring to pass specially the greatest wealth that is possible to come to any creature living and in especial remembering how wretched and unworthy I am in comparison to his highness'. Anne acknowledged that she never deserved by her deeds that he should take 'this great pain' for her, yet she saw daily his 'goodness': 'the daily process of your deeds doth declare your words and writing toward me to be true'. Wolsey would recognise how little it was in her power to recompense him: she could offer him only her good will. But she assured him that once 'this matter is brought to pass', he would find her so bound to him that she would 'look what thing in this world I can imagine to do you pleasure'. He would find her 'the gladdest woman in the world to do it'. Next to the king she made him one full promise, namely 'my hearty love unfeignedly during my life'. She asked him to accept the letter as coming from 'one that is most bound to be your humble and obedient servant'.[23]

It is hard to agree that these letters should be read as dissembling, as 'patently insincere'.[24] Anne repeatedly expressed her deep gratitude to Wolsey for all his efforts. And, given what was known at the time at which she wrote, she was entitled to be hopeful that the king's divorce would soon be secured and consequently to be grateful to Wolsey. Perhaps she was a touch too trusting, too naïvely believing, but for someone with little experience of politics, diplomacy and canon law, that was hardly surprising. Above all there is nothing here to suggest that she in any way regretted not being married to Henry Percy and that she was continuing to bear a grudge against Wolsey for that.

On one matter Anne and Wolsey did disagree: the election of a new abbess of Wilton, Wiltshire. On 24 April 1528 the death of the old abbess was reported to Wolsey. The prioress and nuns would shortly write to him for permission to elect a successor.[25] The majority of the convent favoured Dame Isabel Jordan, the prioress, sister of the abbess of Syon, who 'surely is ancient, wise and and very discreet'. But Thomas Benet, vicar-general of the diocese of Salisbury, warned Wolsey that there would be great labour made for Eleanor Carey, William Carey's sister, supported by a minority of the nuns. William Carey was of course married to Mary Boleyn, Anne's sister. And Thomas Hennage duly reported to Wolsey on 23 June that 'Mr Carre [Carey] humbly beseeches your grace to be good and gracious lord to his sister nun in Wilton abbey to be prioress there according to your grace's promise',[26] a request that

Carey's sudden death from the sweating sickness made the more poignant.[27] And evidently the king promised the vacancy to Eleanor.[28] But then the succession at Wilton became a matter of dispute. Wolsey interviewed the nuns—in the course of which it emerged that Dame Eleanor admitted to having had two children by two priests and had since been kept by a servant of the late Lord Willoughby de Broke. Wolsey consequently refused to agree to her election as abbess, and Henry agreed. He explained the situation to Anne and insisted that he would not 'for all the gold in the world cloak your or mine conscience to make her abbess of a house of so ungodly demeanour'. And if that was not clear enough, Henry added, 'nor, I trust, you would not that neither for brother nor sister I should so distain mine honour or conscience'.[29]

All of this does suggest that Anne had tried to use her influence to further the interests of her sister-in-law; in which case, assuming that Anne knew of her sexual adventures, interesting questions are raised about her own supposed convictions and about claims that modern scholars have made for Anne as a reformer of monasteries that we shall consider later. Here it is sufficient to note that the election of Eleanor Carey would have made a mockery of any attempts to reinvigorate monastic discipline and enforce the vow of chastity.

Henry offered to do Anne pleasure by determining that the prioress should not be elected either, even though the charges of sexual misconduct that had evidently been brought against her too seemed implausible since she was too old for them to be credible. Instead Henry would have some other 'good and well disposed woman whereby the house shall be the better reformed whereof I assure you it had much need and god much the better served'.[30]

Remarkably, Wolsey defied Henry, pretending not to know what Henry had decided and preferred the prioress. Henry was 'somewhat moved', Wolsey was told, since he had sent earlier letters that the prioress should not have it.[31] Henry sent a magisterial rebuke (our knowledge of it is from later notes made for Lord Herbert of Cherbury in the 1640s, as the original does not survive) saying that Wolsey should not have chosen someone whom the king had vetoed. What displeased him even more was that Wolsey cloaked his offence in feigned ignorance, saying that he was not aware of Henry's decision. What could be clearer,

Henry asked, than his words, which he quoted, that no one who had been noted or spotted with incontinence, as the prioress had been in her youth, should be elected? Henry went on to warn Wolsey about gossip that the goods for building his college in Oxford had not been lawfully acquired. But Henry accompanied his rebuke with mercy. If Wolsey acknowledged his fault, there would remain in the king no spark of displeasure.[32] Thomas Hennage, to whom Henry had read his letter, said that Henry treated Wolsey 'as an entire friend and master should do': Wolsey should be comforted and not take this matter 'to your heaviness'.[33] Evidently—judging from another letter that also survives only in the notes made for Lord Herbert of Cherbury—Wolsey made a fulsome apology, explaining that the election of the prioress was only conditional, and whatever the truth of the matter, Henry accepted Wolsey's humble submission, ending his 'rude yet loving letter' with the repeated assurance that 'at this hour there remains no spark of displeasure towards you in my heart'.[34] And Henry then allowed the election of the prioress in November.[35]

Does this show Anne Boleyn intriguing against Wolsey, another episode in a long-running battle of wits? More plausibly, Anne was simply trying to help a relative by marriage, and quite likely doing so without fully grasping all the implications. It is implausible that Wolsey took against Eleanor Carey in order to thwart Anne, not least since at the same time he was evidently working hard to secure the annulment of the king's marriage that would allow Henry to marry Anne: of what conceivable benefit would it have been for Wolsey to have provoked Anne in this way? Much more convincing is the argument that Wolsey was sincerely committed to monastic reform, in other words on insisting that those who held high office should be of impeccable moral virtue, and that, after examining all the nuns, he had come to the conclusion that Eleanor should not be appointed but that the prioress should.[36] It is striking that Henry readily accepted that Wolsey was right about the unsuitability of Eleanor and made it plain to Anne—in one of his love letters—that that was so. The way he put it there does suggest that Anne had been lobbying quite hard; and Henry's initial decision not to support the prioress in order to give Anne pleasure shows that he felt he had to offer Anne some concession. We do not know how Anne felt about the later election of the prioress; maybe once it became clear that Eleanor was not going to be appointed, Anne had no strong feelings about the final outcome. It must have been at much the same time that all this was in the air that Anne wrote Wolsey the effusive letters of thanks already quoted, suggesting that it would be wholly wrong to give the matter of Wilton too much significance.

Relations between Anne and Wolsey were thus largely warm during 1528. Did that change in early 1529? By then it was becoming clear that there would be no speedy resolution of the king's problems. Cardinal Campeggio had finally arrived in the autumn, but doubts were growing whether he had come sincerely equipped with the authority necessary to make a final resolution of Henry's great matter. Henry came to suspect, correctly, that Campeggio, and his master, Pope Clement VII, were not dealing honestly with him. And that suspicion seems to have undermined Henry's confidence in the ability of Cardinal Wolsey to find a way out; and, indeed, led him, most unfairly, even to doubt Wolsey's loyalty.

Did Anne Boleyn steer Henry in that direction? Nothing in any immediately contemporary sources tells us that. Later sources, written with the benefit of hindsight, do give Anne a more prominent role, seeing her as an enemy of Wolsey; but, as we have seen, Anne had frequently expressed her gratitude and devotion to Wolsey. What we may be seeing here, notably in Cavendish's *Life of Wolsey*, is an interpretation that owes a great deal to Cavendish's knowledge when he wrote that Wolsey had spectacularly fallen from office, and his wish to offer some explanation of that fall that avoided blaming Wolsey himself or Henry VIII.

Cavendish is the prime source of much modern interpretation that sees Anne as Wolsey's chief enemy. For Cavendish, Wolsey had upset Anne greatly over her intended marriage to Henry Percy: Anne blamed him for what had happened and from then nursed 'a privy indignation' against the cardinal. Cavendish, of course, had not seen the warm letters Anne wrote to Wolsey in 1528. And Cavendish's account becomes even more fanciful when he presents 'the great lords of the council bearing a secret grudge against the Cardinal' for keeping them low and then 'after long and secret consultation' on how they might 'bring their malice to effect against the Cardinal', realising that the 'great affection' the king bore for Anne Boleyn offered them an opportunity if they could make her 'a sufficient and an apt instrument to bring their malicious purpose to pass'. Anne joined them because of her 'inward desire' to be revenged on the cardinal. It was, as Cavendish presents it, just after the battle of Pavia in 1525 at which Francis I was captured (although a little later in his account this seems telescoped with the sack of Rome in 1527) that the lords of the council joined with Anne, 'their chief', 'to espy a convenient time and occasion to take the cardinal in a brake', but nothing came of it then.[37]

Yet Cavendish does not really bring Anne back into the picture later. He does have Wolsey saying after his fall 'that there was a continual serpentine enemy about the king that would I am well assured if I had been found stiff necked [have] called continually upon the king in his ear (I mean the night crow) with such a vehemency that I should (with the help of her assistance) have obtained sooner the king's indignation',[38] but that can be contrasted with two letters that Wolsey wrote after his fall in which he expressed hopes of securing Henry's favour through Anne's mediation. Modern historians who wish to see Wolsey as Anne's factional victim build on the somewhat shaky grounds that Cavendish appears to offer, making a great deal of the coming together of several noblemen in August 1527, and deducing that this must have been the moment in Cavendish's account when they formed an alliance with Anne against Wolsey. Is it fair to berate 'revisionist' historians as 'blessed with the happy confidence that they understand the past better than those who were alive at the time', while conceding that Cavendish's account is 'too neat and pat', exaggerating 'the extent to which the outcome was planned from the start'?[39] That is to have your cake and eat it. Moreover the line of speculation encouraged by Cavendish founders on the clear evidence that we have reviewed of Anne's gratitude towards Wolsey in 1528.

One contemporary witness appears at first glance to offer some support for the notion that Anne was plotting against Wolsey. On 4 February 1529 Inigo de Mendoza, the imperial ambassador, reported that Anne Boleyn had come to think that Wolsey was reponsible for the delays in securing the king's divorce: Wolsey allegedly feared that if Anne became queen, his power would decline. And in her suspicion of Wolsey's obstructiveness, she was, Mendoza said, joined by her father, Thomas Boleyn, and the dukes of Norfolk and Suffolk who were combining to overthrow the cardinal. As yet, Mendoza noted, they had made no impression on the king, except that Henry did not receive Wolsey at court as graciously as before, and now and then spoke some angry words about him. On the face of it then, Anne was playing a leading part, if an ineffective one.

But if we continue reading Mendoza's letter, rather than stopping with these sentences, we are left with a rather different impression. In a later section, Mendoza wrote that he had just heard that the king had pressed Campeggio and Wolsey so urgently to have the case settled in England that they had given him great hope of a favourable answer: 'This king is so blind with passion that there is nothing he will not do or promise to attain his object'.[40] This suggests that it was Henry, not Anne, who was vigorously pressing the legates to give him what he wanted. If Henry spoke angry words against Wolsey at this time, it is not necessary to see Anne Boleyn as behind them. And du Bellay, the French ambassador, noted at much the same time that Wolsey was in great difficulty: 'things have gone so far that if they do not work out, the king, his master, will go for him'. Du Bellay was pinning the responsibility squarely on the king. He also noted that Anne Boleyn, intervening in favour of a courtier whom Wolsey had sent away from court, used very rude words against Wolsey.[41] But that is not sufficient to make Anne the leader of a faction that would ultimately bring Wolsey down.

How subordinate Anne's role was appears quite clearly in letters sent by Francis Bryan, a trusted courtier, whom Henry had despatched to Italy to report how matters lay. In a series of letters in early 1529, Bryan sent pessimistic assessments of the commitment to the king of both Pope Clement and Cardinal Campeggio. What is revealing is how Bryan always informed Henry first. At the close of a letter to the king conveying disappointing news, Bryan added, 'Sir I would have written to my mistress that shall be'—Anne Boleyn—'but I will not write to her till I may write that shall please her most in this world.' It is interesting that Bryan held back from sending Anne anything but good news and instead kept Henry fully informed. This strongly suggests that day-to-day direction of policy was very much the king's.[42] In April Bryan sent further depressing news, warning that the pope would do nothing for the king. He was sorry to write such news but if he did not, he would not be doing his duty. And importantly for our understanding of Anne's part, Bryan added that while he was also writing 'to my cousin Anne', 'I dare not write to her the truth of this because I do not know whether your grace will be contented that she should know it so shortly or no; but I have said to her in my letter that I am sure your grace will make her privy to all our news.' Bryan, of course, had made it possible for Henry to hide the bad news from her if he wished. Bryan obviously believed that Henry was very much in charge.[43] And when he wrote again, evaluating Henry's belief that Campeggio was working for the king as erroneous, Bryan once again added that 'I dare not write unto my cousin Anne the truth of this matter, because I do not know your grace's pleasure whether I shall so do or no.' Bryan's letters strongly suggest that Anne played no independent part in suggesting ways of pursuing the divorce.[44]

It is unconvincing to read the events of 1529 as the unfolding of a factional campaign against Wolsey. What did for Wolsey was the failure of efforts to secure an annulment of the king's marriage, crystallised in Catherine of Aragon's appeal to Rome which would inescapably lead to long delays. Coming to doubt Wolsey's commitment, in May 1529 Henry even sent Charles Brandon, duke of Suffolk, one of his most trusted advisers, to Francis I to ask the French king whether he believed that Wolsey could be relied upon.[45] And Henry went beyond voicing doubts about Wolsey's loyalty. Why should Henry have humiliated Wolsey as he did in autumn 1529, forcing his resignation as Lord Chancellor, the post he had held since 1515? Because to dismiss a royal councillor who was also a papal legate and a cardinal, in an atmosphere of anti-clericalism reflected in debates and legislation in parliament, was an excellent way of signalling to the pope that the king was utterly serious in threatening to go it alone if the pope refused to give him the annulment of his marriage that Henry believed was rightfully his. And to bully Wolsey, papal legate and cardinal, into confessing that he had committed offences under the fourteenth-century statute of praemunire which prohibited obedience to foreign powers was an ingenious way of placing the church as a whole under continuing threat of legal action, and so eventually securing the acquiescence of churchmen in Henry's divorce. Wolsey quickly became aware of these dangers. Throughout the spring and summer before his fall, he warned the pope again and again that Henry's threats were no bluster but seriously meant: if Henry did not get his way, Wolsey would be the first casualty, followed by the authority of the pope.[46] There is nothing to suggest that any of this was Anne Boleyn's idea, or that she was prominent in, or involved in, either the broad strategic decisions or the detailed elaboration of tactics.

It is interesting that Wolsey appealed to Anne at the time of his fall: he entreated Thomas Cromwell, who was then one of his servants, to solicit the king to be gracious to him, and to urge that the Lady Anne might mediate for him; after Wolsey's letter had been delivered, Anne gave the messenger kind words but would not promise to speak to the king for Wolsey.[47] And Wolsey further implored Cromwell that 'if the displeasure of my Lady Anne be [some]what assuaged as I pray God the same may be, then it should [be devised t]hat by some convenient mean she be further laboured, [for she] is the only help and remedy. All possible means [must be used for] attaining of her favour. I have God knows [great need of friends] now to show charity, pity.'[48] Wolsey, although noting Anne's displeasure, did not see her as responsible for his fall: Anne might, if she chose, show pity on him and act as a mediator between Wolsey and the king. Wolsey had no illusions about the author of his misfortunes: the king.

Against that, du Bellay did report gossip that Anne had made Henry promise he would never give Wolsey a hearing, as she thought that Henry could not help having pity on him.[49] A few weeks later Chapuys, Mendoza's successor as imperial ambassador, reported, incredulously, the opposite: that Anne had sent to visit Wolsey during his sickness and represented herself as favouring him with the king. Chapuys was deeply sceptical, given the hatred that he believed she had always borne Wolsey, and speculated that any such favour meant either that Anne believed that Wolsey was on his deathbed or that she wanted to show off her skills as an intriguer. But maybe it was neither dissimulation nor love of intrigue that provoked Anne but rather some sincere sympathy for Wolsey's plight.[50] Later, on Wolsey's arrest in November 1530, Chapuys would insist that the duke of Norfolk, Anne Boleyn and Anne's father had not ceased to plot against Wolsey, especially Anne, 'who did not stop weeping, lamenting the time she had lost and also her lost honour'. Anne allegedly threatened the king that she would leave him. Henry

went to a good deal of trouble to calm her down; though he pleaded
lovingly with her, even with tears in his eyes, that she should not talk of
leaving him, nonetheless the only remedy was that he should have the
cardinal arrested.[51]

Such speculations, vague and contradictory, are too insubstantial as
props for an overall interpretation that would have Anne playing a dominant and leading political role. Du Bellay, in October 1529, did report
how the duke of Norfolk was made head of the council, the duke of
Suffolk acting in his absence—and 'at the head of all' Madame Anne: but
we would do well not to get carried away by this sort of ambassadorial
remark.[52] If Anne really was the leading force behind Wolsey's downfall,
if Anne was really then 'at the head of all', Wolsey's successor as the
king's chief minister, there would have been much more than such brief
remarks. Anne would have featured in Chapuys's and du Bellay's
despatches as prominently, and above all as regularly, as Wolsey had in
those of the ambassadors in his years of eminence. Never did Anne talk
to the ambassadors, never did she expound government policy, never did
she negotiate. Her position was wholly different. And it is interesting that
ambassadors also offer evidence for that interpretation. In July 1532
du Bellay could state that 'all that the Lady does is by the king's order'.[53]

It has already been argued that it is unlikely that it was Anne Boleyn
who put the idea of a divorce in Henry's head, and now Anne does not
seem to have played a leading part in bringing down Wolsey. Yet some
would even claim that it was Anne who pushed Henry into the break
with Rome and into asserting his royal supremacy. One historian asserts
that Anne 'played a major part in pushing Henry into asserting his head-
ship of the church'.[54] Another claims that Anne and Henry were as one,
but she was 'the bolder one of the pair, the more radical, and arguably,
the more principled'.[55] Modern historians such as these can draw on the
words of John Foxe the martyrologist who asserted that the pope was
driven out of England chiefly by her means; or the words of Chapuys,
that Anne was the cause and principal nurse of the heresies in England,
by which he meant the denunciation of papal authority.[56]

Now there is little doubt that Anne came to be anti-papal, but
given her circumstances, that is hardly surprising. Whether Anne's
anti-papalism pre-dated Henry's infatuation with her, or reflected

independent thinking on her part on the nature of authority in the church, is much more doubtful. If Henry had not sought to marry her and if the pope had not then proved so difficult over the divorce, it is most unlikely that modern historians would be debating the nature of her religious convictions, for no break with Rome would have been necessary. But did Anne push Henry into breaking with Rome? In one fundamental sense, of course, she did, because if Henry had not fallen in love with her, policy would not have taken the turn that it did when it did. But that is not to say very much, simply that as the cause of Henry's search for an annulment of his first marriage, which happened to lead to the break with Rome, Anne was instrumental. Yet this is a chain of events ineluctably but quite arbitrarily set in motion by the butterfly flapping its wings, not the influence of an active driver of policy, which is what many modern historians would claim.

Such claims rest on two stories, one told by John Foxe, and one by John Louth, archdeacon of Nottingham, in 1579. Foxe tells us how Anne was sent a pamphlet entitled the *Supplication for the Beggars*, by Simon Fish, a gentleman-lawyer who had gone into exile after his involvement in an interlude satirising Cardinal Wolsey. Anne's brother George saw Fish's tract, read it and urged her to give it to Henry, which she did; Henry then summoned Fish back from exile and embraced him. But even if these details were true (and their exact chronology is awkward), what Foxe's account shows is that Anne's personal involvement and her theological grasp were limited. It was all rather accidental: there is nothing to suggest that Anne had sought out the tract. In the 1570 edition of the *Acts and Monuments* Foxe offers another account of how Fish's book was brought to Henry's attention. A footman told him that two foreign merchants of his acquaintance could show him an interesting book relevant to his concerns: when the king had the merchants brought before him, they read Fish's tract to him. In this account, Anne played no part.[57]

John Louth, archdeacon of Nottingham in the early years of Elizabeth's reign, is the source for the claim that it was Anne who persuaded Henry to read William Tyndale's *The Obedience of a Christian Man*. Louth does not say in what circumstances Anne obtained the book. We learn that she lent it to one of her servants, from

whom it was taken by one George Zouche. Dr Richard Sampson, dean
of the chapel royal, spotted Zouche reading it, snatched the book from
him and gave it to Wolsey; Anne went on her knees to the king to get it
back. It was then that she allegedly persuaded Henry to read the book;
Henry spoke the famous words, 'this book is for me and all kings to
read', and very soon Tyndale's book opened the king's eyes to the truth
about the pope. On this account, Anne's persuasion of the king was
quite accidental (unless we assume that she had been planning to show
it to the king rather later but that her plans had been upset). Louth set
these details down in a letter to John Foxe in 1579: Foxe did not,
however, incorporate them into the 1583 edition of the *Acts and
Monuments*.[58]

Supposing these stories were true, what would Henry have learned
from these works, if he went on to read them? Both were influenced by
the theology of Martin Luther, but not obtrusively. Fish's pamphlet was
a straightforward anti-clerical polemic, concentrating on the rapacity,
financial and sexual, of the clergy. Tyndale's book is more substantial
but essentially it too was a critique of the abuses and machinations of
the church. Was it only after he had read Fish and Tyndale that Henry
attacked the church? That is unlikely. Neither advocates any of the measures that Henry was taking against the church. Henry's case for his
divorce, especially his insistence that there were certain divine laws from
the penalties of which no pope could grant exemption, had already set
him on a course that would lead to the break with Rome, but even he
had not yet passed the point of no return. By autumn 1529 Henry
was putting increasing pressure on churchmen, most notably accusing
Wolsey of breaking the fourteenth-century statute of praemunire (which
had attempted to prohibit Englishmen from obeying foreign rulers). If
he then read Fish and Tyndale, they would have offered him reassurance
and reinforcement, but not anything essentially new. Any suggestion
that Tyndale's argument that kings had authority over the church was a
bolt from the blue is very misleading.

In the years from 1529 churchmen were subject to repeated attacks
intended to weaken their resistance when Henry eventually broke with
Rome. Eustace Chapuys on occasion saw Anne, her father and her
brother as behind those attacks. In February 1531 Chapuys regretted that

the pope had not sent an order that Anne should be kept away from the king, since, as far as he could understand, Anne and her father had been the principal cause of the king's claim to sovereignty over the church.[59]

When in March 1531, Chapuys tells us, the finest and most learned preacher in England—possibly Hugh Latimer—was detained by the archbishop of Canterbury on suspicion of heresy, he appealed to the king; and Henry sent him away a free man after he noticed that one of the articles of heresy objected against him was that the pope was not head of the church, which Henry remarked was quite certain and true. Chapuys commented that the general opinion was that it was Anne and her father's request that led to his release, since they were more Lutheran than Luther himself, seconded by the king's inclination because the preacher had spoken in his favour against the pope.[60] But the context of Chapuys's remarks about Anne and her father should give us pause: what, for Henry, counted in the preacher's favour was that he was attacking papal authority. Chapuys gives the impression that Anne and her father were committed Lutherans speaking up for a preacher under attack for Lutheran beliefs: but it is more likely that what appealed to Anne and her father was exactly what made the king sympathetic, namely the preacher's effective denunciation of the papal jurisdiction. Chapuys too quickly and too polemically elided rejection of papal authority with Lutheran beliefs. No doubt Henry, Anne and Anne's father were all agreed that preachers who preached vigorously against the pope deserved support, rather than facing charges of heresy. When a year later in March 1532 parliament was discussing the abolition of the authority of archbishops over bishops, so Chapuys reported, though there is no independent confirmation of any such measure, Anne's father was, he wrote, one of the principal supporters of the proposal; and he added the gloss that this was no surprise, since he and his daughter were considered true apostles of the new sect.[61] Anne's father, now ennobled as Viscount Wiltshire, and her brother George, now Lord Rochford, were certainly involved in measures against the church in these years. Rochford was prominent when pressure was put on churchmen in early 1531 to acknowledge that they too had been guilty of offences against the statute of praemunire. At that time Wiltshire had told John Fisher, bishop of Rochester—who presumably then informed Chapuys—that he could prove by the authority of scripture that when God left the world he left neither successor nor vicar.[62] In October 1531 Chapuys wrote that Anne feared no one more than Fisher, as he had always defended Queen Catherine's cause: Anne had now ordered him not to attend parliament, ostensibly so that he would avoid catching any sickness as he had the previous year.[63]

Manifestly Anne, her father and her brother all had a strong interest in the effectiveness of the campaign against churchmen. But that Wiltshire, Rochford and Anne should be seen as the authors of the policy, imposing it on the king, is a very different matter. Here it is pertinent that the Boleyns *père et fils* appear in our sources only now and then, rather than as continuously involved counsellors. Clearly Anne and her father fully supported what was being done in these years, but they do not appear from the evidence to be the driving force behind policy. A letter from Nicholas Hawkins, archdeacon of Ely, to Henry from Mantua in November 1532 in which Hawkins, whose imminent death would be much lamented by Anne, said that it was Anne who had told him that it was the king's commandment that he should seek out such books as could be found there about papal power shows that Anne was fully involved; but there was nothing new in what Hawkins was being asked to do, as Henry had been collecting such materials for some time. Anne was not manipulating the king here.[64] Similarly when, according to Chapuys, Anne gave Dr Edward Foxe—sent to seek favourable opinions on the king's divorce from the university of Paris—benefices and appointed him royal almoner, she was rewarding him and facilitating his task, but there is no need to see her as doing that independently of the king.[65]

Rather than supposing that Anne masterminded the break with Rome, let us look at what our sources reveal of her actions. Anne was undoubtedly becoming more publicly prominent in these years. From the ambassadors we know that Anne was more and more being acknowledged, frequently with Henry, and often resided in designated lodgings at court. We have seen how Anne was sent away during the outbreak of sweating sickness in mid-1528. In December 1528 du Bellay reported that 'Mme Bollan' had at last returned and that Henry had installed her in 'a very fine lodging' which he had prepared for her close to his own. Greater court was now paid to her every day than had been to the queen for a long time. Du Bellay shrewdly added that he saw that 'they meant to accustom the people by small to endure her so that when the time comes to give the big blows, the people will not find it strange'.[66] In a later despatch he reported how that month the whole court had retired to Greenwich where open house was kept by both king and queen, as it used to be in former years. 'Mme de Boulan' was also there, having her own establishment.[67]

That set the pattern for well over a year, a somewhat surreal *ménage à trois*, in which Queen Catherine was still publicly the queen, but Anne Boleyn was never far away. It is clear to us that Henry had fallen helplessly in love with Anne, and that, in modern terms, his marriage to Catherine had irretrievably broken down—not after bitter and protracted rows, but more simply when what had initially been a diplomatic union and an act of youthful assertion had been overwhelmed by the force of Henry's middle-aged passion. But that was not what Henry would say in public. Instead, Henry claimed, most vividly in a speech at Bridewell on 8 November 1528, that he was sorely troubled by his conscience because his marriage was not and never had been valid in the eyes of God. It was therefore essential and indeed urgent that the truth of the matter should be determined by the church. We do not have to believe Henry's protestations that he would have been relieved if the church pronounced his marriage valid—'and as touching the queen, if it be adjudged by the law of God that she is my lawful wife, there was never any thing more pleasant nor more acceptable to me in my life'.[68]

Manifestly what he sought was an annulment. But his public stand would obviously be compromised if he too hastily diminished Queen Catherine's position. And that led to the remarkable way in which, from 1528, Henry continued to act, especially on formal and festive occasions, as if Catherine was indeed his wife and queen. From time to time Henry even took his supper with her in her chamber, though less and less often. In October 1529 he suddenly returned to Greenwich, taking his 'mye' (darling) with him.[69] But as late as Christmas 1529 Catherine presided over the revels as she had always done.[70] If Henry and Catherine were largely apart until April 1530, then Henry rejoined Catherine for their summer progress.[71] Yet James Cliff, a priest, reported in May 1530 that Lady Anne was with Henry and Catherine at Hampton Court.[72] From Chapuys, who strongly disapproved, we know that the Lady, as he often called Anne, was acting 'as defiantly and with greater authority than ever', as he lamented in February 1531.[73] A little later, at Shrovetide, Henry banqueted in company with 'the Lady'.[74]

May 1531 marked something of a turning-point: from then, on the pretext of Catherine's stubbornness in maintaining her appeal to Rome and refusing any compromise, Henry abruptly stopped seeing her, and sent her away from court to one of the smaller royal residences. Not only did Henry never see her again: she would never again set eyes on her daughter Mary.[75] In July Chapuys reported that Catherine noted how Anne spoke with greater confidence than before, expecting that her marriage would take place within three or four months.[76] And from that point, Anne Boleyn more and more took on the role of queen, doing what Catherine would have done. When Giles de la Pommeraye, the new French ambassador, arrived in December 1531, he and his colleague John Joachin de Passano, sieur de Vaux, were feasted by Anne, not by Queen Catherine, who for the first time was absent from the Christmas festivities.[77] By early January 1532 Chapuys could note that 'the Lady' was lodged where Queen Catherine used to be, and was accompanied by almost as many ladies as if she were queen. Nor had Henry sent Catherine any New Year's present.

In the beginning of the twenty-fourth year of the reign, that is in late April 1532, Anne, according to the chronicler Edward Hall, 'was so much in the king's favour that the common people which knew not the king's true intent, said and thought that the absence of the queen was only for her sake'.[78] Was Anne responsible for Henry's sending Catherine away? Chapuys certainly believed so. And it would be easily understandable if Anne had indeed pressed Henry to stop treating Catherine as his queen and to stop seeing her. Unlikely though it seems to us now, Anne can never have been totally sure that Henry would not suddenly change his mind and return to Catherine: the further Catherine was from court, and the less Henry saw her, the stronger Anne might feel her own position to be.

And perhaps at times Anne felt jealous when Henry showed signs of affection for Mary, his daughter by Catherine. On 29 April 1531

Chapuys reported how when Mary, suffering from stomach pains, had written to her father that nothing could do her more good than seeing him and her mother, Henry had refused, in order, Chapuys explained, to gratify 'the Lady'—Anne—who hated her, chiefly because she was aware that the king had some affection for her. When Henry had recently praised Mary in Anne's presence, Anne 'had been very angry and began to vituperate the princess very strangely'.[79] In November 1531 Chapuys reported that some said that it was Anne Boleyn who had had Mary sent away from Richmond to a residence of the bishop of Winchester, forty miles away.[80] In October 1532 Chapuys would report that Henry had met the princess in the fields. It was certain, Chapuys opined, that the king dared not bring her where the Lady was, for she did not wish to see her or hear of her. Chapuys added that Henry would have talked with the princess longer and more familiarly if the Lady had not sent two of her people to listen.[81]

Still, the evidence of Anne's personal vindictiveness against Catherine and Mary comes largely from Chapuys, and we might be cautious in attributing Catherine's misfortunes to Anne alone. Chapuys always saw Anne as responsible. For example, in July 1531, he reported plans to strip Catherine of her title of queen, and deduced that, given Anne's authority, she must have dictated the new policy.[82] But Henry was himself entirely capable of turning the screw, and what happened in these years is readily explicable in such terms. Catherine, after all, was a serious obstacle for Henry and Anne: perhaps Anne at times reinforced the king's irritation. What Henry was concerned to avoid at all costs was that Catherine should become an active leader of opposition to his divorce and measures against the church. Fortunately for Henry, Catherine never took on any such role; defiantly seeing herself as Henry's truly wedded wife, she waited—in vain—for the moment when Henry would realise the error of his ways, repent, and return to her. Undoubtedly Catherine was treated more and more harshly: we shall return to consider how far it was Anne who was responsible for that increasing harshness after she was officially proclaimed Henry's queen.

In these years Henry spent a good deal of money on Anne. The surviving accounts of Henry VIII's privy purse expenses for three years from autumn 1529 give the details.[83] Of course, kings always spent lavishly on their queens and mistresses, and such expenditure is not surprising. But it is unusual to be able to document such gifts in detail. And they vividly testify to the strength of Henry's feelings for Anne. In November 1529 as much as £217 9s. 8d. was recorded for 'certain stuff' 'for maistres Anne'.[84] A month later £110 was delivered 'by the king's commandment' to 'my lady Anne'.[85] Purchases in spring 1530 included saddles and harness:[86] 'an astonishing range of luxurious velvet-covered and gilt horse-furniture' was supplied to support Anne's hunting.[87] Sums of money for the purchase of cloth for shirts and for furs and for the furring of her gowns recur. In June 1532, £4 16s. was spent on twelve yards of black satin for a cloak 'for my Lady Anne', with a further 13s. 4d. on a yard of black velvet for edging the cloak, 16s. on two yards of black lining for the sleeves, 25s. 8d. on twelve yards of Bruges satin to line the rest of the cloak, 2s. on two yards of buckram for lining the upper sleeves, as well as 5s. for labour.[88] Smaller payments included the sum of 6s. 8d. to a servant of the mayor of London in June 1530 as a reward for bringing cherries to Lady Anne and that of 44s. 7d. paid in April 1531 'for garnishing of a desk with laten and gold for my Lady Anne'.[89] More often we depend on chance reports such as that of Chapuys, who noted on 4 January 1532 that while Henry had sent Catherine no present, Anne had given him darts of Biscayan fashion, richly ornamented; in return Henry gave her a room hung with cloth of gold and silver, and crimson satin with rich embroideries.[90] In effect Henry paid for Anne's presents to him: on 17 August 1532, 40s. was paid as reward to a servant for bringing a stag and greyhound to Lady Anne, which she then gave to the king.[91] Anne's gambling losses were met by the king: £5 in groats for 'playing money' was granted her on 23 December 1530, 40s. on 1 May 1531, and £4 on 2 May 1531.[92]

We must leave such glimpses of Anne's daily life, for matters now came to a head. We know that Anne gave birth to a daughter, Elizabeth, in September 1533, so working backwards we can deduce that Henry and Anne were sleeping together at the latest by December 1532 (assuming for the moment that Henry was indeed Elizabeth's father), and, quite likely, a little earlier, given that conception need not have been immediate. This suggests that at some time in the autumn of 1532 Henry and Anne began to enjoy regular and full sexual relations. The absence of any recorded pregnancies earlier (the gossip in Rome in December 1531 that Anne had miscarried seems without foundation)[93] strongly suggests that until this time they had not done so. In an age without reliable means of contraception, pregnancy was the inescapable outcome when men and women made love. Why, then, the change in the autumn of 1532? Why did Henry and Anne begin to sleep together then rather than earlier?

There were significant developments in summer 1532. Henry ennobled Anne as marchioness of Pembroke in the king's presence chamber at Windsor Castle on 1 September, in tail male, that is with the right to pass on the title, with an annuity of £1,000 for life from the manor of Hunsdon, and crown lands in Pembrokeshire.[94] It was a grand occasion: the ceremony took place on a Sunday. The king, the dukes of Norfolk and Suffolk, and several earls and lords attended. Anne was brought in with several noblemen before and officers of arms following her, Garter King-of-Arms carrying her patent of creation. Mary, the duke of Norfolk's daughter, carried on her arm Anne's mantle of crimson velvet furred with ermine and a coronet in her right hand. Anne, in a straight-sleeved surcoat of crimson velvet furred with ermine, followed her, led by Elizabeth, countess of Rutland, on her right and Margaret, countess of Sussex, on her left. Anne was led before the king, who was standing under the cloth of state. Anne made her 'obeyssance' four times, came to the king and knelt down between the two countesses. Garter King-of-Arms gave the king her letters patent which the king took to Stephen Gardiner, bishop of Winchester, the king's secretary, who read them. The king placed the mantle on Anne and then put the coronet on her head and gave her two patents, one of her creation and the other maintaining her estate at £1,000 a year. Anne gave thanks to the king and took her leave, returning to her chamber with the coronet on her head. Gardiner then celebrated mass. The connection between Anne's ennoblement and the French summit is shown by the presence of the French ambassador at the ceremony and by Henry's and the French ambassador's swearing to certain articles; and Dr Edward Foxe preached in praise of the Anglo-French alliance. A choir sang a Te Deum.[95] If Chapuys is to be believed, some councillors—he named the duke of Suffolk and the earl of Oxford—were very uneasy. But Henry pressed on.

The purpose of Anne's elevation was to give her appropriate standing when she accompanied Henry on his visit to meet Francis, king of France, near Calais. Those meetings took place in October 1532. They were of crucial importance. By agreeing to meet Henry and Anne, Francis was in effect recognising their relationship, and implicitly endorsing Henry's stand in his quarrel with the pope over the divorce. That made it plain to Henry that if he went ahead and acted in defiance of the pope, Francis would not be an obstacle. Henry's actions offered Francis an enormous diplomatic advantage: by repudiating Catherine of Aragon, Henry was making any alliance between Charles V and himself virtually unthinkable, greatly strengthening Francis I's position in international power politics. Not surprisingly, Francis offered Henry warm sympathy. How far he knew what Henry planned to do next is impossible to say with certainty. Maybe he still hoped that there would be a solution.

But perhaps Francis was behaving more deviously. Maybe he was encouraging Henry to go further, winking and nodding that he would not only refrain from criticising him but would assist Henry if any measures were taken against him. But once Henry had crossed the Rubicon, once Henry had had his first marriage unilaterally annulled without papal blessing, once Henry had seemingly irrevocably broken relations with Charles V, then Francis, having achieved his aim of an internationally weakened and isolated Henry, would hold back from giving Henry any open and public support, and would instead seem to favour Henry's international critics, knowing that Henry's isolation would make him always look to Francis for friendship.

Henry, of course, realised all these risks, and for that reason had aimed at making Francis pay as high a public price as possible, above all having Francis publicly recognise Anne as, in effect, Henry's queen. And that is the context in which we should consider the meeting of the monarchs in autumn 1532. The crucial event was Francis's coming to Calais on 25 October: he gave Anne a diamond worth 15,000–16,000 crowns and danced with Anne.[96] It was the public recognition that Henry so emphatically sought. There was clearly some diplomatic sparring between the two kings. Initially Anne did not join Henry when he saw Francis at Boulogne on 21 October. But what Henry achieved was sufficient.[97] It is quite possible, as Chapuys wrote in a somewhat convoluted report of his conversation with the French ambassador, that Anne 'had greatly assisted in the promotion of the case and had effected it': that is what the French ambassador had appeared to say, yet this is not wholly dependable evidence, especially given the lack of supporting detail.[98]

The other significant development had been the death in August 1532 of Archbishop Warham. The archbishop of Canterbury had blown hot and cold over the king's divorce and could not be relied upon to pronounce the king's marriage to Catherine invalid. At times he had vigorously supported the king's campaign; at other times, however, he had drawn back and even hinted at his concern. Henry may have been aware of the draft speech prepared in early 1532 but most probably never delivered, in which Warham compared himself to St Thomas Becket. If Henry had gone ahead with his divorce while Warham was still alive, there was a risk, however slight, that suddenly Warham would have found the courage to anathematise Henry. That would have been embarrassing at best, disastrous at worst. It was not a risk that Henry took. Now that Warham was dead, Henry was free from the danger of archiepiscopal condemnation. He could instead exploit the vacancy at Canterbury and present Thomas Cranmer, one of his most trusted advisers throughout the long years that the king had sought his divorce. Henry was not quite there yet—but, unlike in previous years, he could now be more confident that his marriage to Catherine would be declared null and void by the archbishop of Canterbury-to-be and by a majority of English churchmen, and that the new archbishop of Canterbury would refuse to implement any papal censures. Chapuys would report in February 1533 how since being elected Cranmer had dared to say openly that he would maintain—and would be prepared to shed blood for his conviction—that the king might take Anne to wife.[99]

With Francis publicly recognising Anne and with Cranmer about to become archbishop, Henry now felt free to sleep with Anne. Even though not everything had been settled, the attendant risks were by this time small. An alternative reading, of course, is that for the same reasons it was now Anne who yielded to the king and 'allowed Henry to sleep with her for the first time'.[100] But that is less plausible. Quite apart from the objections already set out against such an interpretation of their relationship, if Anne had been holding Henry back all these years until she became queen, she might have been expected to wait just a little longer, until everything was wholly settled: for the moment, even though she had been created marchioness of Pembroke, she had not quite got there; she could still have been discarded. It is much easier to grasp why Henry, with Francis sympathetic and Cranmer about to become archbishop, should have felt empowered to sleep with her.

In August Chapuys reported how 'the Lady' had written to one of her principal favourites that she expected what she had so long ago desired to be accomplished on the journey to Calais:[101] this highlights the importance of the meeting with Francis, but does not settle the question of whether it was Henry or Anne who took the initiative. A letter from Cromwell's agent Stephen Vaughan from about this time—describing how after he had delivered Cromwell's letters, the king showed him a proposed design for a chain, and then called Anne, and showed it to her—offers evidence of a loving relationship, but one in which Henry, though keeping Anne informed, was very much in charge of arrangements.[102]

Just when exactly did Henry marry Anne? It is possible that they were 'privily' married on returning from France, on St Erkenwald's Day (14 November), as the chronicler Edward Hall said.[103] Perhaps it was Anne's pregnancy that drove matters forward. According to Nicholas Harpsfield, the catholic historian of the break with Rome, they were married early in January 1533. Yet in early February Chapuys twice reported the imminence of the marriage: Anne had told a priest who wished to enter her service that he must wait *a little* till 'elle aist fait ses noxces avec le roi'—till she had married the king;[104] on 15 February Chapuys wrote that the Lady within the last eight days, dining in her chamber, had said several times that she felt it as sure as death that the king would marry her shortly.[105] And on the 23rd Chapuys reported that Cranmer had married the king to the Lady in the presence of her father, mother, brother and two of her favourites, and one of his priests,[106] though Cranmer would deny having done that: he learned of it a fortnight later.[107] Quite plausibly, as Chapuys informed Cardinal Granvelle the same day, Henry had hurried because Anne believed that she was now pregnant. She had an insatiable appetite to eat plums that she had never felt before: Henry had told her that was a sure sign.[108] In March Anne took the place usually occupied by the queen at a banquet attended by ambassadors. Later she entertained the king to dinner in her own richly ornamented chamber, sitting on his right hand.[109] On Easter eve, Anne went to mass in royal state, loaded with jewels, clothed in a robe of cloth of gold frieze. The duke of Norfolk's daughter carried her train. Anne had in her suite sixty young ladies, and was brought to church and back with all the solemnities and more that were used for a queen, so Chapuys reported. She had changed her title from marchioness to queen, and the preachers offered prayers for her by name. Henry was planning her coronation with feasts and tournaments.[110]

On 10, 12, 16, 17 and 23 May 1533 Thomas Cranmer, the new archbishop of Canterbury, held a court at Dunstable to pronounce on Henry's marriage to Catherine of Aragon: on 23 May he passed sentence in Henry's favour. Now Henry was officially free—as far as the church in England was concerned—to marry as for the first time.[111]

And so Anne became Henry's queen. On Thursday 29 May Anne came by water from Greenwich to the Tower. The mayor of London, Sir Stephen Peacock, waited upon her with fifty barges, as the king had ordered him to do. The mayor and his brethren were all in scarlet, wearing either gold chains or collars made up of the letter S, if they were knights.[112] Before the mayor's barge was a great dragon 'continually moving and casting wildfire' and 'terrible monsters and wild men casting fire and making hideous noises'. On the right hand of the Lord Mayor's barge was the bachelors' barge with 'trumpets and divers other melodious instruments'.[113] There were two great banners 'rich beaten' with the arms of the king and queen, and the city companies' barges all had music and banners. When these barges reached Greenwich they turned about. And then Anne 'in rich cloth of gold' entered her barge, which was accompanied by many more barges carrying noblemen and bishops. Gunfire greeted her progress: 'to write what number of gunshot . . . and great pieces of ordnance were shot as she passed by in diverse places, it passeth my memory to write or to tell the number of them,' asserted the author of the account printed by Wynkyn de Worde.[114]

It was marvellous sight how the barges kept such good order and space between them . . . the banners and penants of arms of their crafts, the which were beaten of fine gold, illustring so goodly against the sun, and also the standards, streamers of the conisances [badges] and devices ventiling with the wind, also the trumpets blowing . . . the which were a right sumptuous and a triumphant sight to see and to hear as they past upon the water.'[115]

'It was a very beautiful sight,' noted one observer.[116] On landing, Anne was led by the Lord Chamberlain to the king, who received her 'with loving countenance' at the postern by the waterside and kissed her; Anne then turned and thanked the Lord Mayor and citizens 'with many goodly words'. 'But to speak of the people that stood on every shore to behold this sight: he that had not seen it would not believe it.'[117]

On Saturday 31 May Queen Anne rode from the City to Westminster. The streets were gravelled and railed on one side to stop the horses from sliding and causing injury. Cornhill and Graces Street were hung with 'fine scarlet crimson'; the most part of the Chepe with cloth of tissue, gold velvet and many rich hangings which made 'a goodly show'. All the windows were 'replenished' with ladies and gentlewomen beholding the queen and her train as they went by. Twelve Frenchmen, servants of the French ambassador—surely evidence of Francis I's endorsement of the marriage, as was the present of a fine rich litter and three mules that Chapuys would report in late June that he had sent[118]—were at the head of her company going from the City to Westminster, clothed in coats of blue velvet with sleeves of yellow and blue velvet.[119] They were followed by gentlemen, squires and knights, judges—who had been ordered by the king to attend[120]—the knights of the Bath in violet gowns, abbots, barons, bishops, earls and marquesses, the Lord Chancellor, the archbishop of York, the ambassador of Venice, the archbishop of Canterbury and the French ambassador. Then came two squires of honour representing the dukes of Normandy and Aquitaine (it is interesting that the French ambassador did not object). The mayor of London followed; then William Howard, deputy to his brother the duke of Norfolk who was in France, and Charles, duke of Suffolk, High

Constable of England for the day. The lords were mostly in crimson velvet, the queen's servants and officers of arms in scarlet.

The queen herself was parading in a litter of white cloth of gold pulled by two palfreys clad in white damask down to the ground. She had 'a surcoat of white cloth of tissue and a mantle of the same furred with ermine, her hair hanged down'; on her head was 'a coif with a circlet about it full of rich stones'. Over her was carried a canopy of cloth of gold with four gilt statues and four silver bells. Anne was followed by her chamberlain Lord Borough, William Coffin, master of the horse, seven ladies in crimson velvet turned up with cloth of gold and of tissue, and a series of chariots carrying noblewomen and ladies.

Anne was welcomed by a number of pageants.[121] One included 'a costly and marvellous cunning' pageant made by the Steelyard merchants: Mount Parnassus with the fountain of Helicon fashioned of white marble and gushing Rhenish wine, Apollo sitting on the mountain playing his lyre, the Muses on every side playing on 'sweet' instruments, with epigrams in golden letters at their feet, in which every Muse praised the queen. It is likely that Hans Holbein, the painter, designed this pageant: a drawing by Holbein of Parnassus with Apollo and the Muses closely fits the account in Hall's *Chronicle*.[122] Another pageant at Leadenhall presented the fruitfulness of St Anne, 'trusting that like fruit should come of her'. At St Paul's Churchyard two hundred well-apparelled children recited 'divers goodly verses of poets translated into English to the honour of the king and her'. At St Martin's Church a choir of singing men and children 'sang new ballads made in praise of her'. Fountains poured forth wine.[123] Nicholas Udall and John Leland supplied a range of verses, mostly in Latin, for these pageants, praising Anne, as might be expected, making allusions to classical goddesses, but emphasising the qualities and virtues characteristic of any queen— beauty, chastity, fertility, nobility of ancestry—and elaborating the nature of falcons as Anne's heraldic emblem was a falcon, but not saying anything specific that is at all revealing about her.[124]

On Sunday 1 June Anne was crowned in Westminster Abbey. In turn came gentlemen, esquires and knights; aldermen of the City in scarlet cloaks; judges in mantles of scarlet; knights of the Bath with white lace on their left sleeves; barons and viscounts in scarlet; earls, marquesses and dukes in their robes of state of crimson velvet furred with ermine; the Lord Chancellor in a scarlet robe; monks solemnly singing; abbots and mitred bishops; serjeants of arms; and the mayor of London. Then followed noblemen with specific obligations: the marquess of Dorset bearing the sceptre of gold, the earl of Arundel bearing the ivory rod, the earl of Oxford, High Chamberlain, bearing the crown, the duke of Suffolk, Lord High Steward for the day, and Lord William Howard with the rod of the marshalship, followed by every knight of the Garter.

Then came the queen in 'a surcoat and robe of purple velvet furred with ermine' under a canopy. The bishops of London and Winchester 'bare up the laps of the queen's robe'; the queen's train, which was 'very long', was borne by the old duchess of Norfolk. Ladies 'being lords' wives', were followed by 'ladies being knights' wives'.

So Anne was brought to the high place in the middle of the church between the choir and high altar and set briefly in a rich chair. Anne rested and then went down to the high altar and prostrated herself while the archbishop of Canterbury said certain collects over her. She rose; the archbishop anointed her on the head and breast; she was led back up to the high place where, after several orations, the archbishop set the crown of St Edward on her head, gave her the sceptre of gold to hold in her right hand, and the rod of ivory with the dove in her left, and then the choir sang Te Deum Laudamus. This procedure was an innovation: the crown of St Edward had previously been used only for the coronation of monarchs.[125] That done, the archbishop removed the crown of St Edward, 'being heavy', and replaced it with the crown that had been made for Anne. Mass was celebrated.

During the offertory Anne went down to the high altar wearing her crown and made an offering. She returned to her chair until the Agnus Dei, when she went down again and knelt before the high altar where she received the holy sacrament from the archbishop. After the mass was done, Anne went to the shrine of St Edward the Confessor and made an offering there, then withdrawing to a little room on the side of the choir. After a short rest, the queen went crowned, her right hand held by her father, and her left by Lord Talbot, deputy for his father the earl of Shrewsbury. The trumpets played 'marvellous freshly' as she left the sanctuary and entered the palace.[126]

A grand dinner then followed. On Anne's right hand stood the countess of Oxford and on her left the countess of Worcester whose duties included on several occasions during the dinner holding a fine cloth before the queen's face when she wanted to spit.[127] The archbishop of Canterbury sat on Anne's right and the earl of Oxford stood between the archbishop and the countess of Oxford with a white staff all dinner time. The first course was brought in by the knights of the Bath, led by the duke of Suffolk and Lord William Howard on horseback, with the trumpets in the window of the hall playing melodiously. 'As touching the fare there could be devised no more costlier dishes nor subtleties.'[128] The following day there was jousting and dancing.[129]

An openly hostile account says that no one cried 'God save the Queen' as Anne went past; many laughed at the letters H and A, painted in several places. Her crown did not fit well.[130] Similarly Chapuys thought the coronation 'a cold, thin and very unpleasant thing, to the great regret, anger and reluctance not only of the common people but also of all the rest. And it seems that the indignation of everybody about this affair has increased by a half since.' But this reads like wishful thinking.[131] More plausibly, perhaps, Chapuys recorded Anne's irritation with the German merchants who on the day of her entry had set the imperial eagle predominant over the king's arms and hers: that must have struck Anne as a sign of sympathy for Catherine of Aragon.[132] Yet a single example of symbolic subversion, if that was what this was, rather than inadvertence, should not be given too much weight. The sheer magnificence and splendour of the coronation tell their own, rather different, story.

'*The most happy*'

KING HENRY AND QUEEN ANNE

What was Henry and Anne's marriage like? We know the tragic outcome; but was there an accelerating deterioration of relations from the start? Did whatever went so horribly wrong happen only at the very end, or was their relationship more complex than any simple models? The best reading of the evidence is that Henry's relationship with Anne once he had made her his wife and queen was one of sunshine and showers, showers and sunshine. In that respect it seems to reflect the human condition.

It was not wholly smooth, nor was it on a downward spiral from the start, or from an early stage. Moments of anger, and flirtations (and perhaps more) by the king, were matched by sustained periods in which Henry and Anne were reported as 'merry' together.[1] Already in April 1531 Chapuys reported that Anne, becoming more arrogant every day, had used such language to Henry that he had complained about it to the duke of Norfolk, saying that Anne was not like Catherine, who had never in her life used ill words to him.[2] But it would be dangerously misleading to put together a narrative based exclusively on such gossip. Manifestly Henry did not react by rejecting Anne; indeed it may have been Anne's vigorous spirit that in part explains why Henry found her so alluring.

Another tiff reported at this time concerned Sir Henry Guildford, courtier and royal financial administrator. Knowing that he was not very sympathetic to her, Anne had threatened him, going so far as to say that when she was queen she would deprive him of his office of controller. To which he replied that when that time came, he would give up the office himself. He then went to the king to tell him the story and to give up his baton of office: the king restored it to him twice, and said he should not trouble himself with what women said.[3] It is impossible to know how much credence to attach to this: Chapuys was keen to report any examples of disaffection. But it does again show a vigorous Anne—though held in check by Henry.

In February 1533 Chapuys could report that Henry was unable to leave Anne for an hour.[4] Anne was then pregnant. During her pregnancy there were several reports of her well-being, and of the good spirits of both king and queen. In July Sir William Kingston informed Lord Lisle in Calais that the king and queen were in good health and merry.[5] Thomas Cromwell told Sir Anthony Browne in Lyons of the 'prosperity and good health' of the king and queen;[6] in August Sir John Russell wrote to Lord Lisle that that the king was merry and in good health: adding 'I never saw him merrier of a great while than he is now'.[7]

It was in mid-1533 that Chapuys first reported the cooling of Henry's infatuation. In mid-August he noted that Henry had been away from the Lady for a long time.[8] A little later, Chapuys somewhat improbably emphasised the papal sentence against the king as the cause of that cooling, but went on to note that Henry had soon taken heart and remained determined to defy the pope's censures.[9] In early September he reported that Anne was full of jealousy, not without just and legitimate cause, and reproached the king, which he did not like. It is hard to think what Chapuys can have meant other than that Anne was angry that Henry was paying court to other women. Henry retorted that she must shut her eyes and 'endure it as well as those better than her', threatening her by reminding her that it was in his power to reduce her in a moment. And Henry then did not speak to her for two or three days. Chapuys saw all this as 'lovers' quarrels', though he added an 'and yet': and yet anyone who knew what the king was like thought that this might be a very favourable opportunity for the recall of Queen Catherine. Was all that wishful thinking on Chapuys's part? Obviously he was not a witness to any such scene, and was dependent on informants who might have their own axes to grind, or reasons for telling him that things were going wrong for Anne.[10] Or might one rather speculate that as Anne became heavily pregnant in summer 1533, Henry satisfied himself elsewhere? If so, that would not necessarily imply anything for the future of their relationship, except that Henry's passion for Anne was evidently no longer exclusive, and that Anne was angry.

If Henry was hoping for a son, the birth of Elizabeth in September 1533 was obviously a disappointment. But this did not mean that from then on Henry gave up on Anne. Elizabeth's christening was done in great style at Greenwich, in the presence of the mayor and aldermen of London, the king's council, barons, marquesses, earls, bishops, abbots and many ladies and gentlewomen.[11] And there was no reason not to think that Anne would soon be pregnant again.

We do not have as much evidence on how Henry and Anne behaved towards each other as we should wish. But there are some suggestive passing remarks in courtiers' correspondence as well as in diplomatic despatches. In early November 1533 Chapuys, noting gossip about what the pope had sent to the king, reported one of Anne's ladies as quoting Henry saying several times that he would sooner go begging from door to door than ever abandon Anne.[12] In early December, according to Chapuys, Henry had talked familiarly for some time with Christopher Mount, his ambassador recently returned from Germany, making him great cheer, and then, putting his hand on his shoulder, bringing him to Anne Boleyn's chamber—that is, very much showing his commitment to Anne.[13] Henry and Anne were reported as merry by Richard Page on 15 October 1533,[14] and by Sir Thomas Palmer on 29 January 1534,[15] as merry and in good health by George Taylor on 27 April 1534,[16] once again as merry by Sir Francis Bryan on 17 May 1534,[17] and as in good health and merry by Sir Edward Ringley on 11 and 26 June 1534.[18] That points to a more than satisfactory relationship. And Chapuys reported no more gossip casting doubt on Henry's love for Anne until much later.

Early in 1534, not long after Elizabeth's birth, Anne was reported pregnant again.[19] On 27 April George Taylor informed Lady Lisle that the queen 'hath a goodly belly', and added the words 'praying our Lord to send us a prince'.[20] A silver cradle with various images was purchased.[21] If Henry had been disappointed that Anne's first baby was a girl, there was now every reason for him to be hopeful of a son. Henry even showed signs of affection to Princess Elizabeth in these months.

Then in July, when Anne was described as far gone with child, Henry sent Anne's brother Rochford to Francis in France to postpone a planned meeting because of Anne's pregnancy.[22]

But no baby came. Did Anne miscarry, did she give birth to a stillborn child? Or was this a phantom pregnancy? A miscarriage seems unlikely, since if Anne was pregnant early in the year, then she would have been too far gone to have a miscarriage in late summer. One Margaret Chancellor of Bradfield St Clairs, Suffolk, gossiped that Anne had a child by the king which 'was dead born'.[23] Yet if she had a stillborn child, it is highly probable that she would first have taken to her chamber, for which there is no record. In September, Henry, Chapuys tells us, was beginning to have doubts as to whether Anne was pregnant or not,[24] and this has led a medical historian to argue that Anne was suffering from a phantom pregnancy.[25] Did Anne, under immense pressure to conceive and to produce a son, delude herself that she was pregnant? Less likely is that she had sought to deceive Henry from the start, not least since the truth could not be hidden for long. It must all have been at best deeply frustrating, at worst shattering, for both Henry and Anne as it became clear that there was to be no new living royal baby.[26]

And if Chapuys's gossip in September 1534 was well informed, all this had further consequences. Henry, he wrote, had renewed and increased his earlier love for another very beautiful lady of the court: unfortunately for us, Chapuys did not name her, nor make it clear whether she was the flame from the previous year. Anne understandably wanted to drive her away from propinquity to the king. That led to heated words between Henry and Anne: Henry became very angry, telling her she had good reason to be content with what he had done for her and adding, in an unpleasant coda, that if it was to begin—in other words, if he were starting now—he would not do it, and that she should consider from what she had come, and much more. As Chapuys perceptively glossed such gossip, it would not be well to attach too much importance to all this, considering the changeable character of the king and Anne's skill in managing him. But if true, it would be revealing: it would show an Anne prepared to berate her husband for his philandering, and a Henry brutally reminding Anne that it was he who had made her queen.[27] That same month, September 1534, Fernando de Silva, count of Cifuentes, imperial ambassador at Rome, reported news that Anne was in disfavour with the king, who had fallen in love with another lady—but Cifuentes refused to lend much credence to the gossip, and subsequently noted that what he had written appeared to be a mistake.[28] A few weeks later Chapuys reported how Rochford's wife, Anne's sister-in-law, had been banished from court because she had conspired with Anne to procure the withdrawal from court of the young lady whom Henry 'had been accustomed to serve'.[29] That lady had recently sent to Princess Mary to say that her troubles would come to an end sooner than she supposed and that when the opportunity arose she would show herself her true and devoted servant: Anne's credit was on the wane, and so she was visibly losing part of her 'pride and vainglory'.[30] The count of Cifuentes in Rome again picked up on all this: Anne Boleyn was disliked by the lords of England on account of her pride and that of her brothers and kinsmen, and because the king did not like her as much as he once had. The king was entertaining another lady, and many lords helped him, with the aim of separating him from Anne.[31] In late October Chapuys again mentioned the young lady, the king's new mistress, who was quite devoted to Princess Mary.[32] Charles V referred to Henry's discontent with Anne in November 1534.[33] Cifuentes remained sceptical: all this was being said with an object, he warned—and presumably what he meant was that such gossip was being planted in the ears of Chapuys and others with the purpose of deterring Charles from vigorous action in defence of Catherine and Mary. If Charles thought Anne was on the way out, he would simply wait on events rather than contemplate an invasion of England.[34]

In December 1534 Chapuys made a more considered attempt to assess the state of the relationship between Henry and Anne. It was, he wrote, true that the king sometimes showed he was angry with the Lady, but, Chapuys at once glossed, these were but 'lovers' quarrels'. Not much weight should be attached to them, unless the king's love for his new young lady should grow warm and continue some time; on the prospects for that Chapuys declined to speculate, though he noted the king's 'fickleness'. Sir Nicholas Carew, master of the horse, told Chapuys that when Anne complained that the young lady did not do her the reverence she expected either in word or deed, the king went away 'very angry', complaining of her anger and importunity.[35]

All the same, on the face of it there were no fundamental problems: over Christmas the king and queen kept a great house, John Hussee, the agent of Lord Lisle, deputy of Calais, reported.[36] Not much detailed evidence survives about their relationship in the early part of 1535. In mid-February Chapuys reported that the young lady who had been in the king's favour was so no longer; she had been replaced by Anne's cousin-german, daughter of the 'gouvernante'—governess—of Princess Mary. Mary was then being overseen by Anne Boleyn's aunt Anne, sister of her father, married to Sir John Shelton. Chapuys did not specify further and we do not know for certain which of their daughters the king was pursuing. Most likely it was Margaret (Madge) Shelton, one of Anne's ladies-in-waiting, whom we shall encounter again when we consider Anne's fall.[37] Should we play all this down? It has been claimed that 'what Henry had done was to offer his knightly service to a new "mistress" for the game of courtly love' but that this amounted to no more than 'shallow gallantries'.[38] Misunderstandings in such matters are all too possible: Henry may not have had any serious amorous intentions. But Anne was understandably angry. In early May Chapuys reported that Anne, prouder and haughtier than ever, even dared to tell the king that she was the cause of his removal from sin, she had made him the richest king because without her he would not have reformed churchmen.[39] Yet perhaps Anne may have felt the more annoyed because her position as queen was not uncontested. Given the circumstances in which she had become Henry's wife, she could not so readily tolerate her husband's flirtations as a more conventional queen might have done.[40] Catherine of Aragon had evidently turned a blind eye to Henry's affairs and would have continued to do so had Henry not come to the decision that their marriage had always been invalid. Henry's subsequent marriage to Anne was not a typical royal marriage in which a king took as his wife a foreign princess for the dynastic and diplomatic benefits such a union would bring, benefits which were not compromised by any royal dalliances. By contrast Anne's position rested wholly on the love of the king, and anything he did that seemed to cast doubt on the strength of his love for her quickly seemed threatening. And she may well have feared at times that Henry's affections would prove short-lived: a king who had in effect divorced his first wife when he fell in love with another woman could go on to divorce her too.

Henry's occasional threats spoken in anger would- only have reinforced any such anxieties. In June 1535 Carlo Capella, the Venetian ambassador, reported that the king was already tired to satiety of this new queen.[41]

But matters seemingly improved in mid-1535. In June Princess Mary informed Chapuys that the king 'was more infatuated with her than ever before'.[42] After greatly enjoying a staging of a chapter from the Bible in which the heads of churchmen were cut off, Henry sent to Anne that she should come to see the next performance on St Peter's eve (28 June).[43] In the summer and autumn of 1535 Henry, accompanied by Anne, went on progress. And on several occasions they were recorded as merry: Sir Thomas Audley, Lord Chancellor, reported their 'mirth and good health' in September; John Veysey, bishop of Exeter, described them as 'in good health and merry' in October; and Sir Anthony Windsor noted them as very merry in Hampshire the same month.[44] On the whole, then, Henry and Anne's marriage was strong; but there were ups and downs, and all was against the backcloth of the annulment of Henry's first marriage and the consequent break with Rome.

She 'wore yellow for the mourning'
ANNE AGAINST CATHERINE

If Chapuys, the imperial ambassador, is to be believed, then Anne Boleyn constantly campaigned and plotted vigorously against Catherine of Aragon and especially Catherine's daughter by Henry, Princess Mary. Chapuys no doubt exaggerated the wretchedness of the residences in which Catherine was kept in effect under house arrest, but that both Catherine and Mary were put under increasing pressure is undeniable. Again and again, Chapuys highlighted Anne's part in intensifying their misfortunes. Typically he would report some pressures against Catherine or Mary, and then add that Anne was responsible for them. Does that prove it was Anne who 'supplied the emotional drive and energy behind the attacks on Catherine and Mary'?[1]

On 10 April 1533 Chapuys predicted that once this cursed Anne had her foot in the stirrup, there was no doubt but that she would do all the harm she could to Catherine, and also to Mary, which Catherine feared most of all. Anne boasted that she would have the princess as her lady's maid, but that was said, Chapuys believed, only to make Mary eat humble pie, or to encourage her to agree to marry some varlet (rather than the marriage to a foreign prince that her status as a king's daughter would have made more appropriate).[2] On 16 April Chapuys reported pressures on Catherine to renounce her appeal to Rome and accept that Henry's request for an annulment of their marriage could be settled in England. Then she was told that she was no longer to call herself queen, that the king would no longer defray her expenses or the wages of her servants, and that he intended that she should retire to one of her houses (in the country, away from court) and live on a small income that, Chapuys calculated, would not meet the cost of her attendants for more than three months. Henry, Chapuys insisted, was not ill-natured: it was Anne, he said, who had put the king 'in such a perverse and wicked temper, and alienated him from his former humanity'. Anne would never stop until she had seen the end of the queen, as she had that of the cardinal, whom she did not hate so much.[3] Chapuys moreover claimed that no one dared speak a word about the unpleasant way in which Catherine and Mary were being treated for fear of the Lady, Anne Boleyn.[4] On 10 October he reported that Henry had reduced the number of Princess Mary's attendants and expenses: only the importunity and ill will of the Lady could explain why Henry was so quick to treat Mary so meanly.[5] Soon Chapuys again referred to the Lady's importunate insistence that Henry should do more against Mary.[6] On 23 December Chapuys reported that Henry, on the solicitation of the Lady, whom he dared not contradict, had determined to send Catherine to Somersham, ever further away from court. Anne correctly noted, Chapuys said, that once laws were passed declaring Mary illegitimate and revoking Catherine's royal rights, then Henry could confiscate all the queen's goods.[7]

On 17 January 1534 Chapuys reported how Anne complained to Henry that he did not keep Mary in close confinement. Recently interrogated by the king's councillors, Mary had responded rather effectively; Anne remarked (according to Chapuys) that Mary could not possibly have made such answers without having had advice, yet Henry had promised Anne that no one should speak to Mary without his knowing it. What Anne feared, if Chapuys was correct, was the king's 'easiness or lightness': she was nervous that Mary's beauty, virtue and prudence might soften his wrath and lead him to treat her better and allow her to continue to use her title of princess (even though she was now legally a bastard). So Anne—successfully—sent Cromwell and other messengers to Henry to deter him from seeing or speaking with her.[8]

According to Chapuys, Anne had from the beginning resolved to make Mary carry her train—which would have been an exquisite humiliation— but had then thought better of it, as Mary's singular beauty and virtue might, she feared, have moved the king to change his mind about Mary's abasement when he saw her; and once Mary was at court, she would win everyone's heart. So Anne would not have her come.[9]

Anxious about Henry's affection for Mary, Anne plotted unceasingly against her, Chapuys continued to report. Anne had determined to poison Mary: or so Chapuys learned from a gentleman 'who had heard it for true' from the earl of Northumberland with whom Anne had once been entangled. Chapuys reasoned that the earl might know something of it from his 'familiarity and credit' with Anne: he warned Mary to be on her guard.

What Anne feared, and what, Chapuys surmised, might have encouraged her to execute her wicked will, was an eventual reconciliation between Henry and Mary. In the same letter Chapuys noted that the French ambassador had told him how the tears welled up in Henry's eyes when the ambassador had praised her as 'fort bien nourrie'—very well brought up—after Henry had said that he had not spoken to her on account of her obstinacy (over the annulment which had made her illegitimate): Henry could not then hold himself back from praising Mary.

For the moment Anne piled on the humiliations. She ordered Alice, widow of Sir Thomas Clere of Ormeby, Norfolk, who had Mary in her custody, not to allow her to use the title of princess: if she did, Alice was to box her ears as an accursed bastard—or so the gentleman who was Chapuys's informant said. Anne had also ordered that Mary should no longer be served breakfast in her chamber but was now to come to the common table, something of a humiliation for a princess.[10] And shortly afterwards Alice was sharply reprimanded by Lord Rochford, Anne's brother, and the duke of Norfolk, for treating the princess with 'too much honesty and humanity': Mary was to be treated as the bastard she was.[11]

All these accounts of the humiliations and pressures that Mary was subjected to are readily believable, but whether Anne's part in them was quite as independent and as decisive as Chapuys suggested is open to some doubt: Henry may have been as responsible as Anne, perhaps more so. Maybe on occasion 'Anne put out feelers for a better relationship',[12] but such offers should be viewed tactically, and indeed seen as integral parts of the strategy of humiliation. On each occasion what Mary would have been required to do was to yield to Henry, to accept that her mother's marriage to Henry had been invalid and that she was illegitimate, as well as agreeing to the validity of Henry's marriage to Anne. These were not offers that Mary could painlessly have accepted.

For example, in March 1534, when Anne went to see her daughter Elizabeth, she urgently solicited Mary to come to honour her as queen: that, she said, would be a means of reconciliation with the king. Anne further offered to intercede with the king for Mary, promising that she should be as well or better treated than ever. Not surprisingly, Mary replied that she knew no queen in England except her mother Catherine of Aragon, but if Madame Anne de Bolans—as Mary called her— would do her that favour with her father—arranging a reconciliation— she would be much obliged. Anne repeated her remonstrances and offers, and in the end threatened Mary, but could not move her. Very indignant, Anne, Chapuys reported, declared her intention of reducing the pride of such unbridled Spanish blood. She would do the worst she could, Chapuys feared.[13] On this occasion he was not reporting court gossip but what Mary's own messengers had passed on to him about her encounter with Anne. Maybe they exaggerated the boldness of Mary's response, but it is hard to see why this account should not broadly be accepted. And far from 'putting out feelers for a better relationship', Anne was trying to persuade and cajole Mary into unconditional surrender.

Chapuys continued to insist time and again on Anne's malice. He feared that Mary's unwillingness to co-operate would irritate Henry: consequently she would face suffering worse treatment and risk some bad turn at the desire of the Lady, who, he said, 'did not cease day and night to plot the most she could against the princess'.[14]

In spring 1534 both Catherine and Mary were required, but refused, to swear the oath recognising Henry's children by Anne as first in line of succession. Chapuys feared that Henry would in response do them some ill turn, 'at the instigation of his cursed concubine'.[15] Anne had said she would not rest until she had got rid of Catherine. According to certain prophecies to which Anne gave credit, a queen of England was to be burned. Anne wanted that queen to be Catherine so that she would avoid such a fate herself; there was gossip at court about great things to be seen very soon, interpreted by many as meaning that something further would be done against Catherine. Very recently Thomas Audley, speaking in anger to two or three leading foreign merchants, had appeared to say that very great ones—which they interpreted as meaning the queen—would be cut off. Such things were monstrous and difficult to believe, Chapuys continued, yet the obstinacy of the king and the malice of this cursed woman made one fear everything.[16] In 1534 nearly all the gentlemen and ladies of the court went to see Mary, to Anne's great annoyance, Chapuys said, adding that Mary had informed him that Anne was secretly urging those about her to be as rude and annoying as they could.[17] A little later Chapuys reported how one of Mary's young ladies had been put in prison: she had soon been set free but had been forbidden from returning to the princess. Chapuys suspected that all of this was Anne's doing, without the knowledge of the king, since he sometimes showed Mary affection, and had recently sent her his own physician when she was ill.[18]

In June 1534 Chapuys was informed by a person of good faith that the king's concubine had said, more than once, and with great assurance, that when the king had crossed the sea—Henry was contemplating going to France for another summit meeting with Francis—and Anne was left behind as 'gouvernante' (in 1513 Henry had left Catherine behind as regent during the Tournai/Thérouanne campaign) she would use her authority to put the princess to death, either by starving her or otherwise. Anne's brother rebuked her, saying that that was anger the king: Anne replied that she did not care even if she was burned alive for it after. Mary was ready to face death, believing that there could be no better way of reaching paradise and trusting only in God.[19] Can we believe such an account? Was Anne so determined on Mary's destruction that even her brother warned her against angering Henry? Does all that ring true? Chapuys's information must have been indirect: he did not overhear Rochford warning Anne. But if Anne was so bent on eliminating Mary, that would be understandable. Mary was, after all, Henry's daughter. Henry's marriage to Catherine had been controversially annulled. Where did that leave Mary? A month earlier when Chapuys had feared that Henry at Anne's instigation would do

Catherine and Mary an ill turn, 'several thought', he reported, that Henry would put both Catherine and Mary in the Tower when he went to France.[20]

It is striking in this respect that in November 1534 Brion, Admiral of France, sent on a diplomatic mission from Francis I, had asked Henry to sanction the marriage of Mary to Charles, duke of Angoulême, Francis I's third son. Henry was taken aback—had not Francis, after all, been offering him his support in his quarrel with the papacy, and did not such a request cast some doubt on the validity of Henry's divorce, implying that Mary was Henry's legitimate daughter? But Francis's encouragement of Henry had been cynically Machiavellian. With Francis's support, always more tacit than explicit, though at times, as at the meeting in autumn 1532 somewhat more public, Henry had dared to have his marriage to Catherine declared null and void, had dared to wed Anne, and had dared defiantly to break with Rome. Henry had gone out on a diplomatic limb: which was just what Francis wanted, since it diminished the likelihood of an English offensive against Francis in alliance with the Emperor Charles V.

But having isolated Henry, Francis did not wish openly to follow Henry into schism and into principled denunciations of the papacy: a papal alliance was too important a part of Francis's diplomatic policy for him to go as far as Henry would have wanted. Moreover in 1534 Francis was ready to move closer to Charles as opportunities arose, and it was no doubt with that possibility in mind that he sent ambassadors to England to seek a marriage alliance involving Princess Mary, Henry's daughter by Catherine of Aragon, and thus the emperor's cousin. Francis also urged Henry to resume his obedience to the pope. He was not doing this from any moral outrage at Henry's break with Rome and declaration of his royal supremacy: he was rather, in evolving circumstances, weighing the diplomatic gains and losses of an English alliance, knowing that Henry's isolation in 1534–35 was such that Francis could afford to join the critics of Henry's break with Rome without risking turning Henry into an enemy. Of course such unprincipled conduct could come unstuck, but for the moment Francis's diplomacy was proving successful.

How was Henry to respond to Francis's offer of a marriage alliance involving Princess Mary? Three times Henry took Brion's offer as a joke, compelling the ambassador to show him his written instructions under the great seal of France in order to convince him that this really was Francis's suggestion.[21] But when he saw that the proposal was serious, he tentatively countered by agreeing that Mary might marry Angoulême, Francis's younger son—provided that she and her husband-to-be renounced all right to the English crown. And, perhaps recovering his confidence after the surprise offer, Henry more boldly countered by suggesting that if Francis would persuade Pope Paul III to nullify the late Pope Clement's sentence against him, then Angoulême could marry not Mary but—even better—Henry's daughter by Anne, Princess Elizabeth. As part of such a deal Henry was prepared to renounce his title as king of France, as Francis had suggested when Henry and Francis met at Calais in 1532, and as Brion had recently repeated, in exchange, as Francis had then proposed, for Gravelines, Newport, Dunkirk and the duke of Vendôme's lands in Flanders as well as the title of the duke of Lorraine, the dukedom of Brabant and the town of Antwerp, with 'sufficient assistance of the recovery of the same'. Such a grant would have given the king of England a significant block of land on the Channel coast—but it was not Francis's to give, it would have to be fought for, and won, from the emperor. And Francis was unlikely to accept the challenge of securing papal approval for Henry's actions.[22]

That Anne Boleyn was exceptionally sensitive to these diplomatic negotiations appeared in her reaction to Brion's apparent lack of enthusiasm for visiting her daughter Elizabeth in November. When Brion replied very coldly that he would do so if it would please the king, but asked Henry to move forward with the marriage of Mary to the dauphin (he meant Charles, duke of Angoulême, younger son of Francis I), Anne Boleyn, Chapuys noted, was very angry.[23] Anne's frustrations and fears surfaced when she laughed uncontrollably at a banquet in the ambassador's honour: 'what madam, do you laugh at me?' Brion had remonstrated. Anne's (tactful?) explanation was that Henry had told her he would bring the ambassador's secretary to amuse her but, distracted by a lady with whom he got into conversation, he had forgotten.[24]

Henry and Anne were concerned by how Francis would react to Henry's proposals. In early 1535 Francis duly sent Palamedes Gontier, treasurer of Brittany, with his response. Francis had no doubt that since

Henry had given Elizabeth the title of princess, he would take great care
that she would be his heiress. But he added that some way should therefore be found to deprive Mary once and for all of any right to the succession. Henry countered that all that was necessary had already been done
by laws passed by parliament. What Francis should do, Henry yet again
urged, was to persuade the pope to annul the sentence against him. In
response Palamedes suggested that Henry waive the substantial pension
that Francis was paying him: Henry refused.

In a long account of his embassy, Palamedes also described how after
a series of meetings over several days, including one of 'two long hours'
with Henry, in which Henry made 'a very long speech' setting out how
parliament had settled the succession, at one point Thomas Cromwell,
the king's secretary, took him to the queen's chamber, where the king
was also awaiting him. Palamedes paid his respects to Anne, delivered
Brion's letters and set out what Brion had ordered him to say. Anne said
that she was 'astonished', and complained at his long delay which had
raised many doubts and fears in the mind of her husband. Francis, she
said, had to think of some remedy and deal with Henry so that she did
not remain ruined and lost, for she saw herself as very nearly ruined and
lost, and 'in more grief and trouble than before her marriage'.
She ordered him to beg the Admiral to consider her affairs,
of which she could not speak as fully as she wished, on account of
her fears, and the eyes which were looking at her: those of her
husband, and of the lords present. She could not write, or see him
again, or stay longer. Palamedes summed up that 'as far as he could
judge, Anne was not at her ease' because of Henry's doubts and
suspicions.[25]

It would be tempting to build on this to present Anne as a diplomatic
negotiator, even as maker of policy. But the great obstacle to that would
be that Anne was surely behaving in a deliberately contrived manner.
She was emphasising to the French emissary that Henry's alliance with
Francis could not be taken for granted, and even that her own position
as queen was in some jeopardy. She did not say it explicitly, but what
she was conveying was a sense of how urgent it was for Francis to
make concessions and, above all, to give her, Anne Boleyn, continuing
international recognition as Henry's queen and mother of his

daughter Elizabeth. If Francis responded positively to Henry's offer of Elizabeth as wife-to-be of the dauphin, that would greatly reinforce Anne's position and so cement Anglo-French friendship for the long term.[26]

Nothing much came of all this. But this does mean it was not important, or that, for our purposes, it is not revealing. If the French treated Princess Mary as a pawn in diplomatic negotiations—suggesting her as a fit bride for the dauphin—that raised interesting questions about the significance and consequences of Henry's divorce. And, as we have seen, Henry implicitly recognised the point by insisting that Mary renounce all claims to the English throne as part of any marriage alliance and by putting forward Princess Elizabeth instead. All of this made Anne Boleyn's status and the standing of Elizabeth central questions. For Anne, Mary was thus a serious complication, indeed an obstacle, a rival to the claims of Elizabeth. Moreover if diplomacy, however improbably, led to the marriage, or even simply to negotiations for the marriage, of Mary to Francis's younger son, Anne could reasonably fear that she was being upstaged. If Anne felt herself semi-French, thanks to her years at the French court, she might well have felt a touch betrayed by Francis's apparent willingness to afford Mary precedence.

In December 1534 Chapuys, lamenting that the rude treatment of Catherine and Mary was getting worse daily, reiterated his belief that all this was done at the demand of 'the said lady'—Anne—'without', he suggested, 'the king's knowledge'. In justification, Chapuys pointed to the way in which Henry 'from time to time' was affectionate towards Mary, for example when she had recently been unwell. Chapuys, however, also went on to report that when the king's own doctor had told him that Mary would recover more surely if she was sent to live with her mother, Henry had said that that would make it impossible to bring her to do what he wanted. Here, against his intentions, Chapuys showed clearly how it was Henry who was seeking to impose his will on his daughter.[27]

If in early 1535 Anne, after her miscarriage or phantom pregnancy the previous year, despaired of becoming pregnant again, that was understandable. In March Chapuys reported that Anne had forced an unnamed person to say that he had had a revelation from God that she could not conceive while Catherine and Mary remained alive.

Chapuys was sure that Anne talked constantly about it to the king. She always spoke of Catherine and Mary as rebels and traitresses deserving death.[28]

In May 1535 Chapuys returned to the charge. It was to be feared that if the king was getting so inured to cruelty, he would act cruelly against the queen and princess, at least in secret; to which, Chapuys added, the concubine would urge him with all her power. She had lately several times blamed Henry, saying it was a shame to him and all the realm that Catherine and Mary had not been punished as traitresses according to the statutes. Anne was, he said, more haughty than ever, and ventured to tell the king that he was more bound to her than man could be to woman, for she had extricated him from a state of sin; and moreover that he came out of it the richest prince that ever was in England and that without her he would not have reformed the church to his own great profit and that of all the people.[29] Where did Chapuys get that from? Clearly, he was not reporting a conversation, or an argument, that he had overheard. Still, it is plausible that Anne should have complained to Henry that neither Catherine nor Mary had been executed for treason. If she did, it would not say much for her broader political sense: nothing would have done more to inflame the Emperor Charles V than any such executions.

In late July Chapuys recorded how Anne was incessantly crying after the king that in suffering the queen and princess to live he was not acting prudently. They deserved death more than those who had been executed—referring to Bishop Fisher, Thomas More and the Carthusian monks—since they were the cause of all.[30] In November Chapuys informed Anthony Perrenin, Charles V's secretary of state, that 'this devil of a concubine' would never stop till she was freed from these poor ladies, for which liberation she worked by all means possible.[31] To the emperor he wrote that the concubine, who for a long time conspired the death of the said ladies and thought of nothing but how to get rid of them, was the person who governed everything, and whom the king was unable to contradict.[32]

Anne clearly felt little sorrow when Catherine died in January 1536: according to the chronicler Edward Hall she 'wore yellow for the mourning',[33] and Chapuys noted that Henry was dressed entirely in yellow,[34] not the most tactful colour. And no sooner had Catherine of Aragon died than Chapuys feared that Anne would hasten what she had long threatened to do, namely to kill Mary. Chapuys immediately suspected that Catherine had been poisoned: her physician thought it was a slow and subtle poison in some Welsh beer,[35] and confirmed his opinion after hearing from Catherine's confessor the bishop of Llandaff that when her body had been opened, her heart was found to be 'all black and hideous to see'.[36] Anne had, Chapuys insisted, often sworn to bring about the death of both Catherine and Mary, and would never be at rest until she had accomplished her desire.[37] If Mary were reconciled to her father by swearing all the oaths he sought, which was what Henry and Anne were planning in several ways to achieve, then Anne would find it easier than before to poison Mary without suspicion: once Mary had accepted the king's marriage, Anne would no longer appear to have an obvious motive for eliminating her. But, Chapuys mused, she still would because she was all too aware of Henry's fickleness. At the same time, Wiltshire and Rochford, according to Chapuys, lamented that Mary had not accompanied her mother to death.[38]

Much has been made of Anne's subsequent gesture towards Mary. But, just like her earlier 'feelers', what Anne demanded of Mary was her total submission: there was no negotiation, no search for compromise. As Chapuys heard from Mary, Anne threw the first bait to her, getting her aunt Anne Shelton who had charge of the princess to tell Mary that if she would stop being obstinate and obey her father 'like a good daughter', Anne would be the best friend to her in the world, would be like another mother to her, and would obtain anything for her. If Mary wished to come to court, Anne would grant her exemption from the duty of carrying her gown.[39] No doubt Anne was sincere: but the bargain was once more wholly one-sided. And Mary told Anne's aunt that she did not care for the offers Anne had made, defiantly adding that she would rather die a hundred times than change her opinion or do anything against her honour and conscience.

Anne responded by writing a letter to her aunt that Chapuys thought—rather oddly, as it has more the character of a threat—might be called a defamatory libel against Mary; but Mary simply laughed at it.[40] Anne asked her aunt to make no further attempts to persuade Mary to acknowledge the king but leave her to choose her own course of action. Anne insisted that what she had previously attempted had been done from charity, since neither Henry nor she cared what road Mary took, or whether she would change her purpose. 'For when I have a son, which I hope will be soon,' Anne continued, 'I know what will happen to her.' Considering the command of God to do good to one's enemy, Anne had very much wanted to warn her beforehand. She had daily experience of the king's wisdom and so knew that he would not value any 'forced repentance' by Mary for her 'rudeness and unnatural obsti- nacy'. By the law of God and of the king, Mary ought clearly to acknowledge her error and bad conscience—if her affection had not so blinded her eyes that she would see nothing but what pleased her.[41] Was this letter, found in Mary's oratory, deliberately dropped there with the intention of intimidating her?[42] We know of it only from Chapuys's despatch—but it is unlikely that either he or Mary, who evidently informed him, would have made it up.

In his consideration of Anne Boleyn's attitude to Catherine and Mary, Eric Ives, who usually sees Henry as manipulated by courtiers and wives, and especially by Anne Boleyn, questions whether Anne's influence and role in putting Catherine and Mary under pressure was as significant as Chapuys makes out: it was Henry, he argues, who was bent on breaking his daughter's will, as he finally did in June 1536, a month after the execution of Anne Boleyn, but 'it was Anne Boleyn . . . who got the blame'. If it appeared to the world that it was Anne who was the evil genius, then it would be easier for Charles V to remain at peace with Henry and to contemplate an alliance; if it appeared that Anne was responsible for all those petty humiliations, it would be less heart- breaking for Mary than if she thought they came from her revered father.[43] And that is surely right, another example of Henry's political skill at directing policy while allowing others to shoulder public respon- sibility for it. Still, it is entirely possible that Henry and Anne egged each other on. And if Anne did cajole Henry into taking more and more intimidating measures against Catherine and Mary, it is easy to understand why she did. If Anne's language against Mary was 'violent and threatening', quite plausibly such angry menaces sprang 'not from malevolence but from self-defence': at the least, Anne's behaviour was readily comprehensible.[44] If, however, she did go on to talk of having Mary poisoned or executed, as Chapuys insisted time and again—and we have no way of knowing whether he was well informed about what Anne said or intended to do—then she did independently go beyond what Henry would have been prepared to accept.

'I have done many good deeds in my life'
ANNE BOLEYN'S RELIGION

If Anne took against Catherine and Mary, that is not very surprising, though not uplifting. But how far were Anne's actions not just personal but religious in thrust? Beyond the break with Rome and the royal supremacy, was she 'the first to demonstrate the potential there was in the royal supremacy for that distinctive element in the Reformation, the ability of the king to take the initiative in religious change'; was it the case that as an 'active promoter of the gospel', she 'promoted evangelical reform principally in terms of promoting reforming clerics'; was she 'a key element' in the English Reformation, 'a thousand days of support for reform from the throne itself'?[1] Is it convincing to claim for Anne that 'in both her private life and public policy, she was a fervent and committed evangelical'?[2] In short, did Henry VIII's break with Rome and subsequent religious changes owe a good deal to the influence and patronage of Anne Boleyn?

That was certainly broadly the impression given by two men who wrote in the early years of Anne's daughter Elizabeth's reign. William Latymer was one of Anne's chaplains; he was dean of Peterborough from 1560 to 1583. At the beginning of Elizabeth's reign he offered her an account of her mother's life.[3] Latymer's image of Anne was that of a godly lady. Anne helped those who suffered persecution, showing 'constant affection towards the poor gospellers'. She was especially critical of abbots for their 'licentious life'. Monks she saw as 'unprofitable drones' who obstinately refused to follow true religion.[4] Above all, they had sworn obedience to the pope, and especially his 'detestable slight and frivolous ceremonies' as the pillar of their 'fantastical' religion. By contrast Anne was presented as a highly moral queen. She told her council, 'you are commended to be men of great honesty, modesty, wisdom and experience such as wholly embrace virtue and utterly detest and abhor vice': they should show it by their 'virtuous conversation and government'.[5] They should see that her servants 'frequent no infamous places of resort nor yet that they keep no company with evil lewd and ungodly disposed brothers'.[6] Anne deliberately appointed chaplains to be 'the lanterns and the light' of her court, with express instructions to reprove her if ever they saw her 'yield to any manner of sensuality'.[7] That they never had to do. But they watched over her court and they 'reprehended divers and sundry persons as well of their horrible swearing as of their inordinate and dissolute talk together with their abominable incontinency'. When they found certain persons 'incorrigible' they denounced their 'unhonest demeanour' to the queen.[8] Moreover Anne was charitable, giving alms to the poor weekly, including grants to men to buy livestock, and handed out clothing when she went on progress. On Maundy Thursday, humbly 'kneeling on her knees, she washed and kissed the feet of simple poor women'.[9]

The martyrologist John Foxe was even bolder in his encomium of Anne: 'what a zealous defender she was of Christ's gospel all the world doth know, and her acts do and will declare to the world's end'.[10] Already in 1559 he had declared that 'the entire British nation is indebted to her . . . for the restoration of piety [and] the church'.[11] He offered a similar impression to Latymer of Anne's virtue and piety. There was no idleness among her ladies and gentlewomen and 'of her own accord [she] would require her chaplains plainly and freely to tell whatsoever they saw in her amiss'. Foxe presented Anne as an influential patron: she was a 'comforter and aider of all the professors of Christ's gospel . . . her life being also directed according to the same'; she maintained many learned men in Cambridge and brought them into favour with the king; so long as Queen Anne lived, the gospel had 'indifferent' success.[12]

Too readily, these characterisations by Latymer and Foxe have been accepted without much questioning by historians. Yet their polemical purposes must not be overlooked. Neither was simply writing an account of what had happened a generation earlier. Both were trying to influence the developing Elizabethan religious settlement. Neither saw what was set out in 1559 as the final word. Both hoped that Queen Elizabeth would embark on further religious reform. In that quest, what had been aimed at in her father's reign took on a special significance. The more that policy in Henry's reign could be seen as reforming, the stronger the case for further reform under Elizabeth. Such measures could then be presented as continuing what Henry had begun rather than as some revolutionary novelty.

More importantly, in presenting Anne as a modest and virtuous patron of religious reform, Latymer and Foxe were by implication suggesting that so devout a lady could not possibly have been guilty of those shocking adulteries for which she had been condemned. Since Anne's execution, little had been publicly said or written in her support; the accession of her daughter was a good moment to put that right. But if such were Latymer's and Foxe's purposes, perhaps what they wrote was something less than the whole truth; maybe they exaggerated, invented or misinterpreted Anne's religion, and what they wrote about her modesty may have been misleading too.

John Foxe's martyrology is a monumental achievement. It would be unfair to say that his scholarship was corrupted by polemic, but in places there are distortions. In recording and interpreting his detailed evidence of the Marian martyrs in Kent, he 'presented as true protestants and co-religionists men and women who were nothing of the kind but rather rank heretics of a more extreme and eclectic kind'.[13] In his account of the London merchant Richard Hunne, Foxe again offered a confused impression of his religious beliefs.[14] The modern editor of Latymer's life commented that he 'deliberately suppressed all material relating to Anne which is not consistent with Latymer's portrait of a pious and solemn reformer'; 'the author's aims of rehabilitating Anne and advising Elizabeth led him to wander somewhat from the truth on occasion'.[15] Both Latymer and Foxe emphasise the godly living to be found in Anne Boleyn's court. Even an historian who has most forcefully argued for Anne's religious commitment has conceded that Latymer was 'committed to portraying Anne as the archetypal "godly matron" and so very ready to air-brush out anything worldly'.[16] We shall return to this when we scrutinise the charges of adultery brought against her and the rather more fun-loving impression they give of how Anne and her servants lived. Here we shall focus rather on the evidence for Anne's religious convictions and actions. Neither Foxe nor Latymer offers much specific detail about Anne's religion. They stress her pious way of life and they claim that Anne supported defenders of the gospel, but they do not say much about her beliefs.

Was Anne a Lutheran? In her possession she did, it appears, have books by Simon Fish and William Tyndale, both of them influenced by Martin Luther, the German friar whose protests against what he saw as abuses within the church had provoked what we know as the European Reformation. It was, however, anti-clericalism, rather than theology, that was the most immediately striking feature of Fish's *Supplication of the Beggars* and of Tyndale's *Obedience of a Christian Man*, and at a time when Henry was putting pressure on churchmen to support him over the divorce, such anti-clericalism would have struck a chord. But it would be risky to deduce from this that Anne was a Lutheran in the sense that she fully understood and supported Luther's theology. Chapuys repeatedly called her and her brother 'Lutherans', for example writing on 29 April 1536 that the concubine and all her family were such abominable Lutherans.[17] The problem here is that in Chapuys's mind, to break with Rome was in itself evidence of Lutheranism. Because the German princes who had repudiated the pope in the 1520s had done so in the name of Luther's teachings, it is understandable that Chapuys thought that Henry's action was similarly motivated. But Chapuys failed clearly to grasp the distinction between breaking with Rome for essentially personal and jurisdictional reasons, as Henry was to do, and breaking with Rome for more theologically driven reasons. Anne and Rochford seemed 'Lutheran' in his eyes simply because she had precipitated the break with Rome and because they both supported it. Looser still is Chapuys's report of what the French ambassador told him in early 1534. When Henry had denied any intention of following the Lutheran sect, the ambassador had commented that in the end Anne Boleyn would induce him to be worse than Lutheran, as she herself was—though he cited no evidence.[18]

Anne wrote no works of religion from which we might assess her exact convictions. That is to ask a good deal of a queen, it is true, but Catherine Parr, Henry's last queen, would produce several works, notably the *Lamentation of a Sinner*: Anne did nothing of the kind. It is striking that the Frenchman Lancelot de Carles who was resident in the French ambassador's house and who wrote a metrical poem on Anne's fall never describes her as Lutheran or evangelical.

Historians who present Anne as a religious reformer make much of her interest in the Bible: she allegedly had a passionate commitment to the scriptures as the word of God, and her 'central conviction was of the overwhelming importance of the Bible'. This owed much, it has been speculated, to her early residence at the French court and her supposed contacts there with scholars such as Jacques Lefèvre d'Etaples (*c*.1460–1536), translator of the Bible.[19] Latymer noted that Anne was 'very expert in the French tongue, exercising herself continually in reading the French Bible and other works of like effect and conceived great pleasure in the same'. She possessed a copy of the 1534 Antwerp edition of Lefèvre's 1528 translation of the Bible into French.[20]

According to Latymer, Anne often talked about the scriptures with Henry. That is by no means impossible, though Latymer is our only source. Thomas Alwaye, arrested for possessing an English Bible and other banned literature, appealed to Anne, recalling 'how many deeds of pity' she had done 'without respect to any persons, as well to strangers and aliens', poor and rich. He petitioned Anne, perhaps at the end of 1530, to allow unrestricted sales of the Bible: but nothing he said about Anne offers specific evidence of her religious convictions. And that he petitioned her—as his petition survives only in draft, it may not have been sent—need mean no more than that he thought she might be sympathetic and influential.[21] Did Anne help win the king's tolerance of English bibles? The evidence cited for that claim is that three copies of Cromwell's 1536 injunctions to the clergy include instructions to provide bibles in English and Latin in the choir of their churches 'for every man that will to look and read thereon', and present the Bible as 'the very word of God and the spiritual food of man's soul'. And it has been suggested that after Anne's fall, Cromwell removed this article from his injunctions, which is why most of them do not include it. Unfortunately there is absolutely no evidence for the dating of the drafts which do, nor of any involvement of Anne, so it is the merest surmise to see her hand in this.[22]

The central difficulty with such a line of reasoning is that a heightened interest in the Bible was widespread in the 1520s and 1530s and owed as much to Erasmus, who remained within the catholic church, as it did to Luther or Zwingli. It has been well said that to note 'the dominant place in life which Anne Boleyn gave to the Bible is to locate her firmly in the world of Christian humanism'.[23] More is needed convincingly to make Anne out as an 'evangelical' if by evangelical is meant someone who was opening the floodgates to the ideas of Martin Luther or Huldrych Zwingli, the fathers of what came to be called protestantism. Anne's possession of the 1534 edition of William Tyndale's translation of the New Testament is intriguing, but its luxurious form—on vellum, with many woodcuts in full colour and with gilded edges—strongly suggests that it was sent to her as a present, by Tyndale or one of his associates (we know that another reformer, George Joye, would send both Henry and Anne extracts from Genesis the following year). Although it is interesting that Anne did not destroy what was considered an heretical book because of the prefaces and marginal annotations, and in places tendentious translations, that followed Luther's teaching, in no way does this offer convincing proof that Anne herself was a Lutheran. A story told by William Latymer that Anne gave the nuns of Syon prayer books in English, lecturing them on their ignorance, is very doubtful. It ignores the fact that since the early fifteenth century the nuns of Syon had had copies of the *Mirror of Our Lady*, a translation of the Brigittine office made by Thomas Gascoigne with the explicit intention that those nuns who found Latin difficult should understand their religious offices. In effect the nuns of Syon possessed a vernacular primer that in some respects anticipated the Book of Common Prayer, for it included English texts of the Lord's Prayer, the Hail Mary, the Nicene Creed and the Gloria. It is also possible that Syon possessed English bibles. All of this would make it puzzling that Anne should have berated the nuns of Syon.[24] The best detail that can be offered in support of Anne's interest in the Bible in English is a letter she wrote on behalf of Richard Hermon, a merchant and citizen of Antwerp, who claimed to have been expelled from his freedom and fellowship just for setting forth the New Testament in English in Wolsey's time. That hints at some sympathy, but it is hard to know how much weight to give it: Anne's sympathy may simply have been personal.[25]

Several scholars have looked closely at the books and manuscripts that Anne and her brother acquired. They claim that these texts show that Anne was an 'evangelical': 'imported books ... underline her cultural and religious orientation: France and evangelism'; Anne was 'visibly aligning herself with reform through the *reading and display* of these impressive manuscripts'.[26] The term 'evangelical' is somewhat loosely deployed. Historians using it have in mind a set of beliefs no longer wholly orthodox, but not—yet—fully aligned with the teachings of Luther or Zwingli, though somehow pointing the way to protestantism. But that is not how the term was used by contemporaries. When Thomas More called William Tyndale 'evangelical' he meant that he was quite definitely a protestant, that he was was attached to Luther's doctrine of justification by faith alone. When historians use the term they consequently risk confusion since *evangelisch* is the accepted German term for 'Lutheran'. And they do not confront the objection that beliefs and actions they describe as 'evangelical' may well have reflected not some protestantism or proto-protestantism but rather a deeply felt yet entirely traditional ascetic catholicism.[27]

How many such books and manuscripts are there? In effect, these arguments rest on three known texts only. First, there is a manuscript in the Harleian collection in the British Library, Harleian MS 6561, presented to Anne, marchioness of Pembroke. That style dates it to between 1 September 1532, when she was created marchioness of Pembroke, and April 1533, when she was publicly referred to as queen. Anne's heraldic arms appear on the title-page and once later (on the top side of folio 4); and then Anne's heraldic lozenge and Henry's cipher HENREXSL alternate. The text of the work is based on Jacques Lefèvre d'Etaples's *Epistres et Evangiles des cinquante et deux semaines de l'an* (printed by Simon du Bois at Alençon in 1530–32), following the second edition by Pierre de Vingle, of a work first printed in *c*.1525. *Pistelles and gospelles—Epistles and Gospels*—as our text was entitled, comprises some fifty-two readings, one for each week of the year, from the epistles and gospels, each followed by a homily: in this text the homilies, but not the readings, have been translated into English.

It has been argued that Anne Boleyn herself commissioned the translation. In the preface—in the first sentence, which can be read only under ultraviolet light—its author describes himself as Anne's 'most loving and friendly brother' and refers to 'the perpetual bond of blood' between him and his patron. It has been supposed that 'brother' was short for 'brother-in-law' and that Henry Parker, Lord Morley, commissioned it; but it has been argued strongly that there is no reason to doubt that 'brother' means 'brother', not 'brother-in-law' or brother in some looser sense; in other words, Anne's brother George, Viscount Rochford. There is also an unreadable cipher that, it is guessed, contains Rochford's name. The brother declared that 'by your commandment I have adventured to this, without the which it had not been in me to have performed it'. Rochford was fluent in French and it would not have been an intellectually challenging task to have undertaken the translation. Maybe Rochford's later remark, on the scaffold, that men talked of him as 'a setter forth of the word of God', and his lament that 'if I had followed God's word in deed as I did read it and set it forth to my power, I had not come to this', offers a little oblique support: ' "set it forth" may well describe the translating activities he so actively (and learnedly) espoused'.[28] What might give some pause, however, is that there is no other evidence of Rochford's literary activities. A somewhat different impression of his interests is offered by the book of royal privy purse payments between 1529 and 1532. In July 1531 Rochford received £58 for shooting with the king at Hampton Court, and a further £3 7s. 6d. shooting money on 26 August 1531. In January 1532 Rochford was paid £45: he had defeated the king at 'shovillabourde' and also won bets he had placed on the game; he won a further £36 and £5 12s. 6d. the following month. In April 1532 he and his father were paid £9, £32 5s. and £13 10s., won from the king and Mr Bainton at bowls. In June Rochford won £18—'so much money'—from the king 'at the pricks and by betting'. In October Rochford won 45s. from the king for a wager involving a brace of greyhounds.[29] What such payments reveal is that Rochford's interests were more those of a courtier-nobleman than of a scholar. So committed a gamer and sportsman might well have struggled to find the time to translate Lefèvre d'Etaples. While the French of his work is not especially difficult, what must strike any modern reader is the sheer scale of the book, some 202 folios, that is 404 pages. The untranslated extracts from the Bible are far shorter than the translated commentaries. To undertake translations of some fifty-two commentaries, each two or three pages long would be the mark of a dedicated scholar, not some amateur. Of course, it is just thinkable that Rochford applied himself with precisely such scholarly devotion, but on balance it seems implausible that a man revealed in all other sources as a conventional courtier should have spent so many hours on the task. And it might be thought that a brother would not begin a dedication to his sister by declaring that 'our friendly dealing with so sincere and sundry benefits besides the perpetual bond of blood have so often bound me Madam inwardly to love you daily to praise you and continually to serve you'. Would a brother talk of 'friendly dealing' with his sister? Would a brother need to say that he inwardly loved his sister? Would a brother daily praise his sister? Would a brother address his sister quite so formally? It is a matter of judgement, but arguably this is the language of flattery being used by someone who was not that close to the person being praised. His self-description as a 'welwyller' is intriguing in this context too. Referring to his 'experience of your gentleness daily proved', wishing to offer her a gift, he had sent her neither jewels of which she had plenty, nor pearls nor rich stones of which she had enough, but 'a rude translation of a welwyller, a good matter meanly handled'.[30] Is that what a brother would say and do?

Much turns on what this work advocates. Was it a work of protestant, or proto-protestant, piety, going significantly beyond what the church was saying or Henry VIII was doing? The very format of the work—fifty-two readings from the scriptures followed by fifty-two homilies or what we should call lectures, intended in turn for each Sunday of the year—shows an author anxious that the Bible should be read, and, as important, expounded in a distinctive way, to the laity. Such a concern was indeed central to the teachings of Luther and Zwingli, but so it was to those of Erasmus and to a wide range of writers who never broke from the catholic church. Close attention to scripture is not in itself an infallible test by which a protestant or a protestant-in-the-making may be identified. Much of the work consists of rather dense but hardly controversial exposition. There is a good deal of moralising. 'The life of a christian man in this world . . . is but a continual war', that is to say a war against the flesh. 'If you mortify (by the spirit) the works of the flesh you shall live'. We should show charity: 'the faith that we have without charity is no faith for it is but a dead faith an unperfect faith and not lively for the lively faith worketh by charity'.[31] That the work was condemned by the Sorbonne might suggest that it was heterodox. But the Sorbonne took a hard line and condemned much that was generally seen as reformist, so it would be unwise to make too much of that.

In two respects the *Epistles and Gospels* is indeed striking. First, the author undoubtedly emphasises the central role of Jesus Christ.[32]

> Our great advocate. Our mediator is Christ. The true host is Jesu Christ which have suffered death and passion for to save us the which in shedding his precious blood upon us all hath given unto us life hath wholly purged us of sin. . . . He is our shepherd; let us follow him unto the pasture of life. He is our bishop, our mediator, our intercessor, our host. . . . Let us have true faith that none goeth away without being exalted who hath faith in him. There was never so great a sinner but that this host hath satisfied for him if he hath this faith.

Such an emphasis was, of course, in itself far from heretical. It was more the tone that was problematic, hinting at larger implications. Only very occasionally does the writer tease these out. 'It is God and our Lord Jesus Christ that we ought to call upon and not angels or any other creatures and it is he to whom we ought to commend our souls,' urged the writer.[33] More specifically, the writer challenged the elevated status of what was called Trinity Sunday, the first Sunday after Whit Sunday: 'though it be called Trinity Sunday, we ought not to repute it to be a particular feast of the Trinity as is accustomed to make particular holy days for it is an universal feast'; 'there is no particular feast but they be all universal and of God. God is universal.' It was not a particular solemnity:[34]

> if it were understood to be particular, there would be made more greater holy days and solemnities of many other which be under the

name of creatures than of this unto the which is given octaves and not unto this. We must not then put God in the company of creatures or unto the creatures but above them all for ever and universally not particularly.

That was much more explicitly to challenge the church's liturgical calendar. 'Particular holy days'—or saints' days—were an integral and vital part of the practice of worship. The *Epistles and Gospels* flatly ignores them: the readings and homilies are designed for weekly worship on Sundays; the vast number of saints' and holy days simply do not feature. The challenge to the special place of Trinity Sunday apart, nothing is said; but any reasonably devout reader or auditor would quickly realise that something quite radical was afoot. Intriguingly, this anticipates what was to be attempted in summer 1536—after Anne's execution: the abolition of individual saints' days, something to which Henry remained committed to the end of his reign.

And it is indeed what is absent from the text as much as what is present that gives the work its impact. There is nothing about the church as an institution, nothing about the pope, nothing about bishops (only Christ is described as a bishop), nothing about parish priests, nothing about chantry chaplains. There is nothing about saints, nothing about intercessory prayer or purgatory (apart from the veiled remark quoted above), nothing about ceremonies. This is not an openly polemical work attacking or satirising the alleged abuses of the late medieval church. 'We should be none idolators,' the writer says, but without going into condemnatory detail.[35] But it is not a characteristic work of devotion either. The writer has plainly been influenced by the letters of St Paul and Augustine's exposition of them. The renunciation of the world in exhortations such as 'Let us then be poor of spirit seeing nothing in this world nor walking in the world; and we shall finally feed with the glory of God which is a glory above all glories a richesse above all richesses' is striking.[36]

How then should the work be classified, and what does it tell us about Anne Boleyn's beliefs if she did indeed, as the preface states, ask for the work to be translated? It does not show compellingly that Anne was a Lutheran or even that she was moving towards Lutheranism. It does suggest some detachment from 'traditional religion', the devotional practices of the late medieval church, pilgrimages, intercession to saints, monastic prayer. Implicitly it suggests a critical attitude to the institutional church. It may be that the writer was on the move theologically. But equally it may be that the writer was no more and no less on the move than Reginald Pole and his circle in Padua, scholar-theologians who while developing ideas not unlike those of Luther nonetheless remained firmly committed to the unity of the catholic church and abhorred Luther's schism. And for Anne Boleyn to have identified with this, assuming for the sake of argument that she did, and fully understood what was going on, would not make her a protestant or protoprotestant but rather sympathetic to an ascetic strand in late medieval catholicism. Despite the emphasis on Christ as saviour and on faith— 'how then can we attribute to ourselves any goodness and to say that we have done it when Jesuchrist which was all good all mighty all knowing did not attribute any thing to him self but all to his father'[37]—there is no explicit Lutheran-style statement of justification by faith. The striking illuminated image of Christ on the cross on the title-page, with the Virgin in prayer, is entirely conventional. And, incidentally, anyone wanting to see this style of piety as in some way anticipating modern liberal values might ponder the significance of the sentence: 'truth it is also that we ought not to suffer any infidels that were jewes for to enter in among us for whom the apostles did shut their doors'.[38]

Closely linked to this translation is a manuscript called the *Ecclesiaste*, now in Alnwick Castle (Percy MS 465), a copy of a work printed in Alençon in 1530, with the commentary translated into English. The claim that it was 'made for Anne' depends on the presence of her shield of arms at the centre of the front cover. The decorated brass clasps are very probably by Holbein. The first initial has the arms of Henry impaling those of Anne, and elsewhere H or A or HA, together with Anne's motto 'The most happy'. All of this strongly suggests that Anne commissioned the volume, though that heraldic evidence could readily be used in support of the claim that it was Henry who was the sponsor. Both this text and the *Epistles and Gospels* are in the same hand and while the decoration is clearly different, stylistically it is close. It is thus highly likely that this work was indeed commissioned by Anne for herself. And it has been suggested that Rochford was also responsible for this text.

The text derives from a translation into French by Johannes Brenz from Ecclesiastes. Again its content has been used to argue that Anne was an 'evangelical', proto-protestant: the doctrine of this book 'could well have seemed heretical' in England in the 1530s. But once again the emphasis on the need to make scripture available to the layman is not itself compelling proof of heretical tendencies. The remark 'all things without God are vanity' is entirely orthodox, hinting at an ascetic and austere devotion, though later feasts and merriment are defended.[39] There is again nothing about the church, nor about the role of priests, nor about sacraments, which can be read as an implicit critique. All in all, however, it is not a work that offers very specific information on the writer's theology, let alone on the religious convictions of any of its readers.

The question has been asked why Anne, who could read French, should commission her brother (if it was him) to produce part-translations of these texts. These manuscripts were not made for general circulation. Maybe the scribes and illuminators were uneasy at producing the text of the Bible in English; or maybe Anne was so used to the text of the Bible in French that she did not want it translated.[40] Perhaps the aim was to display the works at court, to share them with the ladies of Anne's household. Or perhaps Rochford was just showing off to his sister, offering her a 'rather smart gift', perhaps on the occasion of her marriage to Henry.[41]

The third manuscript associated with Anne Boleyn is *Le Sermon du bon pasteur* or *Le Pasteur évangélique* (perhaps by Clement Marot, or, if a revision is to be believed, by Almanque Papillon). This survives with an additional ending in praise of Henry and Anne, from which (and from Anne's arms on the front) it has been seen as written, or at least adapted, for her. But it may have been intended more for Henry VIII than his queen: the additional final verses (not found in other versions of the text) praise him much more than they do Anne, who, the poet hopes, will conceive a son who will be the living image of his father, the king. One speculation is that it was a coronation gift by the French ambassador, Jean de Dinteville.

Its title, *Le bon pasteur*, implicitly suggests the church is full of wicked priests. It is a commentary on John 10. Was it 'another most persuasive demonstration of Anne's link with French reform'?[42] Yet its exact theological message is hard to characterise as unorthodox. True, it makes an absolute distinction between the Bible and tradition; not a father of the church, not a doctor is cited. But once more, apart from a general sense of the church's need for reform, little that is explicit and detailed can be found here.

In addition to the three manuscripts discussed here, Anne also possessed a copy of the 1534 Antwerp edition of Lefèvre's 1525 translation of the Bible into French. This included the text front and back: 'as all die by Adam, so all will be revived by Christ'. But it would again be difficult to make a great deal of this in considering Anne's convictions.

Intensive bibliographical research into the king's library suggests that the score or so French books published between 1527 and 1534, mostly printed by du Bois, which are now in that collection were originally acquired by Anne and her brother and found their way into the royal collection on Anne's and Rochford's fall. Obviously, if that was the case, it would consolidate the argument for Anne's interest in French theological writing in these years. This is offered some broad support by the remarks, in the early seventeenth century, by Rose Hickman, then in her eighties, about how her father, the mercer William Lock, brought foreign books for Anne: 'I remember that I have heard my father say that when he was a young merchant and used to go beyond sea, queen Anne Boleyn . . . caused him to get her the gospells and epistles written in parchment together with the psalms'. But some of the linkages are rather tenuous. For example, among Anne's books was an illuminated French psalter which had a cipher 'almost certainly' intending HENricus REX. The translation was 'perhaps' by Louis de Berquin, executed (in 1529) for his pro-Lutheran views.[43] This does not tell us very much about Anne's religion, and it is no evidence that Anne was Lutheran.

More problematic, however, is the significance of these works, especially the three manuscripts which can be directly linked to Anne. Most if not all these texts flirt with the concept of justification by faith alone, the central message of Martin Luther that men are saved not through their own efforts but only by the sacrifice of Christ on the cross. Yet these writers most likely reached their position not through the direct influence of Luther, but from their own reflections on the nature of salvation, especially as expounded by St Augustine of Hippo. These were years of theological ferment, and scholars and theologians, especially in northern Italy, were enthusiastically exploring such notions against the background of a general acceptance that the church was in need of moral reform. What such ideas would lead to was not yet settled. Luther was spectacularly schismatic, though as much because the church drove him out as because of any initial wish of his own. But the Italian theologians, of whom Gasparo Contarini was the most formidable, had no wish to reject the papacy or to set up an independent church. Where Lefèvre d'Etaples and the authors and editors of these three texts were heading is by no means sure. They were undoubtedly critical of the church of their day, they wanted reforms, they stressed man's wickedness and the saving grace of Christ in the strongest Augustinian terms. But although some of their works were condemned by the Sorbonne, they remained within the church and in royal favour. It is far from obvious that they supported Henry VIII's break with Rome and royal supremacy or even that their texts supported it or the further reforms that Henry and his advisers were contemplating, notably the dissolution of the monasteries.

Nor is it obvious that Anne Boleyn shared the beliefs expressed in the texts. Under arrest in the Tower in May 1536, Anne asked her gaoler Sir William Kingston, 'shall I be in heaven for I have done many good deeds in my days?'[44] The belief that it is the good deeds you have done that determine whether or not you will go to heaven is poles apart from the emphasis on the saving grace of faith: the belief that it is Christ's sacrifice on the cross that has saved mankind which is found in the works we have been considering. If Anne spoke these words then she simply cannot have been a Lutheran. What she expressed is wholly incompatible with any Lutheran theology of justification by faith alone. Should we give greater weight to Anne's words, as reported by Kingston, or to inferences from sentiments within texts possibly prepared for her? Quoting at length from the translation of Lefèvre d'Etaples and deducing 'if this was Anne Boleyn's experience of faith, then she was an evangelical by conviction and not just by policy' is a risky way of proceeding.[45] Would it not be safer to judge from Anne's own words? According to Chapuys, in February 1533 Anne told the duke of Norfolk that 'immediately after Easter she wanted to go on pilgrimage to Our Lady [of Walsingham] in the event she found that she was pregnant'. That reflects an entirely conventional faith in the efficacy of pilgrimages.[46] Again when in the Tower, Anne was very anxious indeed to receive the host.[47] That was an entirely orthodox attitude. But it was some way removed from the commentary in the *Epistles and Gospels* that 'the true host is Jesu Christ which hath suffered death and passion for to save us'. That Anne was orthodox on the doctrine of the mass is further suggested by her reaction when Tristram Revell, late scholar of Christ's College, Cambridge, wanted to present a translation of Francis Lambertus's *Farrago rerum theologicarum*, which denied the sacrifice of the mass, to her in early 1536: she refused it.[48] It is intriguing that, as we have seen, Anne should have got a man to say that he had had a revelation from God that she could not conceive while Catherine and Mary remained alive: revelations were much more the stuff of medieval religion than of protestantism.[49] So were prophecies such as those to which Anne gave credit, namely that a queen of England was to be burned.[50] And it is interesting that, as has been recently shown, 'there was nothing "protestant" about Anne's coronation'. What was insisted upon was 'the image of Anne as a traditional, catholic queen and the power of medieval precedent'. Nothing was explicitly said about the break with Rome, nor about royal supremacy over the church, nor about any religious reforms: instead the ceremonies of Anne's coronation were 'the most traditional, authentic and correct catholic ceremony that England had ever seen'. If Anne had been the 'evangelical' that so many suppose, it would surely have been possible for her to have found some way of indicating that on such an occasion.[51]

Much has been made of the Book of Hours formerly at Hever Castle in which Anne wrote the words 'le temps viendra/je anne boleyn'—'the time will come/I Anne Boleyn'—below a miniature of the Second Coming and the Resurrection of the Dead.[52] The phrase is the first part of an Old French proverb 'Unq jour qui vient qui tout paie': 'A day that comes that pays for all'. Does this further cement the claim that while Anne was in France she experienced a spiritual awakening? That is possible. Yet fearful anticipation of the Day of Judgment was entirely orthodox, once again reflecting a 'personally-felt ascetic catholicism'.[53] Moreover this may be to overlook the true significance of Anne's possession of a Book of Hours. Her annotation strongly suggests that this was a book she read and used; no such annotations mark the 'evangelical' texts considered above. And using a Book of Hours reflects a traditional catholic piety.

What of Cranmer's exuberant praise of Anne's love of God and his gospel?[54] It is worth noting that Cranmer trusted that Henry would in future bear no less 'interior favour' to the gospel than he did before, 'for so much as your grace's favour to the Gospel was not led by affection unto her'. But that 'favour to the gospel' need mean no more than the break with Rome, the denunciation of the pope, the criticism of smaller monasteries: that is to say, the king's policies to date rather than some supposed protestant or proto-protestant sympathies.

Anne's charitable activity is often presented as unproblematic evidence of her 'evangelism' or proto-protestantism. William Marshall dedicated his study of poor relief in Flanders, *The Form and Manner of Subvention or Helping for Poor People, Devised and Practised in the City of Ypres* (1535), to her with the intention that she should 'be a mediatrix and mean unto our most dread sovereign lord' to establish some such charitable provision.[55] From the fact that Henry came in person to the Commons in support of the poor law of 1536 it might be deduced that Anne had indeed persuaded him; though clearly other explanations of Henry's actions are also possible, most plausibly that he himself recognised the need for statutory provision for poor relief. That Marshall's dedication reflects any informed knowledge of Anne's interests is unlikely: dedicating a work to the queen is no more and no less than a shrewd political calculation. Foxe and Latymer both emphasised Anne's charitable activity. What is not so sure is what drove her charitable impulse. Religious conviction may well have been responsible, though we should be careful in attributing that to protestant conviction, since the medieval church was suffused by the urgent imperative to give to the poor. And there could have been an element of political calculation as well. It may be revealing that Anne should attribute the popularity of Catherine of Aragon to her distribution of alms.[56] Anne Boleyn was not a popular queen, so public and ostentatious charity was an obvious way for her to neutralise that poor reputation, in the manner of an Empress Josephine.

Much has been made of Anne's patronage of churchmen. Wishing to push England into an 'evangelical', or a protestant, direction, she secured, it is claimed, the appointment as bishops, and to other leading positions in the church, of men who were similarly committed to reform. Undoubtedly Anne saw some bishops as especially committed to her: under arrest in the Tower, she would speak of 'my bishops'. And, once again, John Foxe offers an account that sees Anne as influential. But we should be cautious in following him, and, in particular, be more willing to make careful distinctions. Anne's marriage to Henry, and her new status as queen, were, to say the least, controversial. Anne (and Henry) welcomed all the support they could get. When churchmen, and especially learned theologians and canon lawyers, elaborated and publicised Henry's case for a divorce, then both Henry and Anne were obviously appreciative. Once Henry broke with Rome, all churchmen were expected to make the king's case. Some, but not all, of the churchmen who backed Henry over the divorce and the break with Rome were also sympathetic to the religious teachings of Luther and other German and Swiss divines. How far Anne was aware of their evolving convictions in what was very much a period of religious ferment is open to doubt.

When a churchman was appointed to a bishopric in these years it is far from certain that the reason for such preferment was his reforming religious convictions rather than his straightforward readiness to support the divorce, the break with Rome and the king's marriage to Anne. If there is a single strand in all such appointments in these years, it is involvement in the making of Henry's case for his divorce. The most important factor in appointments to bishoprics in the early 1530s was not evangelical or Lutheran doctrine but participation in the diplomacy and elaboration of canon law that Henry's case required. John Stokesley was appointed bishop of London in July 1530. In the previous year he had been sent on a diplomatic mission to the king of France. Earlier in 1530 he had accompanied Anne's father on his unsuccessful journey to negotiate with the emperor in Italy. In September 1531 Edward Lee, the king's almoner, was appointed archbishop of York. He had been sent on an embassy to Valladolid in early 1529. His preferment may have been even more directly related to the king's search for his divorce: Chapuys reported talk that he had been appointed by the king in the hope that he would grant him his divorce, but, once installed, Lee changed his mind.[57] Stephen Gardiner, the king's secretary, had been heavily involved in the campaign for the divorce, his finest hour coming in 1528 when he persuaded the pope to issue a decretal commission that would, if the pope had not quickly had second thoughts, have allowed the commissioners definitively to pronounce Henry's first marriage invalid. He was appointed bishop of Winchester in September 1531. In the following year, however, he resolutely defended the church when the Commons' Supplication against the Ordinaries attacked the church courts, and, most probably, it was for that reason that he was passed over when Archbishop Warham of Canterbury died in August 1532.

It was Thomas Cranmer who was chosen. He too had worked assiduously on the king's case for his divorce. His distinctive contribution was the argument that whether Catherine's first marriage with Arthur had been consummated or not was irrelevant, thus disposing of Catherine's insistence that she had come to Henry a virgin.[58] That was amply sufficient to account for what would otherwise have seemed a startling promotion. Was it, then, Henry who promoted him, as Chapuys reported, or was Cranmer, as is so often said, Anne's man? Was he initially a Boleyn family chaplain? Yet the account in Foxe of how, after Cranmer had at a chance meeting first offered to the king some reinforcement of his case for the divorce, Henry had commended him to the care of Anne's father, does not support such a view. Foxe—unlike Latymer—did not link Cranmer's rise to Anne Boleyn's favour: instead he emphasised his part in the formulation of the defence of the king's divorce and saw his promotion 'as worthy for his travail'. That Cranmer would on Anne's arrest write to the king 'I was most bound unto her of all creatures living' need not mean more than that she had supported him after he had risen to prominence.[59]

The next episcopal appointment after Cranmer was John Salcot or Capon, appointed bishop of Bangor in summer 1533. He too had been engaged in the divorce, securing the opinions of Cambridge divines in 1530, and one of four whom Henry had put forward in July 1531 as neutral judges of the matter.[60] In autumn 1533 Rowland Lee was appointed bishop of Chester and Lichfield: he had worked hard to persuade Cuthbert Tunstall, bishop of Durham, and the Northern Convocation to accept the divorce earlier that year.[61] In March 1534 Thomas Goodrich was appointed bishop of Ely. He had served with other Cambridge divines on a committee pronouncing on the canon law of the divorce in 1530 and had been involved in correcting the king's pamphlet *A Glass of the Truth*.[62] Edward Foxe, the king's almoner, appointed bishop of Hereford in summer 1535, had accompanied Gardiner to Rome in 1528, had been very much involved in persuading the university of Paris to support the divorce in 1530 and 1531, and had then written a treatise on the difference between the powers of the king and the church in 1534, supporting the king's supremacy.[63] John Hilsey, who succeeded John Fisher at Rochester in 1535, had earlier been much concerned with securing the submission to the royal supremacy of the Observant Friars.[64]

In the appointment of all these bishops in the early 1530s it is hard to find much evidence of any direct involvement of Anne Boleyn. If anyone influenced the king, it is more likely to have been Thomas Cromwell, to judge from what scraps of comment on appointments survive. Rowland Lee's elevation was attributed to Cromwell by one of his correspondents who criticised him for it; another wrote that on hearing of Lee's elevation to Chester he would now reckon Cromwell bishop there himself. And it is true that Lee would frequently call Cromwell his friend and had thanked him for an earlier promotion. Salcot thought himself wholly bound to Cromwell for his goodness.[65] But by far the most common factor in these appointments is prominence in service to the king, often in positions close to the king such as secretary or almoner, and involvement in the making of the king's divorce. This leads to the conclusion that appointments to bishoprics were made by Henry himself.

Where does that leave Anne Boleyn? In just three cases some sort of argument can be made for her influence. Anne undoubtedly played a part in appointing William Barlow, who had earlier links to Anne's father, as prior of Haverfordwest. Barlow was then appointed bishop of St Asaph in January 1536 and of St David's in April 1536. But for neither promotion is there any evidence of Anne's role. Barlow was sent on royal diplomatic missions to Scotland in 1534, 1535 and early 1536, in themselves evidence of the king's trust and favour; correspondence shows him working closely with Cromwell. Maybe Anne put in a good word for him with Henry—but no record exists, and Barlow's appointments can readily be explained without bringing Anne's supposed influence into the equation.[66]

Hugh Latimer, raised to the bishopric of Worcester in 1535, was a fiery preacher, frequently summoned by senior churchmen to answer charges that he had provoked controversy, as in Bristol in 1535. John Foxe offers contradictory testimony. In one passage he has Anne placing him in the bishopric of Worcester, in another it was, he writes, 'through the procurement partly of Dr Butts [the king's physician], partly of good Cromwell . . . that he [Henry VIII] advanced him to the degree and dignity of a bishopric', without mentioning Anne. If any individual favoured him it was Archbishop Cranmer, who gave him the chance of preaching before the king in Lent 1534. Once again, it is obviously not impossible that Anne spoke decisively for him. Anne did lend him £200 towards the first fruits that he, like all newly appointed bishops, was bound to pay the king. Clearly she welcomed his elevation, yet Latimer's rise can be explained without invoking Anne's independent patronage.[67]

Finally, Anne also lent Nicholas Shaxton money towards his first fruits after he was appointed bishop of Salisbury in 1535.[68] Shaxton, more than Latimer, had earlier links to Anne: he had served as her almoner.[69] Like so many promoted in these years, he had been involved in the canon law of the divorce. In 1531 he had fallen under suspicion for unorthodox views on purgatory and clerical celibacy. Foxe clearly attributes his promotion to Anne. Yet Shaxton himself, when writing to Cromwell, was mindful of the many kind offices Cromwell had done him, especially in promoting him to the bishopric. Nonetheless it seems very reasonable to suppose that Anne may have played some part in her former almoner's elevation. That conceded, her role in episcopal appointments appears much less central than has become fashionable to assert. And if we see Henry as playing a leading part in the religious politics of these years, it would be even harder to suppose that Anne was acting independently and using her influence to pressurise the king. It makes much more sense to see Anne as engaged, with others, notably Cranmer and Cromwell, in a joint enterprise in which the king was the leader.

And if Anne, when in the Tower, spoke of 'my' bishops when she lamented 'I would to God I had my bishops for they wold all go to the king for me',[70] what is most striking here is not 'evangelical' piety but a rather secular, political, personal, possessive attitude to 'my' bishops. While this could be seen as evidence of a measure of her patronage, it might more realistically be taken as indicating Anne's political naïvety: those bishops who had apparently taken her part during the king's divorce and the break with Rome had not then been supporting her, but rather the king, to whom their primary loyalty was owed. It is interesting that none of these bishops attempted to save her in 1536.

In smaller ways and at lower levels, Anne supported individual priests and scholars. Foxe claims that Anne brought the future bishops Nicholas Heath and Thomas Thirlby to favour with the king; William Latymer said as much for Thomas Goodrich and John Skip.[71] Anne favoured scholars at Cambridge, for example John Aylmer. She had asked the abbot-elect of St Mary's, York, to allow Aylmer, who had also been a candidate for election, to continue his studies at Cambridge, which at that time the abbot-elect was ready to do. But, she now learned, the abbot-elect had not only called him from his learning but had required him to take on 'sundry rooms and offices' in the monastery, 'to the no little disturbance and inquietation of his mind, and to alienate him as much as may be from his said study and learning'. Anne asked the abbot-elect to allow Aylmer to return to Cambridge.[72] But it is hard to make a great deal of this. After all, it was far from unusual for queens to offer patronage, indeed it might be thought intrinsic to queenship. That she supported the petition by the university of Cambridge for exemption from tenths and first fruits suggests no more than a conventional sympathy with learning. What we have are some scraps of evidence of isolated instances of possible interest, intervention, protection or patronage, though these are often open to explanations such as compassion not requiring any specific pious commitment; moreover Anne's apparent interventions were not always effective. To read this as compelling evidence of Anne's supposed 'evangelical' religious

sympathies or her supposed desire to further 'reformed religion' is to
infer too much.

What Anne's patronage and involvement with churchmen more plausibly reflects is her commitment to the break with Rome, denunciation of
papal power and advocacy of the royal supremacy. When Anne
supported the French exile Nicholas Bourbon did she do so because of
his evangelical doctrine—or because he had been imprisoned in France
for 'that he had uttered certain talk in the derogation of the bishop of
Rome and his usurped authority'?[73] When urging Dr Crome to take up
the parsonage of Aldermary which she had obtained for him, she
asserted that the furtherance of virtue, truth and godly doctrine would
be not a little increased if he resided there: here Anne was certainly using
the language of reformers, but what she meant by 'godly doctrine' was
most likely to have been sermons denouncing the pope, and certainly
not Lutheran teaching.[74] And in so far as she did advance individuals'
careers, their needs, rather than any supposed programme of 'evangelical reform', most convincingly explain her patronage. Richard Lyst, a
dissident lay brother at the Observant Franciscan house at Greenwich,
wrote to Anne in February 1533 that he had often spoken and answered
in the king's cause and hers, for which he had been rebuked and
troubled; he had been called her chaplain in derision.[75] Earlier he had
thanked Cromwell for Anne's charitable benefits to himself and his
mother which much bound them to her; he had also informed to Anne
on Father Forest, who would not preach the king's matter; that is, he
refused to support the break with Rome.[76] And later he trusted that the
king and queen would be good and gracious to him.[77] But, significantly
for any perceptions of Anne's religion, what Lyst offered by way of
thanks was to say 100 masses for Anne's prosperous state, spiritual and
corporeal, as soon as he had taken priest's orders.[78] That suggests a very
traditional faith, un-Erasmian and non-evangelical. It is evidence more
of his religious beliefs than of Anne's, yet at the least this shows that he
did not know of her supposed radicalism. Later he wrote: 'I have made
a compound in iii glasses with waters', and said he had sent two of them
to the queen 'for a poor token', sending Cromwell the third. He had
formerly been the cardinal's servant, he went on, and had dwelt in
Cheapside for eight years, 'and made many waters for him, hypocras

also, and served him with spice, as he was both a grocer and an apothecary. These waters will keep their virtue and strength two years.'[79] Not
exactly justification by faith alone.

How keen was Anne on listening to sermons? When Cranmer
informed Latimer that the king was content that Latimer should preach
before him on Wednesdays in Lent, he advised him to prepare himself so
that 'you stand no longer in the pulpit than an hour, or an hour and a
half at the most', since 'by the long expense of time' the king and queen
'shall peradventure wax so weary of the beginning that they shall have
small delight to continue throughout with you to the end', further
suggesting that Henry and Anne were not enthusiastic sermon-
gadders.[80]

There is no evidence that Anne pursued any active and sustained religious policy. There is nothing to suggest a continuing dialogue with
churchmen: no debates, no conferences of divines. If she had been
impressed by Marguerite of Angoulême she did not emulate her. After
all, if Anne was the patroness of religious reform that modern scholars
seek to portray, she was by no means successful. In these years Henry
broke with Rome and asserted his supremacy, but, up to the moment of
Anne's arrest in spring 1536, relatively little in doctrine and liturgy had
changed. James Bainham, Thomas Bilney and John Frith, unquestioned
reformers much influenced by Luther, and in Frith's case by Zwingli,
were burned for heresy in these years.

A summary characterisation offered of what is seen as Anne's
religion—'real spiritual experience, yes; the priority of faith, yes; access
to the Bible, yes; reform of abuses and superstition, yes; but heretical
views on the miracle of the altar, no'[81]—overlooks the extent to which
all of this was essentially Henry's policy, and that in so far as Anne
espoused that (and, as we shall shortly see, over ceremonies she may well
have been more conservative than the king), Anne was following where
Henry led.

And here there is a further twist that complicates the task of those
scholars who would see Anne as 'evangelical' or proto-protestant. In
early 1536, as the bill dissolving the smaller monasteries on grounds of
immorality and abuses made its way through parliament, a group of
bishops had been meeting to determine certain articles and to reform

ecclesiastical ceremonies, studies which were to result in the elaboration of the Ten Articles in Convocation in June. If Anne Boleyn was an evangelical as imagined by modern historians, she might have been expected eagerly to have embraced the reforming tide. She did not. Instead, on 2 April 1536 John Skip, her almoner, preached a quite extraordinary sermon in front of the king's counsellors in the royal chapel at Greenwich. It was explosive. We know of it from a summary which was presumably made on the orders of those most offended and from an interrogatory: a series of questions that were to be put to Skip, casting doubt on his motives.[82]

Skip preached on general themes as well as on specifically religious matters. He began by setting out his criteria of nobility, which 'standeth not in flesh nor blood' but in virtuous living, a commonplace distinction among contemporary humanist writers, and of kingship, namely good government of the commonwealth, again an unexceptionable sentiment. But then he ventured into deeper waters. He drew a contrast between how King Solomon began his reign as 'a very wise and noble king much beloved of his subjects because that he governed them very gently and wisely ever having respect to their common wealth' and how 'in the later end of his reign he became very unnoble and defamed him self sore by sensual and carnal appetite in taking of many wives and concubines. And also by avaricious mind in levying too great or sore burdens and yokes upon his subjects overpressing them too sore thereby'. The contemporary parallels hardly required spelling out.

The interrogatories pointedly asked what the example of Solomon could mean except 'that he intended in his mind to touch the king's grace with the said similitude. Albeit he showed not his mind in plain and express words, but by those words his audience conceived right well the malice of his mind as well by that general example as if he had coined the similitude particularly'. He was to be asked 'whether a preacher speaking generally of any notable crime or vice in such wise as all his audience doth as plainly perceive what person he meaneth as though he specified him by his name, doth slander that person'. In short, was Skip accusing Henry of avaricious exactions and of carnal living?

Skip had continued by telling the story of Rehoboam, Solomon's son, to whom the people turned, asking him to release the great yoke his father had laid upon them. Rehoboam responded by asking them to show patience till he had asked his counsellors: they said that he should indeed lift the yoke. But Rehoboam was himself greedy, and rejected their advice. Instead he 'counselled also with his younger counsellors whom he so had promoted and dangered [?] unto him by his gifts that for that and further promotions which they looked for, they would not advertise him to do any thing but such as they perceived or thought him inclined to'. And as they were struck by how determined he was to maintain the burdens on his people, they advised him to continue to do so, indeed to take even more from them. Such oppression provoked civil war. Not unreasonably, the interrogatories put to Skip asked him whether he had told the story of Rehoboam in order 'to put into the people's head that it were lawful for them if they were overburdened by the prince to fall from him and to rebel'.

Skip had boldly gone on to draw the lesson that 'a king had need to be learned him self and to know the state of his people', and continued, dangerously, to assert that 'his counsel nowadays will move him no otherwise unto any thing but as they see him disposed and inclined to the same'. That was an astonishing charge to make in front of those counsellors. Not surprisingly, the interrogatories asked whether by saying this he meant to accuse the king's council 'as flatterers and deceivers of the king's grace', and bitingly denounced the preacher's anticipated response: 'if he will say that he meant not of the king's council, then was his sermon not meet for the audience, for there were none other councillors of any other king present'. Having implicitly condemned the king's councillors for telling the king only what he wanted to hear, Skip went back to the theme of true nobility with a swipe against the English nobility of the day: any stranger who knew well what true nobility was would, if he came to this realm and saw those who were called noble, 'think plainly that nobility were hence clearly banished'.

And then Skip turned to more directly religious matters, beginning with the clergy. In considering what he said, we should bear in mind the orthodoxy of Anne Boleyn, so often portrayed as an 'evangelical' reformer by historians, and reflect on how compatible that notion is with what Skip, Anne's almoner, preached in April 1536. An 'evangelical' or a proto-protestant preacher would very likely have focused on the abuses and the inadequacies of the clergy, their ignorance, their immorality, especially their sexual immorality, their avarice, their neglect of their liturgical and pastoral duties. And all that would have been suffused with the lesson, implicit or explicit, that the clergy were not really necessary for salvation, because it was Christ who by his sacrifice had redeemed mankind. Just how acceptable such a sermon might have been would have depended on its tone and on how far it toyed with notions of justification by faith alone. After all, there was a long tradition of clerical criticism of the extent to which the clergy fell short of their professed ideals. Too vehement and sweeping a denunciation would, however, have risked provoking charges of heresy from the church hierarchy. Given Skip's moralising criticisms of king, councillors and nobility, one might have expected him to go on to attack the clergy on such lines. Certainly that is what an 'evangelical' or proto-protestant preacher would have done.

But Skip did none of that. Not only did Anne Boleyn's almoner not attack the clergy, he defended them. Christ, he said, had been a lesson to all preachers of God's word that they should live as near as they could without sin. So far, so conventionally idealistic, and potentially reformist. But Skip took another turning. 'Now,' he said, 'the clergy hath been rebuked and is much rebuked daily . . . nowadays many men take upon them to rebuke the clergy very sore far otherwise moved by their malicious mind or else because they would have from the clergy their possessions, rebuking them in every place at the table and elsewhere very sore in so much that if they may spy a great or notable vice or fault in one priest or any of the clergy then they will infame and rebuke all the whole clergy for the same.' That was a remarkable defence of the clergy. More strikingly still, Skip maligned the motives of the church's critics, presenting them as simply malicious, as greedy for church lands, as eager to condemn the whole church when an individual priest behaved badly, and as hypocritical, since they were far from perfect themselves. When Skip then conceded that many of the clergy did deserve to be rebuked, he managed nevertheless to turn that concession into a blow against their rebuker. If Skip on the face of it asserted that even sinners could rebuke the clergy, just as Nebuchadnezzar, 'sent as a minister of God to punish the Jews',

1 Letter from Anne Boleyn to her father, Sir Thomas Boleyn, written at La Vure (Terveuren), near Brussels, *c*.1513–14.

2 *Catherine of Aragon*, artist unknown.

3 Miniature attributed to Lucas Horenbout, thought to be Anne Boleyn, inscribed ANNO XXV (in her twenty-fifth year).

4 The Boleyn, Upton Park, London.

5 Hans Holbein the Younger, *Apollo and the Muses on Parnassus*,
design for a coronation pageant.

6 *Thomas Wolsey*, Papal Legate and Lord Chancellor, artist unknown.

7 Hans Holbein the Younger, sketch of a table fountain.

8 Portrait medal, inscribed A.R. [Anna Regina] 'THE MOOST HAPPI ANNO, 1534'.

9 *Anne Boleyn* by unknown artist, inscribed ANNA BOLINA UXOR HENRI (Anne Boleyn, wife of Henry VIII).

10 *Anne Boleyn* by unknown arist, inscribed ANNA BOLINA ANG REGINA (Anne Boleyn, queen of England).

11 Hans Holbein the Younger, unknown woman.

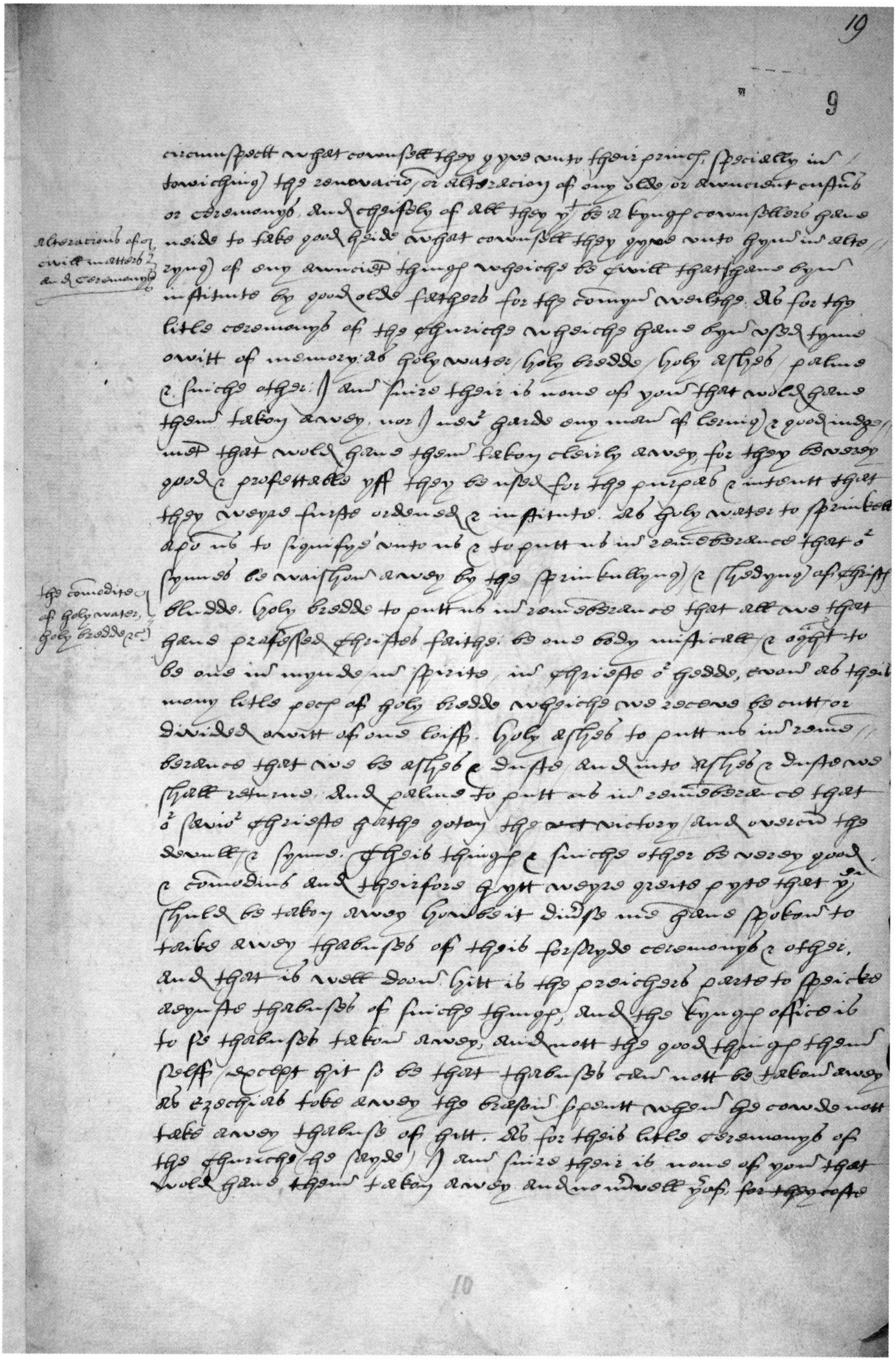

circumspecte what counsell they gyve unto their prince, specially in
touching the renovacion or alteracion of eny olde or auncient custums
or ceremonyes. And chiefely of all they ytt be a kynges counsellers have
nede to take good hede what counsell they gyve unto hym in alte-
ryng of eny auncient thinges whiche be civill that have byn
institute by good olde fathers for the comyn welthe. As for the
litle ceremonyes of the churche whiche have byn used tyme
owtt of memory: as holy water, holy bredde, holy asshes, palme
& suche other: I am sure their is none of you that wold have
them taken awey, nor I never harde eny man of lernyng & good iudge-
ment that wold have them taken clerely awey, for they be very
good & proffettable yff they be used for the purpos & intentt that
they were firste ordened & institute. As holy water to sprinkell
apon us to signifye unto us & to putt us in remembrance that our
synnes be waisshen awey by the sprinkellyng & shedyng of Christs
bludde. Holy bredde to putt us in remembrance that all we that
have professed Christes faithe be one body misticall & aught to
be one in mynde in spirite, in Christe our Godde, even as their
many litle pecys of holy bredde whiche we receve be cutt or
divided owtt of one loiff. Holy asshes to putt us in reme-
brance that we be asshes & duste and unto asshes & duste we
shall returne. And palme to putt us in remembrance that
our saviour Christe hathe goten the victory and overcom the
devull & synne. Theis thinges & suche other be very good
& comodius and therfore ytt were grete pyte that they
shuld be taken awey. Howbeit dyverse men have spoken to
take awey thabuses of theis forsayde ceremonyes & other,
and that is well done. Ytt is the precheres parte to speike
ayenste thabuses of suche thinges, and the kynges office is
to se thabuses taken awey, and nott the good thinges them-
selffs, except ytt so be that thabuses can nott be taken awey,
as Ezechias toke awey the brasen serpent when he cowde nott
take awey thabuse of ytt. As for theis litle ceremonyes of
the churche, he sayde, I am sure their is none of you that
wold have them taken awey and no man well [illegible]. for the reste

Alteracions of civill matters and ceremonyes

the comodites of holy water, holy bredde &c.

12 Part of the interrogation of John Skip, Anne Boleyn's almoner, April 1536.

13 Effigy of Elizabeth Browne, countess of Worcester, St Mary's, Chepstow.

14 Book of Hours, Paris, *c*.1528, inscribed 'Remember me when you do pray/That hope doth lead from day to day/Anne Boleyn'.

15 Hans Holbein the Younger, portrait of Henry VIII, *c*.1538.

16 Attributed to Jean and François Clouet, *Francis I*, *c*.1535.

had done, the sting was in the tail: Nebuchadnezzar was 'damned for his labour'. 'Is it not evident', asked Skip's interrogators, 'that he meaneth that the king's highness, whom he takethe to be a rebuker and punisher of the clergy (as it appeareth by his example of Nebuchadnezzar), shall be therefore rebuked of God as though the preacher knew the will and determination of God?' Skip was criticising Henry's purifying zeal against the clergy.

Skip went on to tell the story of Asseurus (Ahasuerus, or Xerxes, of Persia) and Aman (Haman) to illustrate 'that a king had need to be well wary what he doth after the counsel of his counsellors for some time for the malice that they bear towards many men, or towards one man of a multitude they would have the whole multitude destroyed'. King Asseurus, gentle and tractable, had a counsellor Aman who 'bare all the swing with him'. Aman bore a grudge against the Jews because of a private quarrel; he told the king how the Jews used strange laws and ceremonies and broke the laws of the realm, and said that if they were destroyed, that would enrich the king; Asseurus told him to go ahead; but a good woman—Skip did not name her, but in the biblical story she was Esther, the king's queen—warned the king of Aman's malice and told him that the Jews were innocent.

What was Skip so agitated about? Was it the dissolution of the smaller monasteries? Aman here is Thomas Cromwell, and the Jews are the monks; Anne is the good Esther who steps in to save them.[83] At first glance that looks a neat fit. But it does not work very well. As a protest against the dissolution it was too late: the legislation had gone through parliament. More importantly, that legislation did not aim to *destroy* the monks and nuns. Only the smaller monasteries were being dissolved, and monks and nuns who wished to continue were being offered the option of transfer to larger houses. The measure was being presented as one of reform. If Skip had intended to refer to the monasteries, then his analogy seems misplaced.

And most importantly of all, Skip went on to explain what he was about. In case his allusion was not clear, Skip repeated the need for princes 'to take good heed what counsellors they take about them, and their counsellors had also as moch need to be well wary and circumspect what counsel they give unto their princes *specially in touching the*

renovation or alteration of any old or ancient customs or ceremonies.[84]
And there Skip laid bare what concerned him: reforms that were in the
air to purge the church of supposedly superstitious practices.

That such reforms were undoubtedly on the agenda is confirmed by
Chapuys's report of a pamphlet sent to parliament listing a series of
measures against ecclesiastical ceremonies, images, worship of saints
and purgatory.[85] Just to remove any doubt about his intentions, Skip
went on to list the ceremonies which he was defending and to justify
them. 'As for the little ceremonies of the church which have been used
time out of memory as holy water, holy bread, holy ashes, palm and
such other I am sure there is none of you that would have them taken
away nor I never heard any man of learning and good judgement that
would have them taken clearly away, for they be very good and profitable
if they be used for the purpose and intent that they were first ordained
and instituted.' He then offered detailed justification:

> holy water to sprinkle upon us to signify unto us and to put us in remem-
> brance that our sins be washed away by the sprinkling and
> shedding of Christ's blood, holy bread to put us in remembrance that all
> we that have professed Christ's faith be one body mystical and ought to
> be one in mind in spirit in Christ our head, even as these many little
> pieces of holy bread which we receive be cut or divided out of one loaf,
> holy ashes to put us in remembrance that we be ashes and dust and
> into ashes and dust we shall return. And palms to put us in remembrance
> that our saviour Christ hath gotten the victory. And overcome the devil
> and sin.

Since such things were 'very good and commodious', it would be a 'great
pity' if they were taken away. It was right to take away the abuses of such
ceremonies—but not the good things themselves, unless it was impossible to take away just the abuses. 'As for these little ceremonies of the
churches,' he said, 'I am sure there is none of you that would have them
taken away and no marvel thereof for they cost you little and little ye
shall gain by the taking away of them.'[86]

All that was startling indeed. Skip was making a thoroughgoing
defence of religious ceremonies that he saw as under threat. It is highly

improbable that he would have spoken so forcefully in such a prominent place without Anne's approval. After all, if Anne took a different view, Skip's days as her almoner would surely have been numbered. Let us take it, then, that Skip was expressing Anne's sentiments. What does his sermon tell us about Anne's religious beliefs?

Some scholars have seen Skip as a reformer here because he did not attempt to defend the sacramental functions of these ceremonies, their 'objective sacred power'.[87] Indeed it is true that Skip did not present them as having apotropaic powers. But to read the sermon this way is to miss its tone. Skip was not attacking superstitious understandings of ceremonies: he was rather defending ceremonies, and defending them against those who wished to abolish them outright. Skip's stance was thus that of a conservative trying to block change. Preaching in front of the king's counsellors, he was seeking to persuade them. He sought to win them over by offering pragmatic justifications of these ceremonies, in terms of their stimulus to devotion and their function as reminders of key features of doctrine. This was not the place to treat ceremonies as quasi-sacraments, not least since that was something that many orthodox theologians and bishops had found uncomfortable because too close to superstition. But that should not be misread as offering any support for radicalism. On the contrary, Skip's defence of 'little cere-monies', not as matters indifferent but as positively beneficial, made it manifestly clear that further reformation would be damaging. And if Anne Boleyn shared Skip's forebodings, as seems highly likely, then Anne cannot be regarded as an 'evangelical' let alone a proto-protestant.

Lest there should be even the slightest doubt about Skip's—and Anne's?—hostility to reform, Skip then went on to criticise royal coun-cillors who went about to make 'renovations or alterations in civil matters that have been instituted for the common wealth by good men': that risked provoking complaints from the commons. And Skip, drawing on Demosthenes, told the story of the Locrenses who, much troubled by renovations and alterations in civil matters, by statute upon statute, devised a law that no man should bring into their parliament house any bill for the alteration of any civil matter unless he had a rope around his neck: if when his proposal was read, the people thought the bill against their commonwealth, they could pull the rope and strangle him. As a result they were spared alterations for a hundred years and more, for no one dared bring any bills.[88]

In response, the interrogatories to Skip asked him whether it was not necessary to have the ancient laws of the realm altered and renewed. 'Were not the eldest and most ancient laws of this realm once made new for the reforming of such inconveniences as were used at the time of making of them?' 'May not some ceremonies instituted by the old fathers be altered or be taken away according to the example showed by Christ?' And what was the preacher doing in preaching on civil and worldly matters which were no part of the preaching of the gospel? And was it not the provision that anyone bringing a bill to the parliament should bring a rope about his neck itself a new law contrary to the ancient custom of the Locrenses? 'It were a very good ordinance that such preachers as he is, should bring a rope about his neck into the pulpit that he might be hanged therewith when he falleth to slanderous tales and leaveth the gospel undeclared.' On the evidence of his sermon, Skip was undoubtedly a conservative—and that is how what he said was seen.[89]

Even more pointedly, Skip went on to give what appeared to be his favourable opinion of what went on in parliament. He insisted that nothing was done in 'this high council or court of parliament' except for the commonwealth, in modern terms for the good of the country,

> for there be most noble men of this realm, the most prudent and ancient fathers, the most expert men, the most high learned men ... there is no unquietness, no tumultuous fashion, there is no checking or taunting of any man for showing his mind, there is no man that will stand up and say that it is the pleasure of any person that this or this it should be, there speaketh not past one at once, and if his reason be good it is allowed. And if it be otherwise he is answered with gentle manner and fashion. There is no man speakethe for any carnal affections or lucre of the promotions of this world but all thing is done for zeal of the common wealth.

'This I think', Skip roundly declared, adding 'and other men ought to think the same'.[90]

Nothing, on first reading, could appear more innocuous—until it begins to seem too good to be true, and we realise that we must imagine Skip speaking with a teasing smile, tongue in cheek, for he really thought the opposite of what he was ironically saying. And his interrogators were not taken in. 'What goodness or honesty is in the said preacher to use such ironies or mocks against the parliament?' 'Let the preacher be examined upon his oath whether he spoke not all this sentence ironice [ironically] and mokkisshely [mockingly] in displeasure and rebuke of the parliament'. 'In all ironies', the questioner continued, 'the meaning is contrary to the words' and so the preacher 'meaneth the contrary by his irony': 'And so all the foresaid sentence is to be taken clean contrary to the words'.[91]

All this amounts to a truly astonishing sermon for Anne's almoner to have preached. In attacking innovations he was implicitly attacking much that had been done in recent years: in defending ancient ceremonies he was taking the side of those who did not seek radical reformation. Skip's ingenuity and his choice of time and place leave no doubt that he knew what he was doing and that his sermon was carefully calibrated to influence events. What is remarkable for us is what it shows about Anne Boleyn's religious convictions. If we can take the sentiments of her almoner—who would shortly be continually with her in the Tower as she awaited execution after she had greatly desired to have him there—[92] as approximating to her own, then Anne was no 'evangelical', no Lutheran, no proto-protestant, but deeply attached to the traditional liturgical ceremonies of the church properly defined and practised as aids to devotion and as reminders of the central teachings of the christian church.

That is confirmed by the evidence of Anne's fervent desire to have the sacrament when she was under arrest in the Tower. 'Jesu have mercy on me,' Anne implored, as her gaoler Sir William Kingston reported, and she 'kneeled down weeping a great pace'; then she 'fell to great laughing' and asked him to move the king that she might have the sacrament in the closet in her chamber so that she might pray for mercy.[93] Later the queen, Kingston reported, 'hath much desired to have here in the closet the sacrament'.[94] After her trial she strongly desired to be shriven. This is, of course, utterly conventional, and, given her arrest, in no way surprising. But that, precisely, is the point: there is no hint here of 'evangelical' or proto-protestant conviction. And we have already noted that Anne's question to Kingston, 'shall I be in heaven, for I have done many good deeds in my days?', shows that she had no grasp of justification by faith alone, the central doctrine in Luther's teaching.[95] Relevant here too is Chapuys's account of how when pregnant in July 1533 she solicited the king to ask Queen Catherine for a very rich and triumphant cloth which she had brought from Spain to wrap her children with at baptism.[96]

Anne's scaffold speech has often been considered as evidence of her religious beliefs but the differing versions of her words are rather inconclusive. George Constantyne, recollecting events three years later, claimed that at her execution she had said, 'I do not intend to reason my cause, but I commit me to Christ wholly, in whom is my whole trust',[97] but that could have been a misleading elaboration of the words that the chroniclers Hall and Wriothesley, and the lawyer Spelman more briefly recorded: 'To Christ I commend my soul'.[98] Foxe's rendering, 'O Lord have mercy on me! To God I commend my soul', offers further qualification.[99] It would be risky to use this to support notions of Anne as influenced by Lutheranism. A French poem that we shall be considering in depth later stressed (as did Chapuys) Anne's stoic acceptance of her fate, her denial of her crimes, her appeal to God whether she deserved her death, her regular contemplation of Christ and his passion, her devout preparation for the sacrament and her sure hopes of heaven; but if on the scaffold she asked for prayers to be said to Jesus for her sins so that her soul would not be burdened by them after she died, as the French poem says, that would imply a belief in purgatory.[100] Once again, there is nothing that clinches the case for Anne as evangelical or proto-protestant.

ANNE'S MISCARRIAGE

We saw Henry and Anne many times merry in late 1535. And then Anne became pregnant again before miscarrying in January 1536. Or did she? Ridolfo Pio, bishop of Faenza, and papal nuncio in France, reported gossip in March that she had *pretended* to have miscarried of a son and refused to allow anyone near her except her sister.[1] Anne supposedly invented her miscarried son in order to show Henry that she could still conceive sons and so deter him from leaving her, Dr Pedro Ortiz noted at Rome.[2]

Intriguingly, the Emperor Charles was evidently under the impression that Anne's childbearing days were over: in his instructions to Chapuys at the end of March, he declared that if the papal sentence against Henry were enforced, and Henry then gave up Anne Boleyn, the problem for the imperialists would then be that he might remarry; by contrast it was, the emperor noted, certain that Henry could have no children by Anne. And that maintained the position of Princess Mary. Charles was clearly right in dynastic terms to fear the consequences if Anne fell: when Henry remarried, and Jane Seymour bore him a son, Prince Edward took precedence over Mary.[3] Whatever the implications, it is nonetheless interesting that Charles assumed that Anne would never bear children again. If there was anything in that, it would obviously be thinkable that Anne, incapable of conceiving, again suffered a phantom pregnancy in these months. But more probable is that she did indeed become pregnant. The gossip that she did not is found only in despatches by diplomats far from England. By contrast, Chapuys, imperial ambassador in England, was in no doubt, as we shall see, that Anne had miscarried.

Did Anne's miscarriage in January 1536 mark a turning-point in her relationship with Henry? It must have been especially galling that it happened just days after the death of Catherine of Aragon. Henry had joyfully carried Princess Elizabeth in his arms immediately afterwards, so Chapuys reported.[4] When news of Anne's miscarriage arrived, Henry was undoubtedly dismayed. According to Chapuys, writing on 29 January, Henry now claimed that he had married Anne 'seduced and constrained by spells', as was evident from the fact that God did not allow them any sons: his marriage was thus invalid and he could remarry. Although he reported these fiery words, Chapuys seemed doubtful, glossing that 'the matter is pretty difficult for me to believe, even though it comes from a good place', one of the leading courtiers, whom he did not, however, name.[5] In December 1533 Chapuys had described how this accursed woman 'had bewitched and cast spells over him' so that Henry could neither say nor do except as she wanted and ordered him.[6] Chapuys reiterated Henry's despair a month after the miscarriage when reporting gossip that Henry, who previously could not bear to leave Anne for an hour, had not spoken to her more than ten times in three months. When she miscarried he had scarcely said anything except that he saw clearly that God did not want to give him male children. If Henry had indeed spoken like that, these were not kind remarks. But they ring true as something that a man in emotional turmoil might hurtfully say to his wife. Anne countered by attributing her misfortune in part to news of Henry's fall from a horse in January which left him concussed for a time, and in part to the depth of her love for the king, saying that she was heartbroken when she saw that he loved others. On hearing that, Henry had been very upset.[7]

Such an episode is ambivalent in meaning. It could reflect the accelerating disintegration of a relationship. It could be the first in a series of ever more acrimonious quarrels. But it need not be. It could as easily be just another outburst in a relationship that was undoubtedly difficult at times but rested on a fundamental union. Our glimpses are those offered by Chapuys, who was not well disposed towards Anne, critical of

Henry's cruelty to Catherine of Aragon and Mary, and by no means an intimate eyewitness of what he reported. And his reports were mixed, not offering a single view. He also wrote at this time how Anne consoled her maids who wept after her miscarriage, saying that it was for the best, for she would soon conceive again, and then the son she would have would be born free from any taint since he would have been conceived after Catherine of Aragon's death. It is intriguing that Anne should have implicitly acknowledged a doubt about the legitimacy of Princess Elizabeth, as Chapuys noted.[8] And on the whole Anne came out well—boldly refusing to allow Henry to criticise her unanswered.

Anne's miscarriage has often been invoked in explanations of her fall. We shall turn to the conventional accounts shortly, but first we must examine an extravagant expansion of such an interpretation: the notion that Anne did not simply miscarry in January 1536 but miscarried a deformed foetus, a notion that has proved surprisingly influential even though there is not a shred of evidence to support it. There is simply nothing to say that the foetus was deformed. The most that can be adduced is a passing remark of Nicholas Sander, a catholic exile writing in 1585, long after the supposed event, that Anne gave birth to 'a shape-less mass of flesh'.[9] Supposing for the sake of argument that Sander's information was accurate, his words are too vague to support the notion of a deformed foetus. Sander apart, this hypothesis depends entirely on supposition. Against Sander, there is contemporary evidence that the foetus was not deformed. According to Chapuys, it looked like a male child which Anne had only carried three and a half months.[10] The chron-icler Charles Wriothesley recorded that 'Queen Anne was brought abed and delivered of a man child, as it was said, before her time, for she said that she had reckoned herself at that time but fifteen weeks gone with child'.[11] According to a French poem written in June 1536 (to which we shall return), 'her full belly brought forth its fruit: she gave birth prema-turely to a handsome son who was stillborn over which she shed many tears'. De Carles's description, 'a handsome son', belies any belief in a deformed foetus.[12]

Was Henry's response to this supposed deformed foetus to denounce Anne as a witch? Miscarrying a deformed foetus was, supposedly, char-acteristic of witches. Deformities moreover were, allegedly, evidence of gross sexual misconduct. That Henry was responsible for such a foetus was unthinkable: accordingly, Anne had to be blamed. And so Anne was accused of reckless libertine behaviour—sleeping with five men, including her brother—of which that deformed foetus was the inevitable outcome. Anne's behaviour was more generally seen as that of a witch who had bewitched and seduced the king, afflicted him with impotence and conspired to poison his daughter Mary and his illegitimate son Henry, duke of Richmond.[13]

There is much that is bizarre here. Supposing that the foetus had indeed been deformed, it is hard to understand why giving birth to a deformed foetus should show that the mother was a witch. After all, witches might rather have been expected to have protected themselves from such misfortunes while inflicting them on others. None of the contemporary writers on witchcraft and demonology cited offer support for any such view. One of them tells how witches ripped healthy foetuses from their mothers' wombs or deployed aborted foetuses for evil purposes. The writer reflects on how children—normal children— of convicted witches should be dealt with.[14] Others wrote of witches whose touch alone could kill a foetus in its mother's womb or who could induce impotence or sterility.[15] Yet others discussed the monstrous children that devils could beget; but such children, sometimes monstrous, but sometimes 'tall, very hardy and bloodily bold, arrogant beyond words and desperately wicked', were the fruit of devils' sexual congress not with witches but with ordinary women.[16] There is nothing in any of these writings to support the claim that it was witches themselves who gave birth to deformed foetuses.

And just how seriously did Henry mean his remark about being bewitched by Anne? Chapuys is our source. The gossip was, he said, brought to him on behalf of the marquess and marchioness of Exeter, notoriously unsympathetic to Anne, and, Chapuys himself added, as we have seen, 'the matter is pretty difficult for me to believe, even though it comes from a good place'. But just supposing Henry really did say that he had been 'seduced and constrained by spells', surely his reference to Anne's bewitching him was simply a way in which in moments of anger or regret or despair he referred to his past infatuation with Anne. What he said in no way described her present behaviour, and it strains the evidence past breaking point to see the king as consistently regarding Anne as a witch. It is interesting too that Henry could reason that it was evident that he had been seduced and constrained by spells from the fact that God did not allow them any sons:[17] that was not a very developed understanding of the workings of witchcraft. Chapuys never referred to anything to do with witchcraft again, nor was witchcraft ever mentioned directly anywhere during Anne's fall.

Despite the lack of evidence that Anne miscarried a deformed foetus or that anyone at the time believed that a deformed foetus proved its mother was a witch, we are offered a vague and circular account, claiming first that Anne fell because she miscarried a deformed foetus, and secondly that since Anne's fall was so extraordinary, only a deformed foetus could explain it. Sometimes it appears that it was because she was shown to be a witch that Anne was brought down. Oddly for such a hypothesis, Anne was not charged with witchcraft. To that objection we are told that contemporaries knew that that was the real charge: her alleged licentious behaviour, especially alluring men by touches and kisses, and her afflicting the king with impotence would have readily shown that she was a witch.[18]

But more often we are given the impression that what above all drove Henry on was to prove to the world that he could not possibly have been the father of the deformed foetus. The more men who were accused of having illicit sexual relations with Anne, the more Henry's responsibility for the deformed foetus disappeared. But there is a huge difficulty here. Was a deformed foetus as shameful as this supposes, and was the father, rather than the mother, blamed for it if blame were appropriate? Were not miscarriages and deformities of miscarried or stillborn children seen simply as personal tragedies? On this argument, rather than be seen as the father of a deformed foetus, Henry preferred it to be thought that he had been cuckolded by his wife who had committed adultery with five men. On this argument, Henry even wanted his impotence to be publicly known so that he was not seen as responsible for that supposed deformed foetus. But in fact, Henry was at pains that his impotence should not be made widely known, as we shall see. In my view any man would regard his impotence and his wife's adulteries as far more humiliating than any deformed foetus.

A somewhat different chain of reasoning at one point touched on might more profitably have been developed, namely that 'illicit sexual acts were blamed for the birth of deformed children' and that if a woman miscarried a deformed foetus that was prima facie evidence that she had been sleeping around. If it were claimed that Henry might have interpreted a deformed foetus as evidence that Anne had been unfaithful such a claim would at least have been vaguely plausible.[19] But any claim that it was the suspicions of Anne's fidelity provoked by that supposed deformed foetus that led to a search for her illicit lovers remains undeveloped. Instead the emphasis falls squarely on Henry's determination to deny his paternity. 'The ministers were given the task of identifying several men among her acquaintances who could plausibly be accused of fathering her child, in order to establish that her gross sexual behaviour had caused its deformity.'[20] Yet that claim, implying that those who were condemned with Anne were innocent victims of a royal imperative, is not easily reconciled with the conviction that 'Henry genuinely believed that Anne was guilty of the crimes for which she had died'.[21] Above all, of course, the insuperable problem with all these speculations is that there is no evidence for any deformed foetus.

It is time to set such extravagant notions aside and return to more conventional discussions of Anne's fall. If you are not a specialist historian, if perhaps this is the first book on Tudor history you have read, if your impressions of Tudor history are derived from what you have heard people say or what you have watched on television, then your impression of Henry VIII is almost certainly that of a large, powerful man, a bearded Lothario who ruthlessly and shamelessly exploited his position to bed any young girl who captured his fancy. Such a romantic, indeed sensual, view of Henry makes for compelling television, and there is no doubt something comforting for a society still residually marked by its puritan past in watching sexual rapacity in the belief that what it is seeing reflects not the fantasy of the scriptwriter but what really happened. Yet the surviving sources, on which our knowledge of Henry must be based, lend rather less support to such an image of the king than might be supposed. Henry did indeed take mistresses, as we have already seen, but not as many or as promiscuously as legend would have it—though Anne understandably was far from pleased when he did and told him so.

A more nuanced view of Henry would have him obsessed by the need to father a son so that England would be spared the nightmare of disputed successions that had marked the previous century and led to the civil strife remembered as the Wars of the Roses. There are difficulties with such an approach, not least that Henry's action in repudiating Catherine in itself risked provoking conflict, and indeed in 1553 England would experience a disputed succession, though one that proved mercifully short-lived. A king anxious about the future of his realm would not have embarked on the divorce that Henry pursued, much less the break with Rome. But setting such doubts aside for the moment, on the view that the succession was indeed Henry's driving force, it is straightforward to see how his relationship with Anne could be seen to have turned sour as she failed to provide him with the son and heir he— on this view—so desperately sought. And Anne's miscarriage in early 1536, following whatever had gone wrong in 1534 and the birth of a daughter in 1533, can readily be seen as pushing Henry over the edge and causing him to resolve to ditch Anne. There is, nonetheless, a very serious objection to any explanation that links Anne's fall to her miscarriage in January. It is also a very serious objection to another conventional line of argument to which we must first turn.

That is the popular view that in early 1536 Henry simply fell in love with another woman and consequently decided to discard Anne. Undoubtedly it was around this time that Henry was courting a young lady, Jane Seymour, and what we make of that relationship is pertinent to any assessment of the state of Henry's marriage to Anne. An obvious reading is that Henry was now tired of Anne, increasingly impotent (something we shall hear more of later), disappointed at what he saw as her (not his) failure to produce a male heir, but attracted by Jane who increased his passion by playing hard to get. Determined to have Jane, Henry finally destroyed Anne, falsely accusing her of multiple adulteries, and then took Jane as his wife.

It is a plausible scenario. But we must take care to avoid reading Henry's relationship with Jane with the benefit of hindsight. On 19 May, four days after Anne's execution, Chapuys reported that he had heard that even before Anne's arrest, the king was speaking with Jane about their future marriage. Perhaps this is less strong evidence than it first might seem. Chapuys noted that a day before Anne was tried—though after the four men accused with her had been convicted—Jane was sent for to reside a mile from the king's palace, and then Henry despatched Sir Francis Bryan with news of Anne's condemnation.[22] John Foxe, the martyrologist, saw Henry's marriage, just three days after Anne's execution, as an argument for Anne's innocence ('this also may seem to give a great clearing unto her, that the king, the third day after, was married in his whites unto another').[23] But a more powerful explanation for Henry's speedy remarriage may lie in his need to cover the shame of what Anne had allegedly done to him by committing adultery, and, maybe even more humiliatingly, in talking about his impotence. According to Cromwell, writing to Gardiner, all the noblemen and all his councillors on their knees implored Henry to marry Jane, presumably because they too felt that that would be the best way of drawing a line under what had happened.[24] And Henry's banqueting and late-night merrymaking on the Thames is to be read in that light, rather than as evidence that he had long been set on marrying Jane.[25]

We do not know for sure when the relationship began. We have seen unspecified references to mistresses, and it is just possible that Jane had long been involved with the king, but more plausibly Henry and Jane first met during the king's progress in summer/autumn 1535. Chapuys's letter of 10 February 1536 was the first to name her: Henry had lately given her great presents.[26] In mid-March the new amours of the king with the young lady of whom he had written before still went on, Chapuys wrote, to the intense rage of Anne Boleyn. Much depends on how the purse full of sovereigns that Henry sent Jane at the end of March is regarded. She refused somewhat theatrically. She threw herself on her knees and begged the messenger to pray the king to consider that she was a gentlewoman of good and honourable parents and that she had no greater riches in the world than her honour, which she would not injure for a thousand deaths. If Henry wished to make her some present in money, she begged it might be when God enabled her to make some honourable match. All that marvellously increased Henry's love and desire for her, according to Chapuys.[27] A fortnight earlier Chapuys had reported that Henry had put the young lady's brother into his chamber: this would make it easier for Henry to enjoy liaisons with the lady in question.[28] Now Chapuys reported how Henry had turned Thomas Cromwell out of his room at Greenwich and installed Edward Seymour, Jane's brother, and his wife there, doubtless because there was a private passage from that room to the king's apartments, though the king said that because he wanted to show her that he only loved her honourably, he did not intend to speak to her in future except in the presence of some of her kin.[29] Cromwell at this time told Chapuys that although the king, his master, 'was still bent on paying court and making love to ladies', nonetheless Cromwell believed that from now on 'he intended to live honestly and chastely, maintaining his marriage'. Chapuys felt those words were spoken so coldly that he suspected they had the opposite meaning: but these words were what Cromwell had actually said.[30]

But was it so clear as is often supposed that Henry was tiring of Anne,[31] that Henry was disenchanted with Anne from January, that he was bent on Anne's undoing by all means?[32] Immediately after Anne's arrest, Chapuys claimed that he had been informed on good authority that even if nothing had been found against Anne, Henry had determined to abandon her:[33] but such gossip is dangerously subject to hindsight.

There is one very significant pointer to the contrary. Since he arrived in England in autumn 1529, Chapuys had never recognised Anne, whom he usually called 'the concubine' in his letters, going so far in February 1536 as to say that she showed him no goodwill because he had always told the truth and stood up against her 'damnable obstination'.[34] But in April 1536 Charles V instructed him to negotiate with Henry and not to allow the status of Anne Boleyn to be an obstacle. Accordingly Chapuys went to court on Tuesday, 18 April. Among the councillors who greeted him warmly was Anne Boleyn's brother, George, Lord Rochford, who showed Chapuys 'very good cheer'. Before mass, Cromwell came to ask on the king's behalf if Chapuys 'had any wish to see and to kiss the concubine', saying that would give the king pleasure. Chapuys replied that he was the king's slave but that it would be better not to, and Cromwell apparently agreed that such an encounter might harm relations. Cromwell relayed Chapuys's doubts to the king, who concurred. After dinner, Chapuys spoke at leisure with the king and then with Cromwell and several councillors. Henry received him very warmly, holding his hat in his hand for a while and not allowing Chapuys to be more uncovered than he was.

Then Chapuys went to mass, led there by Rochford. 'As the king came during the offertory, there was a large gathering of people, and part of them to see what expressions the concubine and I would make: she did so courteously enough, for I was just behind the door through which she entered, she turned round to do me the reverence comparable to that which I did her.'[35] In short, at mass, to which Rochford guided Chapuys, many people looked to see how Chapuys and Anne would behave towards each other, and they exchanged reverence—they nodded to each other. The exact details—by no means crystal clear in Chapuys's prose—do not matter. Clearly what happened was staged rather than spontaneous. What, however, is very striking is that Chapuys was expected publicly to recognise Anne and that he did so. That the king wanted Chapuys to acknowledge Anne is highly significant. It strongly suggests that as late as 18 April Anne was totally secure in the king's favour. If Henry was intending to discard or to destroy her, whether because she had miscarried and Henry feared that she would not bear any more children, or because he had fallen in love with Jane Seymour, there would have been no conceivable advantage to him in having her recognised by Chapuys. If Anne was on the point of falling, that would have been an unnecessary and costly demand.

Moreover as late as 25 April Henry was sending instructions to his ambassador at Rome, Richard Pate, insisting on the justice of his case for the divorce from Catherine.[36] I used to think that the setting up of commissions of oyer and terminer on 24 April indicated that by then something was wrong, but I am now persuaded that there is no reason to suppose that these largely conventional commissions need have been set up with Anne in mind. Similarly I am not now sure that the summoning of a fresh parliament on 27 April, barely two weeks after the dissolution of the reformation parliament on 14 April, reflects the need to deal with Anne Boleyn. Nor, as is often suggested, did Henry consult John Stokesley, bishop of London, on 27 April as to whether he might divorce Anne Boleyn: it was long-standing sympathisers of Catherine of Aragon who raised the matter.[37] Right up to the moment of Anne's arrest, then, there is little to show that Henry was anything but fully committed to his marriage.

CONSPIRACY?

If you are not an historian teaching at a university and keeping up with the books and articles written by university historians on Tudor history, you might be surprised that few of them believe that Henry VIII was so dominant a ruler and so forceful a man that he would or could have destroyed Anne Boleyn on a whim, for a new lover. For among such professional historians, much the most pervasive explanation of Anne's fall is that she was the victim of factional conspiracy. On such a view, Henry, seen by them as an essentially weak king and open to manipulation, was readily persuaded that Anne had betrayed him. Two factions have been proposed for this role: first, a group of conservatives, and secondly, Thomas Cromwell.

Let us begin with the conservatives. The argument runs thus. Many courtiers and noblemen had been dismayed by the king's repudiation of Catherine of Aragon, and were resolutely opposed to the break with Rome that had proved essential to allow him to marry Anne Boleyn. They had failed to prevent that marriage. But despite this they continued to hope that, eventually, Henry would discard Anne. And the intrigues of what historians have styled the 'Aragonese faction' allegedly included efforts to tempt Henry, who had had many mistresses, away from Anne. Jane Seymour is seen as their tool.

Such an account is superficially attractive, but it is unconvincing. While it is not difficult to list some noblemen and noblewomen and some courtiers who were indeed critical of the break with Rome and of the treatment of Catherine of Aragon and Princess Mary, it is much harder to find any evidence first that they acted as a coherent political group and secondly that they manipulated the king. Recent writers who make much of this 'Aragonese faction' offer surprisingly little hard evidence to support it. Merely citing family relationships or a single instance of personal dealings is not enough. There is little to suggest that Catherine of Aragon ever acted as a factional leader or encouraged others to indulge in political intrigue on her behalf: and even less in the case of her daughter Princess Mary. Undoubtedly there were some who remained staunchly loyal to Catherine: notably Gertrude, marchioness of Exeter. But whether they were trying or not, manifestly they had failed to stop events moving against them.

But did that change, did the so-called 'Aragonese faction' come close to success in 1536? Was Jane Seymour the conservatives' factional bait to lure Henry away from Anne? 'Anne's opponents took heart. Their leader seems to have been Nicholas Carew.'[1] 'The conservatives in the Privy Chamber and Sir Nicholas Carew in particular . . . used their un-rivalled knowledge of their master's tastes and character to coach Jane on how to behave'.[2] Such claims rest largely on two letters by Chapuys, but little more.

On 1 April, referring to Jane Seymour, he reported that she had been well taught and warned by those of the king's—unnamed—courtiers who hated Anne Boleyn. They told her in no way to give in to the king's fancy unless he made her his queen. And Jane had also been advised to tell the king how much his subjects abominated the marriage with Anne.[3] We shall shortly return to Jane.

In the second letter Chapuys reported a supposed plot.[4] Its co-ordinator was Sir Nicholas Carew; the others named were the marquess of Exeter, Sir William Fitzwilliam, Lord Montagu, his brother Sir Geoffrey Pole, Sir Thomas Elyot and the dowager countess of Kildare. As a list of those sympathetic to Catherine of Aragon and hostile to Anne Boleyn, this is more or less fair enough, though the inclusion of Fitzwilliam, for many years a close servant of the king and not a man of obviously independent views, should give us pause.

The Pole brothers and their kinsman the marquess of Exeter were, we know from depositions made in 1538, unsympathetic to much of what was happening, but there is nothing else to suggest that they were intriguing against the king and Anne, and they would be loyal to Henry during the rebellions of autumn 1536. Henry Pole, Lord Montagu, had accompanied Henry and Anne to Calais in September 1532 and was on the Middlesex commission of oyer et terminer that indicted Sir Thomas More in 1535. His younger brother Geoffrey Pole was more outspoken, meeting Chapuys and telling him how easily Charles V might conquer the kingdom. In autumn 1538, under arrest, his spirit would break and he would confess to damaging recent conversations with his brother and with the marquess of Exeter. Yet there is little in what was alleged against them to suggest that they had been plotting against Henry. And such words as were held against them appear to have been spoken rather later than the fall of Anne Boleyn: after the Pilgrimage of Grace, and when monasteries were being dissolved and pilgrimage shrines were being dismantled. There is nothing to support the notion of the Poles and Exeter as in any sense political leaders in 1536.

Sir Thomas Elyot, scholar and humanist, author of *The Book Named the Governor*, had expressed veiled criticisms of royal policy in his writings but without attracting damaging attention: there is nothing more to suggest that he was involved in political conspiracy. Sir Nicholas Carew, presented as the leader of the faction, was a long-time close servant of the king and gentleman of his privy chamber. Much trusted by Henry, he was sent to Francis I in 1527 and to the emperor and the pope over the king's divorce in early 1530. But he may have been 'ambivalent' about the divorce.[5] In 1535 he sheltered the king's fool who had nearly been murdered by Henry after he had praised Catherine and Mary and called Anne 'ribald'. Of course, that may well have been a purely humanitarian act; it might be unwise to read any political significance into it. And there is little else to inform us of Carew's opinions, though he clearly remained in the king's service throughout these years. Whatever Carew may have privately thought, outwardly he conformed, and in the autumn he would serve against the Pilgrimage of Grace. He often entertained the king in his house at Beddington, including in April 1538. He fell under suspicion when the Poles and the marquess of Exeter were interrogated and tried later that year. A letter was discovered in the marchioness of Exeter's coffer in which Carew told her about conversations in the king's privy chamber. That was clearly a breach of trust, and given that Exeter had just been convicted of treason, it must have looked especially damning. Carew, no doubt hoping for a pardon, confessed and testified against Exeter, notably saying that Exeter had been very melancholy when Queen Jane gave birth to a son. Carew was indicted for having had conversations with Exeter in summer 1538 in which they lamented the change of the world; he had also questioned Exeter's indictment. It is far from clear that Carew ever did anything but talk, but from the king's perspective it must have looked like trust betrayed. However that may be, there is nothing in the sources to justify seeing Carew as an active political figure, a leader of a faction.

The other person named by Chapuys was Elizabeth Grey, the dowager countess of Kildare, whose husband had been executed for his part in a conspiracy in 1534. The countess had an obvious motive for opposition to Henry, but this one mention is the only indication that she was involved in anything.

Was the imperial ambassador here turning gossip into a faction, was he reading organised political intrigue into a list of those whom he knew (though given the inclusion of Fitzwilliam, by no means fully accurately) to be uneasy about the direction that the king had been taking and would welcome the fall of Anne Boleyn?

Let us consider the details of what Chapuys wrote: 'it will not be the fault of Carew if the said concubine is not undermined; he is constantly advising mistress Seymour and other conspirators on how to run against her'.[6] On the face of it, this sounds like a serious plot. And Jane Seymour is specifically referred to. Yet two aspects puzzle. On the same day as he wrote this to Charles V, Chapuys also wrote to Cardinal Granvelle saying that he had nothing of importance to write. Was Chapuys sceptical of the gossip that it was his duty to report?[7] And the date of the letter is important too. When Chapuys wrote, Anne was apparently already under investigation. This letter cannot therefore be taken as proof that there had been a long-term conspiracy. It is suggestive that when Sir Francis Bryan was later examined as to whether he had heard anyone else talk about the prospects for Princess Mary, he replied that upon the disclosing of the matter of the late queen, he had heard Carew, (Sir Anthony) Browne, (Sir Thomas) Cheyney and the rest of the privy chamber talk generally about Mary's prospects.[8] Once Anne was under suspicion, many wondered what the consequences might be, not least for Mary: this does not prove that they had earlier conspired against Anne. Chapuys's letter is thus being made to bear a very heavy weight of factional interpretation. It is impossible to prove a negative, and arguments from silence have their own problems; yet there just does not appear to be enough to substantiate the factional historians' claim of an active, intriguing, manipulating conservative, 'Aragonese' faction.

Nor is the supposed connection between the 'Aragonese faction' and Jane Seymour by any means straightforward. Her brother Edward Seymour, the future Protector Somerset in the reign of Jane's son Edward, seems a somewhat unlikely 'conservative', even in the mid-1530s. If these conservatives were really dangling Jane in front of the king, could they be sure that she, and her family, would be their allies? Were there no young ladies from the families of those named by Chapuys? And how sound a scheme was it? How confident could Sir Nicholas Carew be first that Henry would be interested in Jane Seymour and secondly that if Jane became Henry's mistress, that would lead on to political advantages for the conservatives, especially the downfall of Anne Boleyn?

It is not at all clear that Jane Seymour was the bait carefully prepared by an alleged conservative faction. It is more likely that Henry met her when on progress in Hampshire. Maybe once the king's interest in her was known, courtiers then attempted to exploit the situation, but more for reasons of patronage than policy. It may simply be that Henry entrusted Carew, as a loyal and long-serving courtier, with the responsibility of looking after Jane as she was becoming the king's mistress. After Anne's fall, Jane would be lodged at Carew's house at Beddington. Maybe Carew had already earlier seized the opportunity to encourage Jane to criticise Anne, as Chapuys reported at the beginning of April; or perhaps Carew, whatever he actually did or did not do, boasted to Chapuys that he was coaching Jane to do down Anne, but we should be cautious about believing him. For Jane to tell Henry that Anne was abominated and that his marriage was thought illegitimate would be highly risky. Only someone absolutely certain that the king had already decided to repudiate Anne could confidently say that to him. Yet as late as 18 April Henry was insisting that Chapuys should publicly recognise Anne Boleyn. If Jane Seymour had spoken the words at the end of March that Chapuys says she was being coached to speak, it is likely that the king would have given her short shrift. A few days after Anne's execution Chapuys reported that Jane had suggested to the king that Princess Mary should be restored to her former position: Henry had called her a fool and said that she should look rather to the advancement of their children. How credible is that report? Chapuys could not have overheard any such remarks. Perhaps Jane told Carew what she had told the king—though the king's riposte would hardly have comforted the conservatives. Perhaps it was the king who let the story slip with the aim of putting further pressure, through Chapuys, on Princess Mary.[9]

Such difficulties point to the danger of the conspiratorial approach to history—that it drives the would-be unmasker of plots into a world of speculation in which 'must have' and 'surely' do duty for evidence. 'Many secret meetings amongst the conspirators must have taken place'—how can we say? 'although the evidence is slender, Sir Francis Bryan, long known as a boon companion of the king, was probably a key figure in the liaison between the Seymour faction and Mary's allies in their attempt to effect the disgrace of Queen Anne'—if the evidence is 'slender' how can the historian use the adverb 'probably'? 'Bryan surely had ample opportunity to talk with Henry Courtenay, marquess of Exeter'—'surely'? Far too much in this style of writing rests on mere supposition. More than a list of names linked by supposition is needed credibly to set out an effective political grouping. And it might be noted in passing how malleable and permeable the supposed conservative faction turns out to be. Sir Francis Bryan, seen as a 'key figure' among the conservatives, would in fact briefly be arrested along with the alleged lovers of Anne Boleyn.[10] And it is interesting that the martyrologist John Foxe, who also saw Henry as manipulated, blamed neither Carew nor Exeter but Bishop Stephen Gardiner, one of the 'wily papists' who were 'whispering in the king's ears what possibly they could to make that matrimony unlawful'.[11] No other source includes Gardiner, who was absent at the court of Francis I at this time.

A further puzzle is that more generally these months were hardly a triumph for those conservatively minded. Too much has been made of the election of Nicholas Carew to the Order of the Garter, ahead of Anne's brother Lord Rochford.[12] True, in his letter to the emperor, Chapuys saw that as a defeat for Anne and her brother, and so a portent for their fortunes;[13] but on the same day he informed Granvelle that it was Francis I's support for Carew that had prompted his election.[14] Indeed Francis had put in a plea for Carew in 1533 and had been told in 1535 that the honour had been promised.[15]

In March the bill dissolving the smaller monasteries went through parliament. There were fears or expectations of further religious reforms, not least over images. Catherine of Aragon's confessor, George Athequa, bishop of Llandaff, tried to flee the country, fearing he could not preserve his soul in safety; Henry was reported to be encouraging preaching against ceremonies, images, pilgrimages and purgatory. It is hard here to detect a conservative party in the ascendant, certainly not one becoming so powerful that Thomas Cromwell would have felt it imperative to join with it.

And that is pertinent in any assessment of the part played by Cromwell, seen by most historians as the factional mastermind behind Anne's fall. On their arguments, Cromwell, for reasons of his own, wanted to destroy Anne Boleyn, and successfully poisoned Henry's mind against her by falsely accusing her of incest and adultery: Henry 'allowed Cromwell to strike Anne down'.[16] On the most egregious of the factional historians' arguments, it was when Cromwell saw that the conservatives were making headway that he joined them in attacking Anne Boleyn—but then skilfully neutralised them. 'The conservative plot against Anne, now almost certain to be successful, faced Cromwell with a major political challenge—arguably, in fact, the biggest challenge of his career.'[17] A variant of this interpretation, by contrast, sees Cromwell not only as threatened by the conservatives but also as so threatened by Anne Boleyn that he needed to destroy her. 'Simply to remove the queen would be to invite his own ruin. He had to come to terms with the conservatives first. . . . Somehow he must achieve the gymnastic feat of a double reversed twist, ridding himself of Anne first, with the support of Mary and her allies, and then ditching them too.'[18]

The logic of such a scenario is elusive: on the factional interpretation of politics, Cromwell had risen as the close ally of Anne Boleyn, doing all he could to secure the break with Rome and royal supremacy that would allow the king to marry her. It is puzzling that Cromwell should at this point be seen as ready not simply to abandon her, but to destroy her by the most humiliating of charges. If the conservatives were really rising so fast, then it is hard to see how his position would have been safer without Anne Boleyn. The more powerful the conservatives, the stronger Cromwell's objective alliance with Anne might have seemed: if the queen were removed, he would, in such circumstances, have been highly vulnerable, given his past association with Anne and the break with Rome that her marriage to Henry had required. That Cromwell remained the king's leading minister, that there was no significant pause in the religious reforms, especially the dissolution of the smaller monasteries, and that Princess Mary was compelled to recognise her father as supreme head of the church suggests not that Cromwell joined the conservatives and then trumped them, but rather that, quite simply, there was no 'rise of the conservatives' in spring 1536. There was never any question of the king yielding over his divorce, the break with Rome, his royal supremacy, or the reforms of the church, especially the dissolution of the monasteries, which were then being introduced. Nowhere is any evidence cited to suggest that Cromwell and the supposed members of the 'Aragonese' faction were working together: there is nothing to show that Princess Mary, or Nicholas Carew, or the marquess of Exeter, or any other supposed conservative had any part to play in the fall of Anne Boleyn.

If thwarting the conservatives could not then have been a plausible motive for Cromwell, why else might he have wished to bring Anne down, however improbable a scenario that is? Two rather different sets of explanations have been offered as to why 'by the middle of April . . . Anne Boleyn had become a major threat to Thomas Cromwell'.[19] One line began by explaining Cromwell's disaffection with Anne in terms of diplomacy and foreign policy. Cromwell, on this account, saw the death of Catherine of Aragon in January 1536 as an opportunity to 'normalise' relations with Emperor Charles V. England's interests, he believed, were now best served by a closer imperial alliance rather than the understanding with Francis I, king of France, that had underpinned Henry's break with Rome. On that account, Anne Boleyn was an obstacle to such an alliance. Thanks to her years at the French court, thanks to Francis's support, Anne naturally looked towards France. Any *rapprochement* with Charles V risked undermining her position by reopening the question of the validity of Henry's divorce. And, on that account, Anne was a diplomatic problem because Henry would always defend her interests and insist that she be recognised, thus making a deal with Charles V the more difficult.

There is a good deal wrong with such an analysis. The initiative for an alliance appears to have come from Charles V, never slow to seize a diplomatic opportunity, on this occasion that created by the death of Catherine of Aragon.[20] Chapuys, his ambassador, was sent detailed instructions to negotiate without making the place of Anne Boleyn or the royal supremacy obstacles to agreement. And, as we know, in April Chapuys publicly recognised Anne for the very first time. It is hard to see, then, that Anne's position was in any sense an obstacle to the making of an imperial alliance.

It is true that in bargaining between Chapuys and the king, Henry demanded a great deal from the emperor, but that was the classic way of Renaissance diplomacy; the demands were intended to probe the extent of the concessions that the emperor was prepared to make. The monarch set out what he wanted in lofty terms and in principle; his own ministers then hinted that they knew the king was asking for too much but if they could be offered something, they would do their best to win their master round. If Cromwell seemed to be angry because Henry was apparently demanding immediate recognition of the justice of his divorce and the break with Rome, we must not take that at face value but rather see his anger as calculated and staged, intended to encourage the imperial ambassador to confide in him as they worked together to overcome the king's supposed reservations. The details of diplomatic negotiations must be analysed with great sensitivity: plucking a quotation or a detail out of context and giving it great weight is likely to distort. What we have been evaluating were the preliminary diplomatic skirmishes in a situation transformed by the death of Catherine of Aragon.

We must also take care when evaluating Cromwell's remarks reported by Chapuys. Earlier, in June 1535, Cromwell told Chapuys that Anne would like to see Cromwell's head off his shoulders. Why should Anne have turned against Cromwell? Because, Cromwell implied, of his good relations with Chapuys.[21] In March 1536 Chapuys heard rumours that Cromwell and Anne 'were on bad terms' and that there was talk of a new marriage for the king. Accordingly Chapuys went to see Cromwell, and reminded him of how he had told Chapuys that Anne would like to see his head off his shoulders. Chapuys sincerely wished for Cromwell 'a more generous mistress who recognised what he had done for the king', and warned Cromwell against her attacks.[22] Again, we should be wise not to take all this at face value. Henry and Cromwell were angling for an imperial alliance at the time. Hinting at the dispensability of Anne Boleyn was an astute tactic. Henry and Cromwell knew that Chapuys hated Anne Boleyn, whom he saw as the source of so many ills, especially those that had afflicted Catherine and Mary. They thought he would fall for any suggestions that Anne was on the way out and that Cromwell and Anne were at loggerheads. And consequent hints that Henry might discard Anne and remarry, this time a French princess, were intended to warn Charles not to take Henry for granted but to make him a good diplomatic offer in the complex negotiations then under way.

It is worth looking back to October 1534, when Chapuys had heard from Princess Mary that Anne was secretly plotting with some of Mary's household to cause her all manner of annoyance. Chapuys accordingly went to Cromwell to protest. Cromwell assured him that he had done all in his power to look to the princess's comfort, as, he said, the king had expressly ordered him. It was true, Cromwell added, that sometimes Henry was displeased with Mary's obstinate resistance to his marriage to Anne, but he had told those of his councillors who put forward measures that would disadvantage Mary that he would never agree to them. And Cromwell, raising a corner of the veil, as he put it, went on to tell Chapuys that Henry not only cherished Mary but loved her a hundred times more than he did Elizabeth. Chapuys was sceptical but later in his despatch recognised that Henry had indeed ordered that Mary should be well treated. Cromwell then hinted that Henry 'might change his love', in other words might discard Anne. Chapuys recorded all that at length but although it was, if it could be taken at face value, music to his ears, he immediately remarked that Cromwell 'is very much a man who, to amuse the world, wanted to make people think he believed something even when he himself in fact believed something else'. The phrasing is convoluted but the meaning is clear. Chapuys did not think Cromwell was being straightforwardly honest in what he was saying. In the whole conversation that he recorded, Cromwell was soft-soaping the imperial ambassador, giving him the—misleading—impression that Anne Boleyn's position was weak. We ought to follow Chapuys's caution.[23]

Nothing suggests that negotiations in 1536 were not moving forward smoothly. Nor does Anne Boleyn herself appear in any way to have obstructed these talks. Much has been made of Chapuys's account of how Henry gave him 'a very patient and sympathetic hearing without interrupting me', as Chapuys, gratified, noted. Henry then stated his claims, including that Milan belonged to the king of France, and summoned Audley, the Lord Chancellor, and Cromwell so that he could repeat what he had said. While Henry and Cromwell talked together, Chapuys could see that they were arguing; and eventually Cromwell left the king. Henry then came to Chapuys, explaining that the emperor's proposals were so important that he required them in writing. He insisted that the matter of the pope (his break with Rome) did not affect Charles and was not his business, that the king did not need Charles's help in dealing with the pope, and that he would treat Princess Mary according to how she behaved. What Henry demanded was a letter from the emperor admitting the wrongs he had done him—and Henry berated the emperor for his ingratitude. The emperor, Henry asserted, owed the empire and Spain to him: yet Charles had called Henry schismatic and sought to deprive him of his kingdom. Charles had made peace with France and refused to fight when Francis was a prisoner. According to Chapuys, Audley and Cromwell appeared saddened at these replies. Later Cromwell met Chapuys and 'we both consoled each other very much'. Cromwell assured Chapuys that he was annoyed but that he was still hoping for a good result.[24]

All of this must be handled with great care. It would be credulous to take it as showing that Cromwell was mortified by the extravagant demands of his master and working behind his back to reach a deal with Chapuys. It is improbable that all the councillors got down on their knees the next day to beg the king not to lose an opportunity to establish friendship with Charles. When Cromwell then discussed with Chapuys what

had turned the king's mind, and concluded that 'princes have mysterious
spirits and properties, unknown to all others', we do not have to agree
with Chapuys that by these words Cromwell was covertly revealing his
discontents. Cromwell was engaged in a continuing vigorous process of
bargaining. It is far more likely that Henry and Cromwell were working
in tandem, with one making bold claims and the other hinting at compromise, and the aim of both king and minister was to secure the best available deal. In short, diplomatic relations with Charles V can scarcely have
constituted a motive for Cromwell to seek to destroy Anne. The scenario
in any case lacks plausibility. Would a king's leading counsellor invent
false charges of incest with her brother and adultery with four other men
against the queen, simply because he favoured an alliance with the
emperor and she did not? It would, to say the least, be a risky proceeding.
As a reading of events, it betrays a lack of proportion.[25]

A rather different set of motives for Cromwell's supposed animosity
towards Anne has now been offered: that what provoked Cromwell was
Anne's supposed opposition, revealed in the sermon of her almoner
John Skip that we have already considered, to the dissolution of the
smaller monasteries. That was enough for Anne to become so great a
threat to Cromwell that he simply had to destroy her.

It is not, however, clear that Skip's sermon was about monasteries: he
did lament the wave of innovations, which might possibly be thought to
include the dissolution of the smaller monasteries, but monastic houses
were not mentioned as such. Instead what Skip defended was the traditional ceremonies and images of the church, then under threat. Any
claim that Cromwell's sudden hatred of Anne was provoked by their
supposed disagreement over the dissolution of the monasteries is not
directly supported by Skip's sermon. Another possibility is that
Cromwell and Anne had come to disagree about the desirability of
broader religious reform. If Anne was increasingly hostile to such
reform, especially the reform of ceremonies and images, that calls
into further question any interpretation that sees her as sympathetic
to what modern historians present as evangelical reform and proto-
protestantism. At least a sharp disagreement between royal minister and
queen over religious policy makes some limited theoretical sense, though
such a view does assume, rather questionably, that religious policy was

Cromwell's; if it was not Cromwell but the king who was shaping religious policy, then the plausibility of any explanation of Anne's fall as the result of a quarrel between minister and queen over religion diminishes.

And how likely is it that Cromwell would have thought Anne's opposition to religious policy was so threatening, not just to that policy but to him personally, that he had no option but to attempt to bring her down on false charges of incest and adultery? Was it true that 'Cromwell's very survival no longer coincided with the survival of the queen. She must go'?[26] It would still have been an exceedingly risky strategy, disproportionate to whatever threat Anne might reasonably have been thought to pose. Presumably on these sorts of argument the reason why Cromwell invented charges of incest and adultery against Anne, rather than a reprehensible but less embarrassing offence such as theft or fraud, was that he needed something that would inflame the jealousy of the king and make him want to destroy Anne, rather than giving her the chance to make amends after some mild reproof.[27] But that just illustrates how risky such tactics were, and how vulnerable Cromwell would be if things went wrong for him. And Cromwell would have had to be a true Machiavellian, utterly convinced that the end justifies the means, if he were to combine deep evangelical religious commitment with the ruthless trumping up of false charges of adultery that would cost Anne and five men their lives.

Those brought down with Anne do not constitute an obvious faction nor, indeed, obvious rivals to Cromwell as the king's leading minister. Mark Smeaton, the musician, can scarcely have been thought a rival for Cromwell. George Boleyn, Lord Rochford, Anne's brother, was a man of limited influence: he had been active in 1530–31 during the campaign for the divorce and the pressures on English churchmen, but he had not been prominent since. Francis Weston was too young and junior a courtier to be a political threat:[28] he often played against the king at tennis, dice and bowls, as the privy purse accounts reveal,[29] and since 1532 he had been a gentleman of the privy chamber. At Anne's coronation he was made a knight of the Bath.

Henry Norris, as the king's groom of the stool, might have appeared a more definite threat to Cromwell, yet there is little to suggest that

Norris was at all interested in political matters. Rather like one of his predecessors, William Compton, groom of the stool to 1526, he was more interested in personal enrichment than in public affairs. Both Norris and William Brereton have been treated as threats to Cromwell because of their local interests.[30]

> The Henrician courtiers Henry Norris and William Brereton between them held a nexus of offices under the crown in the three shires of the principality, the royal lordships of the northern marches and the county Palatine of Chester. They belonged to the Boleyn faction at court and in the country, and until Cromwell destroyed them in 1536, the way was not clear for the introduction of ambitious administrative and legal changes such as had been advanced by individual Welshmen and former members of the council in the marches.

Brereton has been seen as 'a proconsul' who 'had little to learn from the text-book "over-mighty" subject', who 'personified all that was amiss' in Wales and the Marches and who was 'in himself a major obstacle to reform' designed to create a unitary sovereign state. 'The only solution to the dangerous isolation they [Brereton and men like him] embodied was the radical one actually under consideration in the last months of his life—the extinction of the politically separate palatinate and marcher lordships and their assimilation into the country at large.'[31]

Yet all that is somewhat exaggerated. Neither Norris nor Brereton was in any sense an 'over-mighty subject'. Norris, groom of the stool, had been appointed chamberlain of north Wales in 1531 and constable of Beaumaris Castle,[32] and so his standing in Wales and the Marches was wholly dependent on that royal favour which had secured him those grants. If, to follow the factional historians' reasoning, it had been thought necessary to remove him from influence there, it hardly seems necessary for him to be accused of adultery with the queen. Why could Henry or Cromwell not simply have dismissed him?

Brereton did have family connections in north Wales and the Marches; it was not, however, any inheritance but rather a series of royal grants that underpinned his influence. From 1528 he was escheator of Chester, from 1530 chamberlain of Chester, from 1532 steward of the lordships of Bromfield, Chirk, the Holt and Yale, and in 1532 he was sheriff of Flint. All depended on continuing royal favour. It was truly said of him that he was 'a man which in the said county of Chester had all the rule and governance *under our sovereign lord the king's grace*'.[33] No doubt Brereton exploited his offices with determination; no doubt his methods were partisan and unscrupulous; very likely his ways made Wales more disorderly than it would otherwise have been. But to go on to say that his rule was so wicked and so dangerous that he had to be removed would be to exaggerate the extent to which he was more ruthless than the early Tudor norm and abused the powers with which he was entrusted.

There is little to suggest that Henry or Cromwell were dissatisfied with him. It is by no means obvious that the momentous reforms of Welsh government in 1534–36 were intended as a challenge to Brereton. The Acts of 1534 (which prohibited the suborning of juries and allowed certain cases to be tried by the council of the Marches) hardly affected him. And in the Act of 1536 which introduced JPs into Wales it is significant that the chamberlain of Chester—Brereton—was to receive estreats of issues and fines from Chester and Flint. (Similar arrangements, it might be noted, were made for Norris.) 'The legislation of 1536 did nothing to limit the power of Chamberlain Brereton.'[34] All that hardly suggests that Brereton was thought to be a problem.

Yet suppose he had gone too far, suppose his tenure of those royal posts was becoming a counter-productive embarrassment, why was he not simply dismissed? After all, Charles Brandon, duke of Suffolk, a great favourite of the king, who had, together with his deputies, ruled effectively if autocratically in those very same lordships of Bromfield, Chirk and Yale which Brereton had come to hold, had been removed in 1525. Admittedly that was not because he was thought dangerously powerful but because his offices could be, it was thought, more effectively deployed as part of a reformed government of Wales. If Brereton was, in the mid-1530s, similarly thought to be providing a less efficient, or a more provocative, rule than might be achieved by other means, why was he not similarly replaced? It hardly seems necessary, let alone sensible, to invent charges of adultery with the queen to secure his dismissal.

Whatever his motives might have been, do the sources support the claim that Cromwell brought Anne down? Once it was all over, Cromwell did indeed claim something of the sort, in a conversation with Chapuys. To the imperial ambassador Cromwell appeared to assert that he had masterminded the whole business. An immediate problem with this is that Cromwell was speaking after the event: what he said is nowhere near as compelling as if he had told Chapuys this in the middle of April. The point of the assertion was that Chapuys should have no doubt about Cromwell's importance. If Cromwell had in fact been taken by surprise by events, this was just the sort of claim he might have made. It is also just possible that Cromwell meant to say no more than that he had been in charge of the trials, not that he had orchestrated all that had happened. Chapuys reported that Cromwell told him that, annoyed at the response that Henry had given Chapuys on the third day of Easter, he set himself 'a fantasier et conspirer le dict affaire'—to invent and to plot the said matter.[35] It is interesting that, according to Chapuys, Henry had strongly emphasised to John Kite, bishop of Carlisle, that 'it was already a good while that he had been aware of the likely outcome of these matters'.[36] To have been taken by surprise would in itself have been damaging.

'A much higher fault'
THE COUNTESS OF WORCESTER'S
CHARGE AGAINST ANNE

The unpersuasive explanations of Anne's fall considered so far—that Henry turned against her because she had failed to provide him with a son or because he had fallen in love with another woman; or that a conservative faction or Thomas Cromwell successfully intrigued against her—share the assumption that Anne was innocent. The charges of adultery, and especially the charge of incest with her brother, were, it is widely believed, so preposterous that no one can take them seriously. But is it so certain that Anne was innocent? Was the evidence against her really so preposterous?

One of the reasons why historians have tended to see the charges against Anne as false is because the legal procedures followed were in many ways a travesty. Modern sensibilities recoil at adultery being in effect a capital offence. Nor was adultery an offence punishable by death in Tudor England. It was a matter that should have been dealt with by the ecclesiastical courts. The capacious treason statutes did not treat adultery committed by a queen as treasonable, though the law was extended to cover that in 1542. It was held against Anne that by committing adultery she had compromised the legitimacy of any children she had by the king: that was fair enough, as modern paternity suits testify, but it hardly warranted treating a queen's adultery as treason.

What the indictments against Anne and her alleged lovers went on to say was that they had sought the destruction of the king. No evidence of any plot was ever referred to; the most that was cited in support of that specific charge was Anne's conversation with Henry Norris in which Anne teased him that he would marry her after the king was dead. We shall return to that, but manifestly it is weak evidence that Anne or Norris or anyone else plotted to kill the king. Somehow Anne's alleged adultery was presented as threatening, as a kind of wishful regicide. This leaves an extremely uncomfortable sense that justice was not done by contemporary norms, that the bloody punishments were wholly disproportionate to the alleged offences. Yet that Anne and her alleged lovers were cruelly punished and that legal procedures were twisted to secure the intended result does not mean that they were innocent of all wrongdoing. It will now be suggested that Anne and at least some of those accused with her were guilty of adultery.

The key source is a poem written in French, first printed in Lyons in 1545, but dated 2 June 1536 and written by Lancelot de Carles, later bishop of Riez, then serving the French ambassador to the court of Henry VIII. The printed poem is entitled *A letter containing the criminal charges laid against Queen Anne Boleyn of England*. There are several manuscript versions, differing slightly but not materially: there is a printed edition in G. Ascoli's book and a summary translation in the *Letters and Papers of Henry VIII*.

De Carles began by referring to 'choses merveilleuses'—extraordinary events—sad for some, joyous for others. No pleasure in this world was lasting; joy and comedy often turned to tragedy. He wrote what he had heard. After giving an account of Anne Boleyn's sojourn at the French court and her ascent to become queen, de Carles emphasised how, protected by the new treason laws, Anne could do as she pleased. And her pleasures included those of the flesh. She could go anywhere, and if by chance she fell in love with someone, she was fully able 'at her pleasure to indulge her friends'. But the king's affection for Anne was cooling, and God wanted to demonstrate that great honours and riches were no more than wind. Anne miscarried—shocked by the news of Henry's fall from his horse when hunting.

And then the poet went on to his central theme, his account of Anne's fall. He describes how one of the king's privy councillors seeing that his sister was giving many signs 'of loving others by dishonest love' ('d'aymer aucuns par amour deshonette')—in other words that she was pregnant—offered her good brotherly warning that she would acquire the reputation of a loose-living and promiscuous woman and greatly damage her honour if she did not stop. Angry, she responded by admitting her actions—she could not deny them to her brother—but claiming that she was not the worst. 'But you see a small fault in me, while overlooking a much higher fault that is much more damaging.' And, thinking that a greater sin would wipe away a smaller one, she went on to accuse the queen. If you do not believe me, she said, find out from Mark—Mark Smeaton, the musician. She then accused the queen's brother. 'I must not forget to tell you what seems to me to be the worst thing, which is that often her brother has carnal knowledge of her in bed.'

Uneasy, the councillor who heard all this did not know what to do: if he told the king he risked the punishment meted out to those who spoke ill of the queen; if he kept it to himself, and it came out nonetheless, he risked being punished for concealing the queen's misdeeds. So he thought it prudent to inform two friends, and they in turn felt it necessary to tell the king, though with no little flattery and foreboding. They made her sound like a common whore: every day she took her pleasures unendingly with several men: as soon as one finished, another came at the appointed time, and then another. When the king left her at night, her minions came. Her brother was not the last. They named Henry Norris, chief gentleman of the king's privy chamber, as well as Mark Smeaton. Anne had incited them by caresses and by gifts. Norris had sworn to the queen that he would marry her.

Astonished, the blood draining from his cheeks, Henry had doubts, thanked them—but threatened them with death if what they reported turned out to be false. The king had Smeaton interrogated; Smeaton confessed that on three occasions he had made love to Anne. That, little by little, persuaded the king that what he had been told was true. At the May Day tournament Henry behaved as if nothing was amiss. When it was over, he ordered the arrest of Norris, told him that he was accused of having slept many nights with the queen, and then offered to spare his life if he confessed. Norris denied it. He was sent to the Tower. The next day Anne and her brother followed him; and then the others were arrested and interrogated.[1]

The merit of this account is that it explains how stories of Anne's behaviour came to light, in a quarrel at court between a privy councillor and his sister. That allegedly loose-living lady who showed many signs of loving others by dishonest love can readily be identified as Elizabeth Browne, wife of Henry Somerset, second earl of Worcester. In a letter written by John Hussee, factotum of Lord Lisle, Lord Deputy of Calais, she was named as the principal accuser of the queen: 'as to the queen's accusers,' Hussee observed, 'my lady of Worcester is said to be the principal.'[2] In another letter Hussee mentioned others—referring to 'the first accuser, the lady Worcester, and Nan Cobham, with one maid more'— but insisted that 'the lady Worcester was the first ground'. The censorious brother in the poem was thus Sir Anthony Browne, a leading courtier and councillor.[3]

What the poet meant by 'showing many signs of loving others by dishonest love' can only be that the countess was pregnant. In what other ways does sleeping around affect someone's appearance? And we do know that the countess was indeed pregnant at this time. Sir William Kingston, Anne's gaoler once she was in the Tower, reported that Anne 'much lamented my lady of Worcester . . . because that her child did not stir in her body'. Asked why that was, Anne replied 'for the sorrow she took for me'.[4] In fact, all was well: we know from the accounts of the bailiff of the earl's manor of Monmouth and Wischam, George ap Thomas, recording payments to his wife for expenses connected with the baptism, that the countess gave birth to a daughter in the year ending Michaelmas 1536, a daughter intriguingly christened Anne, maybe in memory of the queen.[5] But if it was the countess's blurting out what Anne had been doing that had brought the queen to the Tower, it is not surprising that she should be shocked at what she had unwittingly provoked.

The countess was one of the ladies in Anne's privy chamber, evidently close to her. There is a later reference to the countess borrowing £100 from Anne Boleyn. A payment of £4 to the nurse and midwife of 'my lady of Worcester' is recorded in the king's privy purse expenditures for 4 February 1530: and this may reflect Anne's influence.[6] As we saw earlier, the countess of Worcester stood on Anne's left throughout the dinner following Anne's coronation, ready to hold a fine cloth in front of Anne's face whenever she wanted to spit.[7]

None of that, of course, means that the countess of Worcester's accusations against Anne, made in self-justification to her brother, are necessarily true. But the countess's position lends them some credibility. If Anne was indeed sleeping around, then it is very likely that ladies of her chamber would have been aware of it, indeed might have been complicit. And if the countess was herself 'loving others by dishonest love', that would have offered Anne some reassurance that her own behaviour was not likely to be revealed.

Was the countess pregnant by someone other than her husband? Before 1527 she had married Henry Somerset, second earl of Worcester, and all her children were treated as the earl's. Yet when her brother, as we have deduced, pointed to her swelling belly as evidence of her misconduct, that would have made no sense if her baby was her husband's. It is striking that the countess did not deny her brother's charge; she did not counter, 'how dare you, it's my husband's child'. The countess was resident at court for long periods, serving in the queen's household, and her brother would presumably have known that she and her husband had been apart for some time. This is obviously speculative. The countess did not want to destroy Anne: what she said was not premeditated. No doubt she expected that her words would deflect her brother from further accusations about herself: she might reasonably have expected that he would keep what she told him about Anne Boleyn to himself, rather than telling the king.

There is an intriguing further detail. In March 1538 the countess wrote to 'my own good lord' Thomas Cromwell, itself an unusual act for a married noblewoman. A letter from her brother informed her that Cromwell was 'special good lord' to her in the matter of £100 that she had borrowed from Anne Boleyn. She did not doubt that Anne would have been good to her. And for Cromwell's goodness in that matter she most heartily thanked him. She was 'very loath it should come to my lord my husband's knowledge': he was 'utterly ignorant' both of the borrowing and of the using of the £100. She was in doubt how he would take it if he now heard about it so she implored Cromwell to continue his good mind and to be good lord to her.[8] On that evidence, my sometime colleague, the late T.B. Pugh, speculated that the father of the countess's baby in 1536 was not her husband but Thomas Cromwell. If that were true, it would add another dimension to these events. One might then suppose that Cromwell already knew from the countess of the queen's misdeeds but that he kept the knowledge to himself. When, however, the countess blurted them out to her brother, and her brother told two councillors who agreed that the king must be informed, Cromwell (who might have been one of those councillors) would have been in an awkward position: in his anxiety to protect the countess, he would have had an interest in seeing the queen fall. But we do not have to follow T.B. Pugh so far.

What is beyond speculation is that there is strong evidence that it was the countess of Worcester's revelations that sparked the arrests and trials, and that the countess was in a good position to know the truth of what she spoke. The scenario set out by de Carles of the countess defiantly revealing the queen's adulteries when rebuked by her brother deserves to be taken seriously.

Some scholars have claimed that the very idea that a queen could have committed adultery is preposterous—though those of us living in the shadow of the late Princess Diana might find this less implausible. How could she have got away with it? De Carles answers that in general terms by highlighting how Anne, once queen, had the leisure, means and freedom to have her way as she wished, and if she came to fancy anyone, she was wholly free to indulge her friends. Crucially, Anne benefited from the law damning those who spoke ill of the queen: 'through the large liberty that she received from legal protection no one, on pain of martyrdom, dared say anything to the detriment of the queen'.[9]

But how could she have done it in practical terms, would not her ladies have known, how could she have kept it secret, historians have rhetorically asked. Yet if the queen's ladies were indeed aware and complicit, then it becomes easier to see how it could happen, how Anne could get away with it for a time and no doubt hoped to do so for ever, but how in the end her secrets were revealed.

There is one extravagant account, factually wrong in many places, which seems to have come from an old woman, Margaret, in Anne's chamber, who told the whole story when put to torture, we are told. Anne had ostentatiously tried to attract to her service the best-looking men and best dancers to be found. On hearing that in the City of

London there was a young fellow called Mark Smeaton who was one of the prettiest monochord players and deftest dancers in the land (the son of a poor carpenter), she sent for him. Mark played while Anne and Henry Norris danced; then the queen danced with him; and fell in love with him. She gave him money and persuaded the king to give him a salary of £100: she always got him to play for her. When the king went away to Windsor for fourteen days, Anne declared her love to Mark and confided in an old woman of her chamber, who agreed to bring him to her at night. The old woman took Mark to where she slept, in an antechamber next to the queen's room. Here she hid him in a closet in which she kept the sweetmeats and preserves that the queen sometimes asked for and told the queen that once all her ladies were asleep, she should call out to her for preserves. Anne then pretended to be ill and retired to her chamber with her ladies, who went to sleep in an adjoining gallery. Anne called out to Margaret very loudly so that everyone might hear her: bring me a little marmalade. The old woman went to the closet, made Mark undress and took some marmalade to the queen, holding Mark by the hand. The lady who was sleeping in the antechamber with the old woman did not see them. Anne grasped Mark, who was all trembling, by the arm and made him get into bed. He soon lost his bashfulness and remained there that night, and many others. Anne never dined without having Mark to serve her.[10]

All this may be sheer fantasy. Even so, such contemporary fantasies do have the merit of showing what was thought to be within the bounds of possibility. This tale disposes of the argument that Anne's adulteries would have been impossible in an age when queens did not sleep apart from the ladies of their chamber: those ladies, or some of them, could readily connive in the secret affairs of their mistress. Loyalty and self-interest would normally mean that they would keep what they knew to themselves, but it was not unthinkable that in some circumstances they might reveal the truth. For any queen, committing adultery was a risky business—but it was not unfeasible. If things went wrong, however, we might expect to find the ladies of the queen's household at the centre of any investigations; which is exactly what happened here.

That neither the countess of Worcester nor any other of the queen's ladies were charged with any offences, even though on this reasoning they must have been to some measure complicit in Anne's activities, if only by concealing them, does not invalidate this reasoning. Lady Rochford would, it is true, be charged, convicted and executed for her part in conniving in the unquestioned adulteries of Catherine Howard. And no doubt the countess of Worcester and other ladies may well have been in danger in 1536. If, however, they in effect turned king's evidence, offering full and detailed statements, and if their role was more as silent witnesses than as active accomplices—the more probable since Anne was much older and far more experienced in the ways of the court than Catherine Howard would be in 1540–41—then it is quite understandable that they should have been spared.

It is hard to see why the essentials of de Carles's poem should be disbelieved. He was serving as secretary to the French ambassador, Antoine de Castelnau, bishop of Tarbes. The ambassador was following events closely and the sieur de Dinteville, who joined him on 17 May, intervened unsuccessfully (it is not clear why) to try to save Sir Francis Weston, one of those arrested and charged with committing adultery with Anne.[11] It can therefore safely be inferred that de Carles, 'being attendant and near about the ambassador', would have been well informed.

It is of course possible that the French ambassador was deliberately fed misleading information. Explaining events to Stephen Gardiner, bishop of Winchester, and Sir John Wallop, then serving as Henry's ambassador at the court of Francis I, Cromwell declared that the queen's incontinent living was so rank and common that the ladies of her privy chamber could not conceal it. It came to the ears of some of the council, who told the king, although with great fear. And interrogations of members of the king's and of the queen's household made the matter appear evident.[12] That dovetails very neatly with de Carles's account. Was de Carles simply repeating what Cromwell had told him or his master?[13] But if the accounts given by de Carles and Cromwell roughly agree, that might be simply because they expressed what they thought was the truth. It is important here to remember that de Carles's account is supported by John Hussee's identification, in two letters, of 'the lady Worcester' as Anne's first accuser.

More generally, it is difficult to see who might benefit from the story told by de Carles. Why should Cromwell have wanted to give him this story if it were not true? If the charges against Anne were false and were invented, whether by a king bent on destroying her and marrying another, or by Cromwell as faction leader determined to remove a rival, it would have been more pointed to claim that Anne had been caught *in flagrante* rather than umasked by the chance of a quarrel between one of the queen's ladies and her brother. In his poem, de Carles does not generally show Henry in a very flattering light: he criticises the king's cruelty in destroying Thomas More, and his elucidation of the exquisite dilemma facing the countess of Worcester's brother once he had been told of the queen's alleged misbehaviour makes the king appear a tyrant. And de Carles's quoting Princess Mary as saying of Anne, 'if her daughter was the king's', and praising her conduct in adversity, cannot have been welcome. Nor would Cromwell, supposing he were the factional mastermind behind Anne's fall, have been enamoured by de Carles's account, not least his hints that Anne's brother, Rochford, did not lack for enemies. De Carles's account of the denials by Norris, Weston and Brereton further leaves his readers with an uneasy feeling. And his lengthy account of Rochford's self-defence, compared by de Carles to that of Thomas More, in no sense reads like official propaganda on behalf of Henry or Cromwell. It is not surprising that when copies of the text were circulating in Paris the following year, Henry wanted them suppressed.[14]

We must grasp the fundamental and conventional purpose underlying de Carles's account: that of a morality tale showing the fickleness of fortune, the transitory nature of fame and power, one moment worldly success, the next moment worldly ruin. If the first half of de Carles's poem is largely unfavourable to Anne, showing her as successful in worldly terms but highlighting her loose living, the second half portrays her much more sympathetically as a victim, a worldly failure but virtuous, indeed winning popular sympathy because of her desperate plight, resigned to her death, contemplating Christ's passion.[15] So de Carles's purpose is more to draw attention to the fickleness of fortune than to draw out specific implications concerning Anne herself. Thus he presents Anne as teaching her ladies that 'we should despise this world in which all is in vain, broken and transitory in order to aspire to enternal glory'. In this context the details of how Anne's alleged adulteries came to light are in a sense incidental to de Carles's aims, but because of that very marginality they are the more credible. Cromwell's account to Gardiner and Wallop can then be seen as reinforcing what de Carles reports: they both say it because they both believed it to be true.

If the countess of Worcester did make allegations as de Carles says, clearly they could not be ignored: the inquiry they provoked quickly appeared to confirm them, not least once Mark Smeaton, the musician, confessed. And so it becomes easy to understand how and why Henry should have found the charges against Anne plausible, and ordered her arrest.

'You would look to have me'
ANNE'S LOVERS?

Our other principal source for Anne's alleged adulteries is a series of letters written by Sir William Kingston, Anne's gaoler in the Tower of London, reporting the emotional conversations Anne had with him and his wife. Anne was manifestly and understandably under extreme pressure: she talked excitedly, jerkily, extravagantly, sometimes petrified, sometimes confident. When Kingston told Anne that she would go not, as she feared, into a dungeon, but into the lodging she had enjoyed at her coronation, she retorted 'it is too good for me'; imploring Jesus to have mercy on her, she knelt down, 'weeping a great pace, and in the same sorrow fell into a great laughing', and did so many more times.[1] 'One hour she is determined to die, and the next hour much contrary to that.'[2]

She complained that she had been cruelly handled by the king's council at Greenwich, presumably just before she was sent to the Tower: 'to be a queen and cruelly handled as was never seen'. De Carles noted how Anne was transformed in adversity, refused to confess when the king's councillors adumbrated the charges against her, talking to them 'like the mistress', 'like a queen in triumphant honour', which made a strong impression on them.[3] Conveyed to the Tower by Lord Audley, the duke of Norfolk, Thomas Cromwell and Sir William Kingston, on entering Anne had fallen on her knees and beseeched God to help her as she was not guilty of what she was accused of, and asked them to implore the king to be good to her.[4] Kingston's testimony suggests that her confidence ebbed and flowed. She thought the most part of England prayed for her—and she was defiant enough to predict that 'if I die you shall see the greatest [punishment for my suffering] within these vii years that ever came to England'.[5] She marvelled that the king's council did not come to her.[6]

Nowhere did Anne admit to having committed adultery, nor does Kingston offer any direct evidence against her. Kingston's letters are clearly in that sense a secondary source. But it is unlikely that he made up, or even exaggerated, what he claimed Anne said. And indeed he reported Anne's asserting her innocence—'I am as clear from the company of man, as for sin I am clear from you, and am the king's true wedded wife'—and her question 'Shall I die without justice?' and her laughter at his reply that the king's poorest subject had justice.[7] 'Shall I have justice?' she later asked Kingston, who assured her that she should have no doubt about it. But Anne responded, 'if any man accuse me I can say but nay, and they can bring new witness', illustrating the difficulty she faced in proving a negative.[8] If he had wanted to incriminate Anne, Kingston could have invented her saying much more definitely damaging things than on his accounts she did. The very tantalising nature of Kingston's letters does rather enhance their credibility. What they reveal about Anne is obviously open to interpretation. At the very least, as we shall see, they show Anne behaving somewhat indiscreetly, enjoying conversations and relationships that went far beyond the formal conventions. Even her protestation of innocence was colourful: 'I hear say, said she, that I should be accused with iii men, and I can say no more but nay without I should open my body, and there with opened her gown.'[9]

Anne told Kingston about Mark Smeaton, the musician. 'Mark, thou art here too,' she lamented on coming to the Tower.[10] 'He was never in my chamber but at Winchester'; she had sent for him there 'to play on the virginals for there my lodging was above the king's'. But, Anne insisted, 'I never spoke with him since', except on the Saturday before May Day (29 April), 'and then I found him standing in the round window in my chamber of presence'. She asked him why he was 'so sad'; Mark replied that it was no matter; and Anne said 'You may not look to have me speak to you as I should to a nobleman because you are an inferior person'. 'No, no, madam,' Mark, rejoined, 'a look sufficed me, and thus fare you well.'[11]

In those exchanges Anne certainly did not offer any compelling grounds for supposing that she had committed adultery with Mark Smeaton. That she should ask her musician why he looked so sad hints at some sort of friendly relationship. Her disdainful reproach—dismissing him as 'an inferior person'—suggests that she was trying to distance herself from him, to show her gaoler how little she had thought of him. Maybe the impression she leaves of a musician besotted by his mistress is right. Perhaps Mark was hopelessly infatuated with Anne, and perhaps his confession that he had three times made love to her reflected his desperate wishful thinking. But it is also entirely possible that Mark and Anne had indeed had a brief affair. Maybe Anne was here dissembling; maybe it was Anne's hasty bringing the affair to an end, fearful of detection, or with her affections transferred elsewhere, that provoked Mark to confess, despite the horrendous consequences.

More substantially, Anne admitted to remarkably flirtatious talk with Henry Norris, Henry VIII's groom of the stool. Kingston reported how Anne, having opened her gown, added, 'O Norris, hast thou accused me; thou are in the Tower with me and thou and I shall die together.' The next day Anne talked with Mistress Coffin. The previous Sunday (30 April) Norris had, Anne declared, told the queen's almoner (John Skip) that 'he would swear for the queen that she was a good woman'. Mistress Coffin, not unreasonably, asked why any such matters should be talked about. Anne said, 'I bade him do so, for I asked him why he did not go through with his marriage'. He had replied that he would tarry a time. Anne—on her own account—had then retorted, 'You look for dead men's shoes, for if anything came to the king, you would look to have me'. Norris, Anne said, had replied that 'if he should have any such thought, he would his head were off'. Anne then jibed that 'she could undo him if she would'; and then—she said—'they fell out both'. Anne then told Kingston that she feared Sir Francis Weston because he had said that Norris came more to her chamber for her than he did for Anne's cousin and lady-in-waiting, Margaret Shelton, to whom Norris was betrothed but whom he was not hurrying to marry, as Anne had noted.[12]

What can reasonably be read into all that? Anne admitted joking—or perhaps it was more than joking—with Norris that if anything happened to Henry, Norris would seek to have her. Any married woman who talks like that about her husband is surely playing with fire, especially if that husband is the king.[13] And in the context of Norris's delaying his planned marriage, Anne's remarks take on a stronger resonance. Norris could be forgiven for deducing that Anne was interested in him. Why did Anne indulge in such conversation? If—for example—she thought Henry might not live long and she would indeed have liked to marry Norris, then clearly she would want to deter him from marrying another, and to keep his hopes of marrying her alive. Nothing here proves that Anne and Norris were already lovers. Norris denied it when pressed by the king. It is, nonetheless, pertinent that Norris had affirmed his willingness to swear that the queen was a good woman. That conversation was singled out by Sir Edward Bainton in a letter to Sir William Fitzwilliam as especially significant.[14] Why, as Mistress Coffin pointedly asked, should anything like that be talked about? Anne said that she had asked him to say this. But she would have done so only if there was much talk about it. Her request implies gossip in which Anne and Norris were talked about as lovers. Gossip is often fanciful; but sometimes gossip is true. When Anne feared that Norris had accused her, what did she fear that he was accusing her of?

Anne admitted to Kingston that she had talked on similar lines to Sir Francis Weston. She feared him more than she did Norris, she said, though she did not elaborate on what she feared. Did she fear that Weston might testify against her, for example on the frequency with which Norris came to her chamber? According to Kingston, Anne told him that she had talked to Weston about his marriage 'because he did love her kinswoman', her cousin Margaret Shelton. And Anne had gone on to tell him that he did not love his wife. Weston's riposte to her reproaches was to declare that 'he loved one in her house better than them both': when Anne asked who that was, he replied 'it is yourself'. Anne's response, as she told Kingston, was that 'then she defied him'.[15]

Once more, this is scarcely evidence of adultery. Yet a woman who talks to a man about his marriage, and tells him that he does not love his wife, is, at the least, inviting misinterpretation of her intentions. Anne might have been playing the role of a counsellor, offering advice on how to restore a damaged relationship; or she may quite simply have been flirting.

All in all, what Kingston's letters revealed about Anne was far from flattering. Such conversations were sure to be regarded as inappropriate for any married woman, and *a fortiori* for a queen. Anne had been behaving like the young lady-in-waiting she had long been, not with the dignity and restraint befitting her new status. What she said does not offer definite or detailed support for the charges of adultery brought against her. But through her indiscretions she made herself look guilty in the eyes of the king.

What other evidence was or could be deployed against Anne and her friends? The indictments against Anne and her alleged lovers survive. But there are no extant records of the trials. Presumably evidence was collected in support of the charges, and, most likely, it included testimony from the queen's ladies—but we do not know. That nothing survives is not in itself suspicious, though it is conceivable that the records were destroyed later, perhaps in Queen Elizabeth's reign. Or it may be that no witnesses were called during the trial.

Much has been made of the details of the indictments. As we have seen, Anne and those who were accused with her were alleged to have committed offences on specified dates and at specified places. There are puzzling features. Two sets of indictments survive: the dates of the alleged offences differ. Those in the indictment found at Deptford are in one case a month earlier and in the other four cases a month later than in the indictment found at Westminster. Anne allegedly had sexual relationships with Henry Norris in October or November 1533, with Sir William Brereton in November or December 1533; with Mark Smeaton in April or May 1534; with Sir Francis Weston in May or June 1534; and with her brother in November or December 1535. Moreover there is something rather formulaic in the details: in each case Anne is alleged to have seduced her lover on a specific day and then to have been 'violated' three, five, six, twelve or fourteen days later.[16]

An obvious response is to dismiss these indictments as wholly worthless inventions. Some historians have gone to some trouble to show that the dates and places of the alleged offences were quite impossible: other sources show that Anne and her supposed lover simply could not have been together on that day in that place. Only six of the twenty dates and places in the indictment studies were even theoretically possible, it has been suggested; for the rest it can readily be shown that Anne or her alleged lover could not have been at that place or on that day.[17]

Maybe such reasoning is not wholly watertight: secret and speedy journeys were by no means impossible; and clerks might have made errors of transcription, for example writing Greenwich when they should have put Hampton Court. It is possible to fit the dates into what we know of the relationship between Henry and Anne, but it may be mistaken to take these indictments altogether at face value. The charges against Anne and her alleged lovers were by their nature most unlikely to be documented. Unless Anne and her lovers had been caught in the act, and there is no indication that that was the case, those responsible for framing the indictments would have been dependent on the testimony of those who first brought the alleged offences to the attention of the king. And it is improbable that the countess of Worcester, the first accuser, would have been able to offer exact dates and places for so many alleged offences. Some people have exceptional recall of when they did something, but most have no more than a rough recollection of even the most dramatic days in their own lives.

Thus it is not an unreasonable surmise that those who were entrusted with these prosecutions found themselves in an awkward position. From the countess of Worcester's outburst, from Mark Smeaton's confession, and from the king's own interrogations, enough had emerged to have convinced Henry of Anne's guilt. But the lawyers had to set out the charges in due legal form. It was not possible to accuse Anne of having committed adultery in general: according to law, the offence had to be specified. So dates and places were attached to the alleged offences, chosen by informed guesswork rather than because there was any concrete evidence for them. Thus to dismiss the indictments because the dates and places are impossible is to miss the point. These details were included because details had to be included; the details themselves, however, were not independent evidence, and those bringing the indictments did not bring specific evidence in support of each and every one of them. And the indictments do also include a catch-all phrase, 'diversis aliis diebus et vicibus antea et postea' (in and on various other dates and places before and after), further suggesting that the dates and places given were intended as specimen charges. It may be that the details of dates and places are indeed fabrications. But that does not mean that the charges themselves were fabrications. Those who drew up the indictments believed—or had been instructed by those who believed—that Anne and those accused with her were guilty. They had the unenviable task of working out just how to secure convictions in court, so they then made rough and ready guesses as to when and where the offences had taken place. If the indictments had been drawn up at the behest of a king or leading minister who knew that the charges were entirely false, one might have expected greater care to be taken over the precise details. That the details are as they are does rather suggest that it was on the basis of the testimonies, necessarily imprecise on dates and places, that we have been considering that Henry was persuaded of his wife's guilt and then ordered preparations to be made for the trials.

Our knowledge of the trials comes largely from the despatches of Eustace Chapuys, the imperial ambassador. He wrote how the principal charges against Anne were that she had 'cohabite' with her brother and the others, that Anne and Norris had promised each other that they would marry once the king was dead, a promise taken to mean that they had hoped for his death, not least because Anne had given Norris some medals (Chapuys does not specify further), and that Anne had poisoned Catherine of Aragon and was plotting to do the same to Princess Mary. Henry had apparently claimed that she had determined to poison both Mary and Henry Fitzroy, duke of Richmond, Henry's illegitimate son.[18]

Anne totally denied all of this and gave what Chapuys described as 'plausible' responses to each charge. De Carles described Anne as defending her honour soberly, not saying a great deal, but impressing by the way she looked.[19] Wriothesley's *Chronicle* reports Anne as making 'so wise and discreet answers to all things laid against her, excusing herself with her words so clearly as though she had never been faulty to the same'.[20] Anne did admit, Chapuys continued, that she had given Sir Francis Weston money and that she had done the same to several other young gentlemen.

What should we make of this? There is nothing elsewhere to suggest that Anne was supposed to have poisoned Catherine of Aragon: was Chapuys, once more, indulging his hatred of Anne and repeating malicious gossip rather than what was officially alleged against her in her trial? Chapuys had earlier been reporting that Anne was plotting to poison Mary: perhaps he could not resist including that among Anne's alleged offences, though it is hard to see why he did. However that may be, the other charges confirm what we know from the indictments, but nothing Chapuys says amounts to detailed supporting evidence. Anne's gifts to the young courtiers are obviously intriguing, but could readily be seen as no more than might be expected from a queen.

More striking is what Chapuys said about Anne in connection with her brother. It was held against Anne and Rochford that they often made fun of the king and of his clothes: in several ways she showed that she did not love the king and was 'ennuyee de lui'—bored, or perhaps more strongly, irritated by him. If that was true, then it would supply a context in which committing adultery was thinkable; but it hardly amounts to proof. Rochford was accused 'by presumption', Chapuys said, of having committed incest with his sister: the grounds, Chapuys added, were that he had been once found a long time with her. Frustratingly, Chapuys also refers to 'certain other little follies', but without specifying. So well did Rochford reply that several of those present were confident enough to want to bet at the very unattractive odds of 10 to 1 on (i.e. they would risk 10 to win just 1, plus the return of their stake) that he would be acquitted, particularly since no witnesses were produced, as was usual, especially when the accused denied the charge.[21] Much the same was reported in Wriothesley's *Chronicle*: Rochford answered the accusations 'so prudently and wisely . . . that marvel it was to hear, and never would confess anything, but made himself as clear as though he had never offended'.[22] According to Chapuys, who expressed himself more convolutedly than usual, it was also held against Rochford that his sister had told his wife that the king 'nestoit habille en cas de soy copuler auec femme at qu'il nauoit ne vertu ne puissance' ('that the king was not physically capable of copulating with women and that he had neither virtue nor power')—in other words, Henry was impotent and unable to make love. Rochford went on to cast doubt on the paternity of Anne Boleyn's daughter, Elizabeth: was she the king's daughter? To that highly damaging charge of calling into doubt the succession to the throne, Rochford—according to Chapuys—made no response at his trial.[23]

If Henry was indeed impotent, at least at times, it could explain why Anne should have slept with others, if she did. For the queen and her brother to talk of such matters at all was to run huge risks, especially if discussing the king's impotence led them to question whether Princess Elizabeth was really the king's daughter. It is not hard to believe that all this made Henry very angry. But none of it amounts to compelling evidence that Anne and her brother slept together. If a sister talks to her brother about her husband's impotence, does that mean that they sleep together? Was T.B. Pugh perceptive in remarking that 'a woman never mentions her husband's impotence unless she is willing to take a lover'? Did Henry consequently think that Anne despised him for his lack of virility?[24]

Relevant here is the conversation that Chapuys had with the king in April 1533, if we can believe Chapuys's account of a remarkable exchange. When Henry told him that he wished to have children, Chapuys retorted that Henry was not sure of having them. Henry responded by asking Chapuys three times 'if he was not a man like other men'. Were both Chapuys and Henry coyly alluding to his alleged impotence?[25]

Chapuys's account of the trials remains tantalisingly brief in what it reveals. And Chapuys himself, however pleased he was at the downfall of Anne Boleyn, declared that, Mark Smeaton—who admitted his guilt—apart, the others were condemned 'upon presumption and certain indications, without proof or valid confession'.[26] On the eve of Anne's execution, moreover, Chapuys referred to her as 'the unblemished concubine'.[27]

The notes of the judge Sir John Spelman state that 'all the evidence was of bawdery and lechery, so that there was never such a whore in the realm'. Unfortunately what details of 'bawdery and lechery' were presented at the trial we do not know. Maybe we should read this as judicial scepticism, that the charges were so over the top as to be fanciful, showing that Spelman 'dismissed the evidence',[28] but it might be prudent to keep an open mind and to allow the possibility that these comments should be taken at face value as a reflection of sincere horror at what was revealed.[29]

De Carles also gave an account of the trial in his poem. Anne denied the charges, appealed to God, and won the sympathy of those who had

come to hear her. Rochford swore that the charges were false and maliciously contrived lies. When he replied point by point to the charges, not
even More—said de Carles—had been more eloquent.[30] Once again,
however, we are left to imagine the details of what Rochford said. A
month later Cromwell would inform Gardiner in France that he had
written as fully as he could without sending the very 'confessions'—he
does not specify whose confessions—'which were so abominable that a
great part of them were never given in evidence, but clearly kept secret'.[31]

Nothing is more difficult in historical study than imagining evidence
that does not survive, not least since such efforts at imagination are by
definition unverifiable. But manifestly some considerable evidence of the
alleged misdeeds of Anne and those accused with her was prepared before
the trials, even if, as Chapuys says, no witnesses were called at them. And
whatever we do not know, we can be certain that Anne and her brother
were declared guilty by their peers. That is worth further comment. The
peers who convicted Anne were Charles Brandon, duke of Suffolk, Henry
Courtenay, marquess of Exeter, William Fitzalan, earl of Arundel, John de
Vere, earl of Oxford, Henry Percy, earl of Northumberland, Ralph
Neville, earl of Westmorland, Edward Stanley, earl of Derby, Henry
Somerset, earl of Worcester, Henry Manners, earl of Rutland, Robert
Radcliffe, earl of Sussex, George Hastings, earl of Huntingdon, John,
Lord Audley, Thomas, Lord De la Warr, Henry, Lord Montagu, Henry,
Lord Morley, Thomas, Lord Dacre, George, Lord Cobham, Henry, Lord
Maltravers, Edward, Lord Powys, Thomas, Lord Monteagle, Edward,
Lord Clinton, William, Lord Sandys, Andrew, Lord Windsor, Thomas,
Lord Wentworth, Thomas, Lord Borough and John, Lord Mordaunt.
With the exception of the earl of Northumberland who was suddenly
taken ill, the same peers found her brother guilty.[32] Four noblemen were
not there: the earls of Shrewsbury, Essex and Cumberland, the first two
both ageing, and the earl of Wiltshire, Anne Boleyn's father (who,
Chapuys reported, wanted to take part).[33] The duke of Norfolk who
presided over the trial as Lord High Steward was in tears as he passed
sentence if we believe the later account by George Constantyne, Henry
Norris's servant.[34]

Why did the peers reach the verdict they did? James Froude, the great
Victorian historian of Tudor England, whom I follow in giving the names

of all the noblemen who convicted Anne and her brother, defended the trials on the grounds that they could not possibly have been party to what, if Anne was innocent, would have been an unimaginably grotesque miscarriage of justice. 'If there was evidence, it must have been close, elaborate and minute; if there was none, these judges, these juries and noblemen were the accomplices of the king in a murder perhaps the most revolting which was ever committed.'[35] On what we have gleaned from Chapuys's account of the trials, it is indeed intriguing that they convicted Anne and her brother. One additional factor that may have swayed them is that Anne and Rochford were tried on 15 May, three days after the commoners Mark Smeaton, Sir Francis Weston, Henry Norris and William Brereton had been tried and found guilty by two juries of twelve. If they were guilty, then it would be impossible for Anne not also to be guilty in at least some measure. But the conviction of the commoners would not have reinforced the case against Rochford. According to Spelman's notes, the judges present at the trial 'murmured' at the judgment against the queen, but what they murmured at was not the verdict of guilty but that the judgment was 'disjunctive', in other words offering the king the choice of what punishment the queen should endure: burning or beheading.[36]

Senior churchmen were not involved in the trials, but it is striking that Archbishop Cranmer should evidently have accepted the truth of the charges against Anne. He was clean amazed by the news, he wrote to Henry, but he thought the king would not have gone so far if she was not guilty. Summoned by the king's councillors, he was sorry that such faults as they reported could be found against her. Cranmer's tone has perceptively been described by Rowan Williams as 'unhopeful defence': hoping against hope that the charges would prove to be false. As Williams notes, Cranmer was 'a constitutionally timid man struggling to be brave', determined to express his amazement. But he was also 'a man uncomfortably capable of believing himself deceived', Williams goes on: Cranmer thought that he had known Anne Boleyn, but now he could see that he had not really known her.[37] Nicholas Shaxton, bishop of Salisbury, lamenting that by her misconduct she had 'sore slandered' the honour of God, went on to regret that 'she hath exceedingly deceived me'.[38] None of the bishops and churchmen whom Anne had allegedly favoured now defended her. Maybe they were cowed; maybe they believed that the charges against her were true.

According to de Carles, on conviction Anne appealed to God: 'You know if I have deserved this death.' Turning to those who had judged her, she said that she did not want to say that their judgment was unjust, but she insisted that 'I have always been faithful to the king'.[39] According to Chapuys, Anne 'put on a brave face', and asserted that what most troubled her was that those named with her were innocent.[40] On the eve of her execution, Anne—if Chapuys was rightly informed— having received the holy sacrament, had declared on the damnation of her soul that 'she had not misused herself with her body towards this king'.[41] Sir William Kingston reported that 'this morning she sent for me that I might be with her at such time as she received the good Lord to the intent I should hear her speak as touching her innocence always to be clear'.[42] Much has been made of this: 'it argues mightily for inno- cence'.[43] Would Anne have said all that if she were in fact guilty, would she not have been jeopardising her immortal soul if she were lying? Unfortunately these are just the circumstances in which a man or woman might lie. If Anne had indeed committed adultery, then what she faced in the world to come was already dire: she might thus risk another untruth. Why should she do that? If she asserted her innocence, on the sacraments, in the presence of her gaoler, there was still the chance, however small, that the king would respond by deciding to believe her, and would spare her life. If she confessed that she was guilty, even that small ray of hope would disappear. And Anne was still 'in hope of her life', saying that she would go to a nunnery, on 16 May, so Sir William Kingston reported.[44] Moreover if Anne's plea of innocence were believed, that would save not just her, but also those accused with her. If she was guilty, then she was lying when swearing her innocence: but in lying, a guilty Anne could nonetheless be seen as acting not wholly self- ishly but also with a degree of altruism. To deduce that because Anne did not confess but rather swore her innocence means that she was indeed innocent is a step too far. Anne's oath provokes sympathy, but it raises acutely all the uncertainties of the case. In itself it does not amount to evidence, let alone proof, that she was innocent. Similarly the remarks attributed to her by Chapuys, that she did not think that she was condemned by divine judgment except for having been the cause of the ill-treatment of Princess Mary and having conspired her death, add little.[45]

Nor is the letter to Henry dated 6 May and purportedly written by Anne at all likely to be hers.[46] In it Anne refused to confess in exchange for royal favour: Henry should not imagine that his poor wife would ever confess a fault which she never, ever imagined. Never had prince more dutiful wife than Henry had in Anne Boleyn—with which name and place she would have been willingly content if God and Henry had so been pleased. Anne insisted that in her exalted state—as queen—she never forgot herself but always looked for such a transformation of her fortunes as had now occurred. She asked for a lawful trial; if Henry had already determined that her death and an infamous slander would bring him his desired happiness, then she prayed God to pardon his great sin and her enemies, the instruments thereof. Her innocence would be known at the Day of Judgment. She asked that she alone should bear the burden of the king's displeasure, not those poor gentlemen imprisoned with her.

The handwriting plainly is not Anne's. Could this be an Elizabethan copy of a genuine letter? If it is genuine, does this reinforce Anne's oath and show that she was not guilty? Or is it open to doubt? The defiant tone may reflect injured innocence. But if Anne was guilty, she would have had every interest in writing in the same way. And that defiant tone does raise some doubts. Would Anne, if innocent, not have done better to adopt a more conciliatory note, to insist that there had been serious misunderstandings, to express her love for the king? Was it more an appeal to posterity than to the king?[47] Even if this letter is genuine—and that must be seriously questioned—it does not clear Anne.

On the scaffold Anne, if de Carles was correct, refused to go into the details of why she found herself there, but simply asserted that the 'judge of the world' knew everything, asked him to show compassion on those who had judged her, and recommended 'your good king in whom I have seen such great humanity and the acme of all goodness: fear of God, love of his subjects'.[48] The account offered later by George Constantyne was similar. Anne declared that she did not intend to reason her cause but committed herself wholly to Christ, and asked all present to pray for the king, 'for he is a very noble prince and full gently hath handled me'.[49] Wriothesley's *Chronicle* presents Anne as pliant: 'I here humbly submit me to the law as the law hath judged me, and as for mine offences, I here accuse no man, God knoweth them.' She beseeched Jesus to save the king, 'the most godly, noble and gentle prince that is', words spoken with 'a goodly smiling countenance'.[50] Hall presents Anne as coming to die, 'for according to the law and by the law I am judged to die and therefore I will speak nothing against it'. She would accuse no man, but prayed God to send the king long to reign over them, 'for a gentler nor a more merciful prince was there never'; to her he was 'ever a good, gentle and sovereign lord'.[51] Again all this makes for a deeply moving picture, but neither Anne's words nor her demeanour offer any compelling evidence that might take this inquiry further.

Thus far, we have approached the question of Anne's innocence or guilt by looking in turn at the key sources—de Carles's poem, Kingston's letters and Chapuys's account of the trial. Now we must review the charges again, looking one by one at those who were accused with Anne. And before that, we should not overlook those who fell under suspicion but were not charged. Sir Thomas Wyatt, the poet, Sir Francis Bryan, courtier and diplomat, and Sir Richard Page, another courtier, were all in danger. According to John Hussee, Page, sent to the Tower in early May, would be banished from the king's presence and from court for ever, but he would not be punished more severely;[52] and, despite rumours, he was not tried.

Sir Francis Bryan's involvement we know about from the testimony of the abbot of Woburn in 1538. The abbot described how Cromwell had in great haste sent for Bryan 'as a worldly lucifer'. After Bryan returned home unharmed, the abbot expressed his delight that Bryan had not been charged. 'Sir in deed as you say I was suddenly sent for marvelling therof and debated the matter in my mind why this should be,' Bryan replied. Knowing his conscience was clear of any possible offence, he had gone first to Cromwell, and then to the king, and there was 'nothing found in me, nor never shall be found but just and true to my master the king's grace'.[53] As we have seen, three hours after Anne's condemnation, Bryan was sent by the king to inform Jane Seymour.[54]

More remarkable still was the experience of Sir Thomas Wyatt, sent to the Tower in early May. By 10 May, however, Cromwell was assuring Sir Henry Wyatt, his father, that he would not be charged, and so it proved. Wyatt's earlier dealings with Anne, discussed above, no doubt raised suspicions.[55]

But what is revealing is that Wyatt was not destroyed. Nor were Page and Bryan. This strongly suggests that when allegations of Anne's adulteries came to light, they were carefully investigated. And when nothing incriminating was found, men were set free. In turn, this should encourage us to take seriously the charges against those who were tried and convicted. It is also interesting that when Wyatt (according to his fellow diplomat Edmund Bonner who wrote critically about him to Cromwell in summer 1538) recalled his imprisonment in the Tower, which he did 'often' in communication with Charles V—it 'seemeth so to stick in his stomach that he cannot forget it'—he declared 'God's blood, was not that a pretty sending of me, ambassador to the Emperor, first to put me in the Tower and then forthwith to send me hither? That was a way indeed to get me credit hither. By God's precious blood, I had rather the king should set me in Newgate than so do.' In those words, Wyatt clearly saw the king as responsible for his incarceration.[56] And it would have been odd that Cromwell should have had Wyatt first arrested and then released.

Mark Smeaton, the musician, confessed, pleaded guilty and never retracted his admission. Was he tortured? De Carles explicitly denies it, George Constantyne, testifying a few years later, recalled 'the saying' that Mark had been 'first grievously racked', which, he added, 'I could never know of a truth'; he had begun his account by saying that 'I can not tell how he was examined'.[57] Mark admitted to sleeping with Anne on three occasions. Why should he have confessed if it was untrue?

One extravagant speculation can be discarded: that Smeaton was the lover of Anne's brother Lord Rochford, and, because of his humble background, supposedly especially susceptible to blackmail and humiliation over his sexual behaviour. The evidence cited for their relationship is that Rochford gave Mark a music book (now BL, Royal MS 20 B xxi) inscribed 'Thys boke ys myn George Boleyn 1526' on folio 2 and 'a moy

m marc S' on folio 98. It is not immediately obvious why such a gift—
entirely explicable for professional reasons, for Mark was a musician
and Rochford and Anne were his patrons—should be thought to have
sexual significance. Nor is the case strengthened by saying that Rochford
and Mark 'had a common interest in music, for his lordship wrote
poetry, which was often sung to old refrains'.[58]

A more convincing explanation for Mark's damaging confession is
that he was angrily jealous. The *Spanish Chronicle* is, as we have seen, a
somewhat colourful source. But the writer's suggestion that Mark's relationship with Anne made Henry Norris and William Brereton jealous
does not seem unreasonable. Anne's response was to offer her favours on
successive nights to Norris and Brereton rather than to Mark, offering
Mark a purse full of gold sovereigns as some sort of compensation. The
Spanish Chronicle then offers a rather different account of how Mark
came to be interrogated, an account that is not easy to square with other
sources, but the sense it gives of Mark as jilted and jealous lover rings
true. Is it unreasonable to speculate that by confessing he intended to
cause the greatest damage to both Anne and his rivals? And he may have
hoped that by confessing, and in effect turning king's evidence, he might
be spared the worst torments of punishment—indeed he was beheaded
before being quartered—and even that he might, in return for his
evidence, eventually be allowed to go free. Henry VIII was too ruthless
a king for that. It remains possible, of course, that Mark's claim that he
had made love to Anne three times was sheer fantasy, the invention of an
unrequited lover, but if he was in the business of invention it would
surely have been more profitable for him to have told tales of Anne's
adulteries with others rather than admit his own. It is somewhat less
credible that Mark was compelled to confess to offences that he had not
committed, especially offences of this kind. It is theoretically possible
that he was racked to the point where he would confess anything. Yet
there is little to confirm that torture of this kind was employed in early
Tudor England. And it is difficult to understand why Mark should not
have retracted his confession if it had been made under duress, or in the
misplaced hope that if he confessed his life would be spared; or why he
persisted in his words, as de Carles put it, on the scaffold. After all, the
others charged with him denied the charges and pleaded not guilty: this

was not one of those show trials in which all the accused admit their offences. Mark's confession that he had on three occasions made love to Anne remains an important stumbling block for those who think Anne wholly innocent. Lamenting all who died with Anne, Thomas Wyatt nonetheless did not mourn them equally: in Mark's case he pointedly asked

Ah, Mark, what moan should I for thee make more
Since that thy death thou hast deserved best.

It was, however, Mark's vain ambition to rise above his station that prompted Wyatt's criticism, so these tantalising words cannot safely be taken as evidence that Wyatt thought Smeaton guilty.[59] But nor can Anne's irritation that on the scaffold Smeaton had not cleared her name be taken as evidence that his confession was 'false', as, according to de Carles, Anne claimed.[60]

That Anne committed incest with Rochford, her 'sweet brother',[61] is the least probable of all the accusations. We have seen Chapuys's doubts about the case that was brought against him. The *Spanish Chronicle* has Rochford arrested for going on several occasions to his sister's room wearing only a dressing-gown; Rochford did not deny this but explained that all he had done was to speak with his sister when she was ill. But suppose that Rochford had behaved unconventionally in calling on his sister in her chamber when he was not fully dressed, suppose that Rochford and Anne had talked about the king's impotence and made fun of his clothes, as Chapuys reported, suppose Rochford had questioned whether Henry was the father of Anne's daughter Elizabeth: none of that justifies convicting Rochford of incest. But perhaps more compelling evidence was brought than now survives. De Carles's poem lamented that 'par ladvis seulement d'une femme' (by the testimony only of a woman) Rochford was thought guilty: was that woman the countess of Worcester? Or did Rochford's wife give evidence against him? If Rochford, as de Carles suggests, declared that the charges against him were false, 'maliciously contrived lies',[62] maybe it was his wife whom he had in mind. We cannot say, and Rochford's conviction remains a conundrum.

When on the scaffold Rochford lamented that 'if I had followed God's word in deed as I did read it and set it forth to my power, I had not come to this', was he recognising his guilt in the charges against him or simply presenting himself as a man of sin like others? If the dedication to Anne in the preface of the *Epistles and Gospels* was written by Rochford, does what was 'an exercise in the conventions of courtly love', despite being an introduction to scriptural readings and homilies, offer anything to tell against Rochford? The author asks the dedicatee 'patiently to pardon where any fault is, always considering that by your commandment I have adventured to do this, without the which it had not been in me to have performed it. But that hath had power to make me pass my wit, which like as in this I have been ready to fulfil, so in all other things at all times I shall be ready to obey'. As has intriguingly been observed, 'if one did not know these were a brother's words, one could easily mistake them for those of a hopeful suitor'.[63] Could Rochford have been both brother and suitor? However that may be, it was probably Rochford's conduct that did for him. According to George Cavendish, writing much later, Rochford was a notorious womaniser:[64]

My life not chaste, my living bestial,
I forced widows, maidens I did deflower
All was one to me, I spared none at all,
My appetite was all women to devour.

That reputation may have coloured responses when Rochford was accused of incest. So might his excessive pride, noted by Thomas Wyatt in his poem on those who perished in May 1536:[65]

Some say, 'Rochford, hadst thou been not so proud,
For thy great wit each man would thee bemoan'.

Rochford's behaviour during the trial may have contributed to sealing his fate. If no compelling, detailed, evidence was brought against him, if much rested upon circumstantial evidence such as Rochford's presence, half dressed, in the queen's chamber, then those who had to give a verdict were very likely to make up their minds on their sense of

Rochford's character. Courts often faced the challenge of determining the truth of charges which depended on the word of one person against another, or on chains of more or less plausible reasoning. In such cases, the impression that a defendant made on those judging him or her was crucial: the jurors' estimate of character, of sincerity, of trustworthiness, was crucial, indeed potentially more important than their judgment of 'the facts' presented to them, not least since their sense of the trustworthiness of the defendant could influence their interpretation of those facts, often ambiguous, incomplete and circumstantial evidence.[66] At one point in the trial Rochford was shown some evidence in writing. That was unusual: the standard practice was for everything to be presented orally. He was also ordered not to disclose what he had been shown. Despite so specific an instruction, Rochford brazenly read out its contents in open court. They related to the king's impotence. Manifestly Henry and his advisers had not wanted that to be made public. They clearly expected that Rochford would silently read what he had been shown and then respond to it without divulging its contents, whether by agreeing with it or by denying it. Rochford, however, thwarted their intentions. Yet that action may well have damaged him in the eyes of his peers. By telling the world that the king was impotent, by defying those who were organising the trial, Rochford risked giving those who would determine his fate every reason to think the worst of him. His effrontery made stories that he had gossiped mockingly about the king's impotence and cast doubt on the paternity of Princess Elizabeth all too credible. From there it was not such a long way to concluding that he was also guilty of incest with his sister.

That leaves three men convicted of adultery with Anne. William Brereton's fate provoked Norris's servant, George Constantyne, to assert a few years later, 'By my truth, if any of them was innocent, it was he.' It was because he had appeared to imply his innocence on the scaffold that Constantyne believed it. We know very little that is pertinent. The doubtful *Spanish Chronicle* says that Mark Smeaton named Brereton in his confession, but there is no supporting evidence; it also includes Brereton among those to whom Anne showed great favour. Brereton was a rising landowner and royal office-holder in north Wales; he was married to the sister of the earl of Worcester whose wife, if de Carles's poem is correct, had revealed Anne's adultery: had the countess of Worcester also named Brereton? That Brereton was nearly fifty, and therefore 'no gallant fluttering about Anne',[67] does not in itself acquit him. Maybe Brereton was especially unfortunate to be caught up in this affair simply because his name had cropped up and because, unlike Wyatt, Page and Bryan, he had been unable to clear himself. Wyatt, in his poem, noted that the 'common voice doth not so sore thee rue' as Norris or Weston, and it may be that it was Brereton's unpopularity, his reputation as a hard man in north Wales, that had affected how the suspicions against him were now treated. What we do know is that Anne knew Brereton; and it is just conceivable that their relationship was more intimate than was prudent. Are there 'credible grounds for suspicion' that he had committed adultery with Anne? These grounds, however, are essentially circumstantial, resting on evidence which shows that William and his brother Urian were certainly close to Anne. Urian hunted with Anne in September 1530; Anne named her lapdog Urian. William may have been a witness of Henry and Anne's marriage. And in June 1533 Sir Edward Bainton reported that William Brereton had been in Anne's household. That in itself does not seem very damning, but we shall shortly consider what Bainton reported about 'pastime' in the queen's chamber.[68]

Sir Francis Weston is also hard to assess: 'a rather shallow young man caught out of his depth' is one verdict.[69] It is interesting that his mother and his wife, Anne, daughter of Sir Christopher Pickering, appealed to the king to spare his life, as did the bishop of Tarbes, the French ambassador, and Jean de Dinteville, sent to join the bishop on embassy. There was some gossip that Weston would go free; but Henry was unyielding. We know from Anne Boleyn's conversations reported by Sir William Kingston that she had feared him. What Anne feared, most likely, was that he would break under pressure, confess, and give evidence against her. Anne, as we have seen, teased Weston that he loved her kinswoman Margaret Shelton but did not love his wife. Weston retorted that he loved one in the queen's house better than both of them, and when Anne asked him who that was, he replied 'it is yourself'. Such banter certainly does not prove that Weston slept with Anne; but if Weston did commit adultery, it may have been not with Anne but with Margaret Shelton.

Nonetheless in the context of the trial such talk would not seem altogether innocent. Weston sent his father, mother and wife a letter asking them to discharge his debts and, significantly, 'to forgive me of all the offences that I have done to you, and in especial to my wife, which I desire for the love of God to forgive me. And to pray for me for I believe prayer will do me good.'[70] It is hard not to read that as an admission of adultery—what other offences could he have committed against his wife?—but it might be that his lover was Mrs Shelton. Later George Cavendish in his *Life of Wolsey* would remember him as one 'that wantonly lived without fear and dread . . . following his fancy and his wanton lust'.[71] On the scaffold Weston declared, 'I had thought to have lived in abomination yet this twenty or thirty years and to have made amends'.[72]

Finally, we turn to Henry Norris, chief gentleman of the king's privy chamber. Riding back to Westminster after the May Day jousts at Greenwich, Henry—according to both de Carles and George Constantyne—offered Norris a pardon if he confessed and told the truth about everything. According to de Carles, Norris refused to confess and insisted that he could prove that the charges against him were false; according to Constantyne, Norris did confess, but quickly retracted his confession, saying when it was laid before him that he had been tricked into doing so by Sir William Fitzwilliam.[73] Anne's words in the Tower, reported by Kingston, reflect at the least some imprudently flirtatious conversations. For Anne to tease Norris that he looked to marry her if anything happened to the king was remarkably indiscreet. Chapuys reported that Archbishop Cranmer had declared that Princess Elizabeth was Anne's bastard by Norris, not the king's daughter.[74] Here Chapuys was wrong, but his error itself may be revealing. A little later Chapuys implicitly corrected himself, reporting that Elizabeth had been declared a bastard: not because she was Norris's daughter, as might more honestly have been said, Chapuys commented, but because Henry's marriage to Anne had been invalid from the beginning owing to Henry's previous sexual relationship with Anne's sister.[75] De Carles's poem has Princess Mary implicitly doubting Elizabeth's paternity. Does that and Chapuys's gossip imply a long-standing relationship between Norris and Anne? There is nothing that offers conclusive proof, but that

Norris and Anne were lovers is by no means a far-fetched interpretation of the fragmentary sources available to us. Thomas Wyatt's poem stops intriguingly short of an assertion of Norris's innocence and alludes instead to his actions:[76]

> To think what hap did thee so lead or guide,
> Whereby thou hast both thee and thine undone. . .

'Incontinent living so rank and common'
WAS ANNE GUILTY?

If adultery was a crime and all this was presented in a court of law, the only fair response would be the Scottish verdict of not proven. There simply is not sufficient evidence to conclude beyond reasonable doubt that Anne, her brother, Norris, Weston, Brereton and Smeaton were guilty. Courts that dispense justice and that can deprive men and women of their freedom, indeed of their lives, must properly operate according to the most exacting and demanding standards of proof. But to conclude that it would, on what we know, be unfair to convict them does not mean that they were all innocent. The Scottish verdict of not proven is not the same as the English verdict of not guilty.

Historians can legitimately reason at different levels of proof. What historians seek to do is to understand what happened in the past. Inevitably the surviving sources are fragmentary and in varying degrees affected by the perspectives of those who produced them. Historians are thus well used to developing their arguments from documentation that is often much less full than would be desirable. But that we cannot know as much as we should wish, or with the certainty that we should wish, about the past does not invalidate our proceedings. Anne Boleyn either did or did not sleep with the men accused with her. Lacking divine omniscience, and in the absence of compelling eyewitness descriptions of illicit lovers caught *in flagrante*, we are left to weigh a range of possible explanations that make the best sense of the inadequate sources that we do have. Most historians have too quickly decided that the very notion that a queen could have committed adultery, and with five men, is so preposterous that it is hardly worth considering seriously. But their alternative explanations, as we have seen, have been unconvincing, contradicted by our sources read carefully, and falling foul of elementary tests of plausibility. If we do not begin with the assumption that Anne must have been innocent, but instead allow a measure of controlled inference, it is possible to offer a reading of events that makes her downfall appear very understandable indeed.

Let us suppose that Anne was naturally flirtatious—and that it was her vivacity that had originally captivated and infatuated the king. Henry clearly fell head over heels in love with her. But it is unlikely that Anne was ever quite so much in love with him. She may have been much more involved with Henry Percy, the future earl of Northumberland, and with Thomas Wyatt. Once Henry's wish for an annulment of his marriage to Catherine of Aragon became generally known, Anne Boleyn was widely criticised. How far was such denunciation a true reflection of her character and behaviour? When the abbot of Whitby said that the king 'was ruled by one common stud whore Anne Bullan',[1] when a Warwickshire priest, Ralph Wendon, said that Anne was a 'whore and harlot',[2] when another priest, James Hamilton, asked, 'who the devil made Nan Bullen, that whore, queen',[3] when one Robert Borett called her 'a whore',[4] when one Burgyn's wife of Watlington said that Anne was 'a whore and a harlot of her living',[5] when Margaret Copland called her 'a strong whore',[6] when John MacDowell or Maydland, a Scottish Dominican friar who preached at the London Blackfriars in 1534, called her 'that mischievous whore',[7] when Margaret Chancellor of Suffolk called her 'a goggyll-eyd hore', a 'naughty whore',[8] were they simply attacking the woman who had undermined the king's first marriage? Would any woman who had won the king in such circumstances have been dismissed as a whore, whatever her personal characteristics? Burgyn's wife had explicitly and unfavourably compared Anne Boleyn to Queen Catherine.[9] None of those who denounced Anne had, it may be assumed, had any first-hand knowledge of the queen's private life, though of course they may have heard gossip, and gossip is not necessarily false. Mistress Amadas, wife of the king's goldsmith, and something of a prophetess, said that Anne should be burned because she was a harlot. Did she know more about Anne? Interestingly she also said that Norris acted as bawd between the king and

Anne.[10] In late 1534 the duke of Norfolk, after a quarrel with Anne, called her 'a great whore'.[11] The law of treason was revised in 1534, with anything 'to the prejudice, slander, disturbance and derogation' of the king's marriage to Anne Boleyn being treated as treason (25 Henry VIII c. 22): it is interesting that such measures should have been thought necessary and suggests that the perception of Anne as a whore was widespread. Gossip in Flanders in September 1533 had it that 'the king is abused by the new queen, and that his gentlemen goeth daily a playing where they will'.[12] When the king told her she must put up with his affairs, he said that she must shut her eyes and endure as well as more worthy persons: what did Henry imply by his use of the phrase 'more worthy persons'?[13] When instructions to Nicholas Heath and Christopher Mount, sent on embassy to the German princes in 1534, insisted on Anne's 'excellent virtues', and listed them as 'the purity of her life, her constant virginity, her maidenly and womanly pudicity, her soberness, her chasteness, her meekness, her wisdom . . .', maybe the king was protesting too much.[14] According to Ridolfo Pio, bishop of Faenza, the papal nuncio in France, Francis I spoke in summer 1535 of 'how little virtuously she has always lived and now lives'.[15] Anne's choice of New Year's gift to the king in 1534 was 'a goodly gilt basin, having a rail or board of gold in the midst of the brim, garnished with rubies and pearls, wherein standeth a fountain, also having a rail of gold about it garnished with diamonds; out thereof issueth water, at the teats of three naked women standing at the foot of the same fountain'. Was this unusually risqué, hinting at what might be called a liberated, certainly an un-puritan, attitude to sexuality?[16] If, as Chapuys reported, she told 'someone she loved well but whom the king had thrown out of the court from jealousy'—could that have been Wyatt?—that she thought she was pregnant in early 1533, did she not risk being seen to be behaving flirtatiously?[17]

There is a remarkable description of Anne's court in June 1533 by her chamberlain Sir Edward Bainton. Since he was writing to Anne's brother, it is hard to see why what he said should be doubted. Sounding like Don Alfonso in Mozart's *Così fan tutte*, Bainton reported that[18]

as for pastime in the queen's chamber, [there] was never more. If any of you that be now departed have any ladies that ye thought favoured you and somewhat would mourn at parting of their servants, I can no wit perceive the same by their dancing and pastime they do use here, but that other take place, as ever hath been the custom.

Was it then the case that, as has been suggested, '"pastime in the queen's chamber" does seem to have got somewhat out of hand' and Anne's 'loss of control within her household' made Anne 'vulnerable'?[19] Not surprisingly, John Foxe, the martyrologist, would be at pains in his description of Anne's godly household to insist that Anne's ladies would have no leisure 'to follow such practices as daily are seen nowadays to reign in princes' courts'.[20] Foxe leaves the impression, perhaps deliberately, that so pious a queen could not possibly have been behaving so badly. There is a pervasive and tenacious assumption that those who are devout must and do live moral and chaste lives; and an equally pervasive and tenacious assumption that those whose lives, at least at times, are dissolute, or who, at least at times, defy or show little respect for the teachings of the church, cannot be, at least at times, sincerely devout.

Any hints of the contrary are often treated by modern historians as a problem. That Anne and Henry exchanged love notes in a Book of Hours does not mean that they were not pious. 'Remember me when you do pray/That hope doth lead from day to day,' wrote Anne; 'If you remember my love in your prayers as strongly as I adore you, I shall hardly be forgotten, for I am yours, Henry R. forever,' responded Henry; to which Anne added, beneath a miniature of the Annunciation, 'By daily proof you shall me find/To be to you both loving and kind.'[21] The commitment, if not the place in which these words were written, was entirely proper. Were the lavish bindings of several of the books in what is seen as Anne's library evidence of her love of beautiful things, and does it show 'elements of the "frivolous butterfly" . . . whose household was a centre of elegant artifice, who owned and proudly flaunted her beautifully crafted, jewel-like books, "gorgiously" bound'?[22] Should that be contrasted with her piety? Or was it not necessarily incompatible with being personally pious? That is surely the case. Human nature, and especially human sexuality, is more complex than that, and men and women all too often behave in ways that go against ideals that they have themselves upheld. 'The evidence of many a christian life suggests that the same person may be capable both of expressions of piety and personal dissoluteness: Anne Boleyn may well have been both flirtatious and fearful of the Doom; her brother's French influence may have extended to kissing as well as piety.'[23] Moralising sermons denouncing the temptations of the flesh may well, paradoxically, have been attractive to those who felt, and succumbed to, such temptations all too often. Obviously it is in imaginative literature that we find the most subtle and penetrating explorations of the human predicament, but it would be wrong to suppose that in this respect works of fiction do not vividly illuminate the dilemmas of life as it is and was lived.

Let us imagine Anne, naturally flirtatious, but during the long years in which Henry pursued his divorce, loyally and patiently waiting while Henry held back from full sexual relations until everything was officially regularised. Let us imagine Anne at last married to Henry, and now crowned queen of England, but continuing to enjoy dancing and pastime in her chamber, served by ladies who readily acquired new suitors. Let us imagine that Henry, for all his expressions of love for Anne, found himself at least intermittently impotent, yet tempted, perhaps more auspiciously, by others. Let us imagine a defiant Anne, resentful of Henry's continuing affairs ('And often I felt some jealousy towards him', de Carles's poem presents Anne as saying; and remember Chapuys's remark about Anne's jealousy in 1533),[24] prepared, in 1536, to encourage her almoner, John Skip, to offer barely veiled criticism of Henry's philandering in a sermon preached in the royal chapel. Let us imagine that mixed with Anne's defiance was her awareness of the king's expectation that she should produce a son for him. Let us imagine Anne consequently enjoying relationships with her courtier servants that went far beyond the contemporary conventions of courtly love, the platonic gallant courtship of married women. Chapuys, the imperial ambassador, appeared somewhat sceptical at the charges presented against Anne at her trial, but nonetheless reported gossip that after the 'new bishops' had told Anne that she had no need to confess, she had grown more audacious in vice; they had persuaded her that it was lawful to seek aid elsewhere, even from her own relations, when her husband was not capable of satisfying her.[25] Henry Norris, chief gentleman of the king's privy chamber, was an obvious suitor, and Norris and Anne may well have enjoyed a quite lengthy relationship. It was contemporaries who gossiped that Elizabeth, Anne's daughter born in September 1533, was Norris's child, not the king's. And let us imagine Anne flirting at times with Weston, Brereton and Mark the musician, and allowing her brother to come to her chamber. Anne was playing with fire. Of course such behaviour was foolish and reckless. But such is human nature and such is the force of sexual desire that men and women do take risks and behave in ways that onlookers not so driven might well think extraordinarily imprudent. All the time Anne was Henry's queen and if their relationship in these years was one of sunshine and storms, no more than those of Henry did Anne's affairs and flirtations prevent their being reported, on several occasions, as 'merry' together.

When Anne and the others were indicted, the adulteries were alleged to have been committed on specified dates. Let us, for the sake of argument, suppose that the dates given were broadly correct. Anne would then have committed adultery with Henry Norris in October/November 1533 and with William Brereton in November 1533, just after what was for Henry the disappointment that Anne's child born in September was a daughter rather than the hoped-for son and heir, and just after Henry's interest in another lady had provoked Anne, if Chapuys is to be believed. Anne was then accused of having committed adultery with Mark Smeaton in April/May 1534 and with Sir Francis Weston in May/June 1534. If Anne was indeed pregnant in those months, that would be highly improbable; but suppose Anne knew that she was not pregnant, but experiencing a phantom pregnancy, then maybe such affairs could be seen as an attempt to become pregnant by someone. And Anne's alleged incest with her brother in November/December 1535 could just be seen as an ever more desperate attempt at pregnancy: and an early miscarriage in January could be seen as her body's swift rejection of an unnatural pregnancy. All that, of course, is vastly speculative, but it does at least offer some sort of explanation for Anne's apparently reckless behaviour: both defiance of Henry's affairs, and increasingly desperate attempts to get pregnant. And if Henry was not so much impotent as intermittently impotent, it offered Anne both a problem—her chances of becoming pregnant by Henry were dwindling—and an opportunity—she could try to become pregnant by someone else without Henry having any reason to doubt that the baby was his own.

Of course that was terribly risky. But unmasking, if always a danger, was not inevitable. Those who gossiped about Anne's relationship with Norris 'knew' they were lovers, but that is not to say that they could have proved it in law, and unless something happened to force them to speak out, they would do no more than gossip. Courtly love derived its charge precisely from its ambiguities and uncertainties. 'Madame X might have been "known" to be the mistress of Chevalier Y', but who could be sure that such a relationship was sexual rather than simply a friendship? 'Do they or don't they?' would be the mostly unspoken subtext of court gossip and banter in a society in which religion laid down demanding ideals of sexual restraint.[26] The 'double standard' by which men's affairs were tolerated while women were expected to remain pure and faithful added a further burden[27]—against the hypocrisy of which Anne Boleyn may well have felt she was protesting. But were she to be found out, her reputation would be destroyed.

Mary, Anne's sister, offers a vivid illustration of how the 'double standard' worked. She had been banished from court when she became pregnant out of wedlock by Sir William Stafford in 1534, even though they then hastily married.[28] He was young, and love overcame reason, Mary explained to Cromwell, three months after their clandestine marriage. She saw so much honesty in him—and we should pause to note that the word 'honest' was often used as a synonym for chaste—that she loved him as well as he did her. She felt she was in bondage: for her part she saw that all the world did set so little by her. By contrast he set so much store by her that she felt she was to be at liberty: 'I thought I could take no better way but to take him and forsake all other ways and to live a poor honest life with him.' If they recovered the favour of the king and queen she was sure that they would be able to do so. 'For well I might have had a greater man of birth and a higher, but I assure you I could never have had one that should have loved me so well nor a more honest man.' She begged Cromwell to put her husband to the king's grace—did she mean to intercede for her husband, or to allow her husband to speak directly to Henry?—and persuade the king to speak to Anne, 'who is rigorous against them'. That might be thought to be somewhat unkind of Anne. Her brother, George, and the duke of Norfolk were 'so cruel against us'. And Mary repeated herself, insisting that she had found so much honesty in her husband that 'I had rather beg my bread with him than to be the greatest queen christened'. That cut rather close to the bone. After all, Mary Boleyn had for a time been Henry's mistress, and, perhaps, the mother of two of his children.[29]

It was the accident of a quarrel between one of the queen's ladies and her brother that brought Anne's conduct into the open. What was then crucial was the attitude of the king. If he had been told such things in the early stages of his relationship, he probably would have dismissed them, so deep was his infatuation, especially if the tales rested on hearsay rather than directly observed evidence. When Wyatt had warned him that Anne was a bad woman, Henry's reaction was to reject the tale out of hand and to ban Wyatt from court for two years—or so the *Spanish Chronicle* tells us. But by 1536 Henry's passion had cooled, and while he continued, politically, to defend Anne as his lawful wedded wife, he was pursuing Jane Seymour. This does not mean that he would inevitably have discarded Anne; more likely, Jane would have been just another in a long line of mistresses. But against that background, if stories of Anne's relationships with Norris, Smeaton and others were to surface, Henry would no longer be certain to dismiss them. Now Henry would probe and test the evidence, interrogate those under suspicion, and, once persuaded, strike hard.

And what Henry learned was, it has been suggested here, not only plausible, but also persuasive. The countess of Worcester, as one of the queen's ladies, was in a good position to know what the queen had been doing: her testimony carried weight. Mark Smeaton's confession would have taken some disbelieving. Much must have hinged on Henry's confronting Norris with the charges: evidently Norris's denials failed to convince the king. What Kingston reported from the Tower that Anne was saying can only have reinforced the king's conviction that Anne and the others were guilty: in short, it was not unreasonable for Henry to have believed what he heard. And it is hard to think that he would have been anything but angry to learn that Anne was gossiping about his impotence.

Not surprisingly given the seriousness of the charges, anyone known to be acquainted with Anne would now fall under suspicion. In his anger and frustration, Henry declared that Anne had been unfaithful with more than a hundred men.[30] According to the indictments, Henry 'took such inward displeasure and heaviness', from Anne's malice and adultery especially, that 'certain harms and perils have befallen his royal body': the shock had made him ill.[31] But that Wyatt, Bryan and Page were first imprisoned and then released shows that Henry's reactions were not indiscriminate but rather that he was making real efforts to grasp what was going on and who was involved. Misunderstandings were, of course, not impossible in such circumstances, and some of those charged with Anne may in fact have been wholly innocent but unfortunate enough to have said or done something that now looked irrefutably suspicious. That might explain how William Brereton, and even Anne's brother, came to be involved, if we conclude that they were innocent. It is unlikely that the countess of Worcester would actually have seen Anne and her lovers *in flagrante*. But if they did come to the queen's chamber, if among them Anne's brother, somewhat unconventionally, came to her chamber as well, all sorts of inferences, but also misunderstandings, were possible.

Also just possible, of course, is that *everything* we have considered was no more than a series of misunderstandings in response to 'unguarded speech and gossip', 'a lot of smoke but precious little fire'.[32] After Anne, in the Tower, told Kingston about Mark Smeaton, her mother rebuked her: 'such desire as you have had to such tales has brought you to this'.[33] It is just about possible that the countess of Worcester had herself read too much into what she thought she had seen, not just in the case of Anne's brother, but of all she spoke of. It is also just about possible that Anne's burblings in the Tower could be innocently explained away—but, crucially, that what Henry learned was amply sufficient to make him, reluctantly but reasonably, conclude that, alas, it was all true and then seek furiously to deal with those who had wronged him. Was it that, although there was no evidence that Anne was guilty, enough had been said to make Henry understandably and sincerely believe that she was?[34] Yet the countess of Worcester was in absolutely no doubt about Anne's behaviour—and she was in a very good position to know the truth. If what she said was wholly wrong, we should have to believe either that she deliberately invented the charges she brought against Anne or that she utterly mistook what Anne was, and was not, doing in her chamber. It is far more plausible that the countess was not totally wrong and that if, perhaps, she read too much into George Boleyn's visits to his sister's chamber, there was still a good deal of truth in what she declared about Anne's behaviour. And so it remains my own hunch that Anne had indeed committed adultery with Norris, probably with Smeaton, possibly with Weston, and was then the victim of the most appalling bad luck when the countess of Worcester, one of her trusted ladies, contrived in a moment of irritation with her brother to trigger the devastating chain of events that led inexorably to Anne's downfall.

EPILOGUE

The Anne Boleyn presented in this book is not the Anne Boleyn to be found in most accounts of her life. Here the characteristic view of Anne Boleyn as the woman who captivated Henry VIII but refused to sleep with him for six years until he made an honest woman of her, as the inspiration for the break with Rome and royal supremacy, and as the patroness of protestant reformers, in short as the *fons et origo* of the Henrician Reformation, has been rejected. Nor has Anne been seen as the innocent victim of a king who tired of her or of rival political factions who brought her down with malicious and false accusations: here it has been suggested that those charges were at least credible, and, quite probably, in part true.

If, like so many, you hold the traditional view of Anne, then this book might seem to have diminished her standing, since Anne no longer emerges as such a leading player in the politics and religious ferment of the late 1520s and 1530s. But I did not set out to write this book with the intention of belittling Anne. My concern, quite simply, has been to recover the historical Anne Boleyn. It was by asking questions, especially in the course of teaching, by going on to examine how securely founded that traditional view of Anne was, that I came to doubt it, and then to suspect that Anne's life had too unthinkingly been incorporated into a triumphalist account of how a formidable woman sparked off the English Reformation. I came to my sceptical view not from any prejudice against Anne, much less any prejudice against queens, and certainly not any prejudice against women, but because the sources simply do not seem to me to support that conventional image.

It has been a careful review of the evidence that has led me to the conclusions that it was not Anne but Henry who held back for years from full sexual relations until he could marry her and father children of unimpeachable legitimacy, that it was Henry, not Anne, who developed the ideas that led to the break with Rome and the assertion of the royal supremacy, that it was Henry, not Anne, who worked with churchmen to purify the church, and that it was neither Henry nor political factions that brought Anne down, but her own actions, or at least justified perceptions of her own actions.

If your view of Anne has been close to the claim that she was 'that Tudor rarity, the self-made woman ... [who] was where she was by virtue of her own abilities and what she had made of herself, not by virtue of wealth or family',[1] or that vividly expressed on a website devoted to discussion of Anne, that

> she was a truly amazing woman, strong, independent, intelligent, witty, seductive, ambitious, determined and fiery. She changed the world she lived in by taking an undesirable situation (Henry VIII wanting her for his mistress after seducing and discarding her sister Mary) and moulding it into what she wanted (refusal, leading to the break with Rome, Reformation, Queenship)

then the portrait I have offered here may well be deeply unsettling, rather like coming back to a landscape you thought you knew, only to find all the trees in different places, indeed to be told that the trees had never been where you thought they were. That will be all the more the case if, like the poster of those thoughts on the website, you see Anne as a role model for women: 'I believe it's something we girls should learn from; we should not sulk when things don't go our way, we should change it.'

With those admirable sentiments on how to live a life, I have no quarrel at all. But I do question the use of men and women from the past, indeed the present, as role models of that sort. Much better to work out what to do in its own terms; and important to remember that most men and women are mixtures of good qualities and not-so-good qualities. Models are not necessary. To the lament, 'Unhappy the land that has no heroes', Brecht's Galileo replied 'Unhappy the land that needs heroes'. Men and women should not need to study the life of Anne Boleyn, or modern 'celebrities', to learn that if you do not like your lot in life, you should do what you can to improve it. Anne lived too long ago, and her circumstances were so extraordinary, that they can have little direct bearing on the lives we lead today. Yet if the reasoning deployed in this book leads to a very different Anne, it still leaves her as a significant figure. If Henry had not become infatuated with her, events would have unfolded very differently—'this business', an ostler of the White Horse, Cambridge, allegedly said, 'had never been if the king had not married Anne Bullen'[2]—and for that reason alone Anne's life demands scholarly attention. If it was not Anne who gave Henry the idea of breaking with Rome, once all that was done, Anne may, as Chapuys suggests, have encouraged Henry to treat Princess Mary more harshly. Anne undoubtedly took an interest in religious developments, but not as a proponent of protestantism, whether embryonic or fully fledged. And if she did sleep around, and commit at least some of the adulteries with which she was charged, she may well have done so boldly, in a spirit of defiance of the pervasive double standard that allowed men but not women to take lovers. The Anne that this book seeks to present is not an insignificant and submissive mistress. If the Anne to be found in the sources, scrutinised and questioned rigorously as they have been here, is neither the Anne of protestant legend, nor Anne as a modern heroine, she nonetheless remains one of the most important figures in Tudor history.

Appendix: The Portraits of Anne Boleyn

What did Anne Boleyn look like? The only indisputable image created during her lifetime is a now somewhat damaged medal (in the British Museum) bearing the date 'Anno 1534' and inscribed 'A.R.'—for Anna Regina—and the motto 'The Moost Happi'. Anne's nose has been unflatteringly flattened; the medal is consequently not that helpful as an indication of her appearance.

Two near-identical miniatures, one in the collection of the duke of Buccleuch and the other in the Royal Ontario Museum, Toronto, have been claimed as portraits of Anne, though they lack any identifying inscription. The Toronto portrait bears the date 'ano xxv', implying that the sitter was twenty-five years old. If Anne had been born in 1501, then this portrait would have to date from 1526–27. Some scholars think such a date rules it out as a portrait of Anne Boleyn as it would be a touch too early if we are to assume that the painting was commissioned by Henry VIII after he had fallen in love with her and she had agreed to be his mistress; others accept its authenticity as a portrait of Anne and indeed treat it rather as independent evidence for the timing of Henry's infatuation with Anne. On grounds of style these miniatures have been attributed to Lucas Horenbout, who was in England from 1526, or to his father Gheraert.

More widely associated with Anne Boleyn are two portraits, one at Hever Castle, Kent, and the other in the National Portrait Gallery, London, both bearing inscriptions—'Anna Bolina Angliae Regina' and

'Anna Bolena Uxor Henrici Octavi' respectively—which proclaim the sitter as Anne Boleyn, queen of England and wife of Henry VIII. There are several other versions of this image, mostly in country house galleries. The Hever and National Portrait Gallery images are certainly striking, though lacking the astonishing vividness characteristic of Hans Holbein's portraits (for example his Thomas More or his Thomas Cromwell, both now in the Frick). On grounds of such connoisseurship they are generally taken to be later sixteenth-century copies—because the outlines of the faces are clearly defined without signs of reworking, implying dependence on a standard pattern—of a now lost original from the 1530s—because the dress and position of the sitters are like those of portraits undoubtedly from that decade. One suggestion is that the original was painted by Lucas Horenbout. Another possibility is that it was indeed by Holbein, who was in England from 1532 and could easily have painted Anne.

It is possible that Holbein at least drew Anne Boleyn. There are two surviving chalk and pen drawings by him, part of a book of drawings acquired by Henry VIII after Holbein's death, inscribed 'Anna Bullen Regina' (formerly at Weston Park, now in the British Museum) and 'Anna Bollein Queen' (in the Royal Collection, Windsor Castle). Whether they are images of Anne Boleyn has, however, been a matter of controversy. They do not really seem to be of the same woman, and while the British Museum image is not altogether unlike the Hever/NPG portraits, though the lips are larger, the Windsor image is of a woman with a double chin, her head-dress is informal, and she is apparently wearing a nightgown. It has been suggested that the listing in his privy purse payments of a gift from Henry to Anne of a nightgown clinches the identity of the sitter as Anne, but that does not seem compelling. Another possibility is that the drawing is unfinished and what appears to us as informal could have been intended to be worked up into a more conventional image. The inscription on the Weston Park/British Museum drawing dates only from 1649 and could be misinformed. The caption on the Windsor Castle drawing is most likely the work of John Cheke, tutor to Edward VI, who identified all the drawings in a book acquired by Henry VIII after Holbein's death. That it was thought necessary to write the names of the sitters on the drawings implies that there was already some uncertainty about their identities. Still, Cheke was in a good position to know. But the reliability of the current inscriptions is called into question as they may not be Cheke's originals but copied from originals which it is thought may have been on separate mounts.

More speculatively, in Holbein's *Solomon and the Queen of Sheba*, Solomon does plausibly bear some resemblance to Henry VIII: should we see the queen of Sheba as Anne, and go on to see Anne Boleyn as Holbein's patron? The difficulty with that, of course, is that the queen of Sheba was only a visitor, not Solomon's wife; and, for anyone interested in Anne's appearance, the details of the queen's face are unrevealing.

Again, a reading of Holbein's *Ambassadors* which links it to Anne's coronation—the French ambassadors stand on a Cosmati pavement, clearly referring to the sanctuary of Westminster Abbey where Anne was anointed—and concludes that Holbein's first royal patron was Anne Boleyn, rests on a chain of circumstantial reasoning, does not explain why Anne rather than Henry should have commissioned it, and does not throw any direct light on the question of whether Holbein ever portrayed Anne.

Finally there is a ring now at Chequers with two enamel portraits. One is clearly of Queen Elizabeth; the other, it has been claimed, is of Anne Boleyn. It is not easy to think of what other woman would have been a suitable companion for Queen Elizabeth in such a pairing, but obviously such reasoning is not conclusive. More telling is that this image is comparable to the portrait medal of Anne Boleyn of 1534, and to the portraits at Hever and in the National Portrait Gallery. That was, it can be deduced, what, in the reign of Elizabeth, Anne was thought to have looked like.

Of course, it is possible that it was a case of mistaken identity. The sheer number of portraits of Tudor monarchs and their queens raises questions here. From some point, maybe the middle of the century, more probably from the middle years of Elizabeth's reign, it became fashionable for noblemen and greater gentry to display portraits of kings and queens in their houses, especially in halls and long galleries. Many of these portraits are not works of the highest quality and it is easy to suppose that those who produced them were working from stock images. The reliability of any of the details of faces in such confections becomes moot: copyists may well have produced what they believed their patrons wanted rather than a scrupulously accurate copy. Confusion was readily possible. What was long taken as a portrait of Lady Jane Grey has, for example, been identified as a portrait of Catherine Parr.

Recently it has been claimed that all the panel portraits of Anne Boleyn, including the Hever and NPG portraits, are in fact copies or variants of an original portrait not of Anne Boleyn but of Mary, Henry VIII's sister, briefly married to Louis XII, king of France, and then to Charles Brandon, duke of Suffolk. By the time they were made, in the later sixteenth century, the confusion of identity had occurred and from then on when copyists thought they were reproducing an image of Anne Boleyn they were in fact depicting Mary. In circumstantial support it is suggested that the brooch in the form of a B that the sitter wears was unlikely to have been used to signify Boleyn: much more likely that it signified Brandon. That is not, however, conclusive: in his love letters to Anne Henry used her initials AB. And it is not at all obvious that Mary, as the sister of the king of England and widow of the king of France, should have thought it appropriate to identify herself with the by no means socially distinguished family name of Brandon. More intriguing, perhaps, is that the woman in the NPG portrait is portrayed with brown hair and brown eyes, not entirely corresponding to the few contemporary written descriptions of Anne. Perhaps specific documentary evidence may yet come to light.

More hopefully, the National Portrait Gallery *Making Art in Tudor Britain* project, in the course of which NPG portraits are being subjected to intensive technical study, including dendrochronology, promises to yield compelling evidence of dating. Early findings suggest that many panel portraits of Henry VIII's courtiers date from the late sixteenth or early seventeenth centuries. The NPG portrait of Anne Boleyn is due to be examined in 2010.[1]

Given the uncertainties, there remains ample scope for guesswork. And my guess is that the Hever and NPG portraits, if they are not original (and until dendrochronology offers a definite date it is not entirely clear why they cannot be original), were based on an original painted from the life by Holbein.

Yet it would be as well to be cautious, given that the identity and dating of most of these portraits is uncertain, and given that a remarkable feature of scholarship in this field is that many a portrait has been variously identified by scholars, first as one queen, then as another. Above all we must take care not to erect elaborate psychological explanations of Anne's character on the tantalisingly fragile evidence of these images.

NOTES

Abbreviations

BL	British Library
BN	Bibliothèque Nationale
Cal. S.P.	*Calendar of State Papers*
Hall, *Chronicle*	Hall, E., *Chronicle* (1809 edn)
LP	Brewer, J.S., J. Gairdner and R.H. Brodie, eds, *Letters and Papers, Foreign and Domestic, of the Reign of Henry VIII* (21 vols in 36, 1862–1932)
RSTC	Pollard, A.W., G.R. Redgrave, W.A. Jackson, F.S. Ferguson and K.F. Pantzer, *A Short-Title Catalogue of Books Printed in England, Scotland and Ireland, 1475–1640* (revised edn, 1986)
State Papers	*State Papers of Henry VIII* (11 vols, 1830–52)
TNA, PRO	The National Archives, Public Record Office

Chapter 1: 'These bloody days have broken my heart': the fall of Anne Boleyn

1. T. Aymot, 'A memorial from George Constantyne to Thomas Lord Cromwell', *Archaeologia*, xxiii (1931), p. 64.
2. I quote from the translation in J.S. Brewer, J. Gairdner and R.H. Brodie, eds, L[etters and] P[apers, Foreign and Domestic, of the Reign of Henry VIII], 21 vols in 36 (1862–1932), X 876 (TNA, PRO, KB8/9 9–11) for originals of indictments.
3. BL, Cotton MS, Otho C x fo. 226 (*LP*, X 792).
4. John Foxe, *Acts and Monuments*, ed. J. Pratt (8 vols, 1877), v. 136.
5. 'Does any historian seriously believe these charges?' asked Joel Hurstfield: *English Historical Review*, xcvi (1981), p. 614.

Chapter 2: Who was Anne Boleyn?

1. TNA, PRO, SP3/2 fo. 8 (*LP*, VIII 324).
2. BL, Cotton MS, Vitellius B xiv fo. 68 (*LP*, VII 148).

3. Cf. J. Gairdner, 'The age of Anne Boleyn', *English Historical Review*, x (1895), p. 104.
4. *LP*, IV i 1. I rely on the *LP* transcript from Cambridge, Corpus Christi College, MS 119 fo. 21.
5. H. Paget, 'The youth of Anne Boleyn', *Bulletin of the Institute of Historical Research*, liv (1981), pp. 162ff.; quoting *Correspondance de l'Empereur Maximilien Ier et de Marguerite d'Autriche*, ed. A.J.G. Le Glay (2 vols, Paris, 1839), ii. 461 n. 2.
6. *Correspondence of Matthew Parker*, ed. J. Bruce and T.T. Perowe, Parker Society (1853), p. 400, cit. E.W. Ives, *The Life and Death of Anne Boleyn* (Oxford, 2004), p. 3.
7. *LP*, III I p. 1539.
8. 'si bien addresse et si plaisante suivant son josne eaige': Paget, 'Youth of Anne Boleyn', pp. 164–5, from *Correspondance de Maximilien Ier et Marguerite*, ii. 461 n. 2.
9. Paget omits this: 'Youth of Anne Boleyn', p. 164.
10. Ibid., p. 165.
11. Ibid.
12. *Correspondance de Maximilien Ier et Marguerite*, ii. 461 n. 2.
13. Ives, *Anne Boleyn*, pp. 26–7; Paget, 'Youth of Anne Boleyn', p. 167.
14. Ives, *Anne Boleyn*, pp. 27–8.
15. G. Ascoli, *La Grande Bretagne devant l'opinion française depuis la guerre de cent ans jusqu'à la fin du XVIe siècle* (Paris, 1927), includes the edited text of L. de Carles, *Anne Boullant, Epistre contenant le process criminel faict a l'encontre de la royne Anne Bovllant d'Angleterre* (Lyons, 1545) (I have consulted the copy in Paris, BN, Res. Ye. 3668, and the MS versions in BN, Fonds francais, nos 1742, 2370, 12795). The passage cited is De Carles, *Anne Boullant*, p. 234. De Carles's poem will be discussed below, pp. 152–6.
16. *LP*, IX 378.
17. *LP*, VII 958.
18. De Carles, *Anne Boullant*, p. 234.
19. *LP*, III ii 1994.
20. *Calendar of State Papers, Spanish, Further Supplement*, p. 30.
21. *LP*, III i 1004.
22. *LP*, III i 1011.
23. *LP*, III i 1011, ii 1628; BL, Cotton MS, Galba B vii fo. 142 (*LP*, III ii 1709); *LP*, III ii 1718; BL, Cotton MS, Galba B vii fo. 52 (*LP*, III ii 1762).
24. BL, Cotton MS, Galba B vii fo. 52 (*LP*, III ii 1762).
25. *LP*, III ii p. 1559; E. Hall, *Chronicle* (1809 edn), pp. 631–2. Hall says that there were eight ladies beneath the castle but gives only seven names, as Sydney Anglo noticed, listing the seven 'and one unnamed', but without specifically drawing attention to the discrepancy: S. Anglo, *Spectacle, Pageantry, and Early Tudor Policy* (Oxford, 1969), p. 121.
26. George Cavendish, *The Life and Death of Cardinal Wolsey*, ed. R.S. Sylvester, Early English Text Society, ccxliii (1959), p. 29; D.M. Loades, ed., *The Papers of George Wyatt*, Camden Society, 4th ser. v (1968), p. 143.
27. Cavendish, *Life of Wolsey*, pp. 30–34.
28. Vienna, Haus-, Hof- und Staatsarchiv, England, Karton 7, Korrespondenz, Berichte, 1536, fo. 100 (*Cal. S.P., Spanish*, V ii no. xlviii p. 107).
29. *Wriothesley's Chronicle*, ed. W.D. Hamilton, Camden Society, 2nd ser., xi (1875), p. 41.
30. TNA, PRO, SP1/46 fos 231–6 at 234–234v (N. Pocock, *Records of the Reformation* [Oxford, 2 vols, 1870–71], i. 22ff: too briefly summarised in *LP*, IV ii 3686 [1, 2].
31. *LP*, III ii 3321.
32. TNA, PRO, SP1/34 fos 71–72v (*LP*, IV i 1201), TNA, PRO, SP1/39 fos 167–8 (*LP*, IV ii 2523). D. Starkey, *Six Wives* (London, 2003), p. 277, has made a case that a list of

household expenses beginning on 23 August in the eighteenth year of Henry VIII's reign, that is 1526, proves that 23 August 'must have been the date, on or shortly after their wedding day, when they had set up house together'. If that reasoning is valid, the wedding took place in 1526. But these surviving accounts need not have been the first annual set; they may have been the second, as Starkey himself surmises, in which case the marriage, took place in 1525—or perhaps the third or fourth set, thus dating the marriage back to 1524 or 1523. And the document is incomplete. Although the surviving first folio does indeed begin with 23 August 1526, the document in its entirety may well have begun on an earlier date, as Richard Hoyle has suggested to me. So it does not offer conclusive proof of the date of the marriage.

33. *The Life and Letters of Sir Thomas Wyatt*, ed. K. Muir (Liverpool, 1963), p. 23.
34. Thomas Wyatt, *Sir Thomas Wyatt: Complete Poems*, ed. R.A. Rebholz (1978), p. 96, no. liv, lines 1–2; cf. p. 374.
35. Ibid., p. 77, no. xi, lines 12–14.
36. Ibid., lines 1–2.
37. Ibid., p. 96, no. lv, line 1; p. 151, no. cxix, lines 1–2; p. 241, no. clxxxiii, lines 1–2.
38. S.W. Singer, ed., *The Life of Cardinal Wolsey* (2 vols, 1825), pp. 185–7.
39. M.A.S. Hume, ed., *Chronicle of King Henry VIII of England* (1889), p. 68.
40. Vienna, Haus-, Hof- und Staatsarchiv, England, Karton 5, Korrespondenz, Berichte, 1533, fo. 23.

Chapter 3: 'Whose pretty dukkys I trust shortly to kiss': Henry VIII's infatuation with Anne

1. De Carles, *Anne Boullant*, p. 234.
2. *Cal. S.P., Venetian*, iv no. 824 p. 365.
3. *Cal. S.P., Spanish*, IV ii (i) no. cmlxvii p. 473.
4. *LP*, VI 585.
5. N. Sander, *Rise and Growth of the Anglican Schism*, tr. and ed. D. Lewis (1877), p. 25.
6. Ibid.
7. De Carles, *Anne Boullant*, p. 234.
8. Paget, 'Youth of Anne Boleyn', pp. 169–70.
9. Cavendish, *Life of Wolsey*, p. 29.
10. *LP*, III ii p. 1539.
11. A. Hoskins, 'Mary Boleyn's Carey children: offspring of Henry VIII', *Genealogists' Magazine* (Mar. 1997).
12. TNA, PRO, SP1/92 fo. 37 (*LP*, VIII 567).
13. TNA, PRO, SP1/46 fos 231–6 at 234–34v (Pocock, *Records of the Reformation* i. 22ff: too briefly summarised in *LP*, IV ii 3686 [1, 2].
14. TNA, PRO, SP1/93 fo. 68 (*LP*, VIII 862 (2); Pocock, *Records of the Reformation*, ii. 468).
15. BL, Cotton MS, Cleopatra E iv fo. 99v (pencil foliation) (*LP*, VI 923).
16. TNA, PRO, SP1/125 fos 202–6, 207–9v; fos 211–11v (*LP*, XII ii 952 (1), 953); G.W. Bernard, *Power and Politics in Tudor England* (Aldershot, 2000), pp. 12–16, for Throckmorton.
17. TNA, PRO, SP1/92 fo. 31 (*LP*, VIII 565 [2]).
18. Quotations are from the facsimile edition—photographs and transcripts—provided by T. Stemmler, *Die Liebesbriefe Heinrichs VIII an Anna Boleyn* (Zurich, 1988).
19. *LP*, IV ii 3218; Stemmler, *Liebesbriefe Heinrichs VIII*, pp. 92–3.
20. Ives, *Anne Boleyn*, p. 85 agrees, as does Starkey, *Six Wives*, p. 274.
21. Brewer, *LP*, IV i p. cclviii.
22. *LP*, IV ii 3140.
23. TNA, PRO, SP1/45 fos 229–30 (*LP*, IV ii 4322).

24. Hall, *Chronicle*, p. 707, interpreted by Starkey, *Six Wives*, pp. 272–4.
25. *LP*, IV ii 3219; Stemmler, *Liebesbriefe Heinrichs VIII*, pp. 88–9; cf. Starkey, *Six Wives*, for a recent attempt.
26. *LP*, IV ii 3326; Stemmler, *Liebesbriefe Heinrichs VIII*, pp. 96–7.
27. Quoted Starkey, *Six Wives*, pp. 287–8.
28. *LP*, IV ii 3220; Stemmler, *Liebesbriefe Heinrichs VIII*, pp. 84–5.
29. *LP*, IV ii 3325; Stemmler, *Liebesbriefe Heinrichs VIII*, pp. 104–5. From the fact that Anne's gift was 'une etrenne'—a New Year's Day gift, Starkey (*Six Wives*, pp. 281–3) dates this letter to early 1527, just a few months before Henry publicly sought an annulment of his marriage to Catherine: Ives disputes the meaning of 'etrenne', suggesting that it need mean simply a gift, not a New Year's gift, and going on to postulate that 'etrenne' was anyway a metaphor for 'virginity: what Anne was pledging was her body. And that makes the likeliest date for Ives the early summer of 1527: Ives, *Anne Boleyn*, pp. 86–90.
30. Ives, *Anne Boleyn*, p. 91.
31. Starkey, *Six Wives*, p. 283.
32. TNA, PRO, SP1/46 fos 231–6 at 234–234v (Pocock, *Records of the Reformation*, i. 22ff); too briefly summarised in *LP*, IV ii 3686 [1,2].
33. Le Grand, *Histoire du divorce de Henry VIII* (3 vols, Paris, 1688), iii. 325 (*LP*, IV ii 5679).
34. Hall, *Chronicle*, p. 759.
35. *LP*, IV ii 4597; Stemmler, *Liebesbriefe Heinrichs VIII*, pp. 136–7.
36. Vienna, Haus-, Hof- und Staatsarchiv, England, Karton 7, Korrespondenz, Berichte, 1535, sealed to fo. 47 (*Cal. S.P., Spanish*, V i no. clxxxiv, p. 520; *LP*, VIII 1106 (ii)).
37. *LP*, IV ii 3990; Stemmler, *Liebesbriefe Heinrichs VIII*, pp. 112–13.
38. *LP*, IV ii 4984; Stemmler, *Liebesbriefe Heinrichs VIII*, pp. 148–9.
39. *LP*, IV ii 4597; Stemmler, *Liebesbriefe Heinrichs VIII*, pp. 136–7.
40. *LP*, IV ii 4537; Stemmler, *Liebesbriefe Heinrichs VIII*, pp. 108–9.
41. *LP*, IV ii 4742; Stemmler, *Liebesbriefe Heinrichs VIII*, pp. 144–5.
42. Le Grand, *Histoire du divorce de Henry VIII* iii. 137 (*LP*, IV ii 4391).
43. TNA, PRO, SP1/48/fo. 199 (*LP*, IV, ii 4408).
44. Le Grand, *Histoire du divorce de Henry VIII*, iii. 143 (*LP*, IV ii 4440).
45. Le Grand, *Histoire du divorce de Henry VIII*, iii. 164 (*LP*, IV ii 4649).
46. *LP*, IV iii app. 206.
47. *LP*, IV ii 4440.
48. *LP*, IV ii 3221; Stemmler, *Liebesbriefe Heinrichs VIII*, pp. 100–1.
49. *LP*, IV ii 4403; Stemmler, *Liebesbriefe Heinrichs VIII*, pp. 116–17.
50. *LP*, IV ii 4383; Stemmler, *Liebesbriefe Heinrichs VIII*, pp. 120–1.
51. *LP*, IV ii 4410; Stemmler, *Liebesbriefe Heinrichs VIII*, pp. 128–9.
52. *LP*, IV ii 4477; Stemmler, *Liebesbriefe Heinrichs VIII*, pp. 124–5.
53. *LP*, IV ii 4537; Stemmler, *Liebesbriefe Heinrichs VIII*, pp. 108–9.

Chapter 4: 'The King's Great Matter': Henry's divorce and Anne

1. *LP*, IV ii 3140, 3422, 3643.
2. *LP*, IV ii 3913.
3. TNA, PRO, SP1/82 fo. 19v (*LP*, VII 21); BL, Cotton MS, Vitellius B xiv fo. 68 (LP, VII 148).
4. *LP*, IV ii 4597; Stemmler, *Liebesbriefe Heinrichs VIII*, pp. 136–7
5. *LP*, IV ii 4648; Stemmler, *Liebesbriefe Heinrichs VIII*, pp. 140–1.
6. BL, Harleian MS 419 fo. 104v (*LP*, IV ii 4251).
7. BL, Cotton MS, Titus B i fo. 299 (*LP*, IV ii 4409).

8. *LP*, IV ii 4742; Stemmler, *Liebesbriefe Heinrichs VIII*, pp. 144–5.
9. *LP*, IV ii 4984; Stemmler, *Liebesbriefe Heinrichs VIII*, pp. 148–9.
10. Cavendish, *Life of Wolsey*, pp. 74–5.
11. TNA, PRO, SP1/42 fos 147–147v (*State Papers of Henry VIII*, i. no. cix p. 194; *LP*, IV ii 3217).
12. TNA, PRO, SP1/42 fo. 227 (*LP*, IV ii 3302); P. Gwyn, *The King's Cardinal: The Rise and Fall of Thomas Wolsey* (London, 1990), p. 515.
13. Gwyn, *The King's Cardinal*, pp. 515–16.
14. TNA, PRO, SP1/44 fos 38–47v at 40v–41 (*LP*, IV ii 3400).
15. TNA, PRO, SP1/44 fo. 76 (*LP*, IV ii 3422).
16. TNA, PRO, SP1/44 fo. 79v (*LP*, IV ii 3423).
17. TNA, PRO, SP1/47 fos 54v–55 (*LP*, IV ii 4005).
18. TNA, PRO, SP1/47 fo. 111 (*LP*, IV ii 4081).
19. TNA, PRO, SP1/48 fo. 101 (*LP*, IV ii 4335).
20. BL, Cotton MS, Vitellius B xii fo. 4 (*LP*, IV ii 4360).
21. BL, Cotton MS, Otho C x fo. 218 (*LP*, IV ii 4480).
22. BL, Cotton MS, Vespasian F iii fo. 34 (*LP*, IV iii app. 197).
23. BL, Cotton MS Vespasian F xiii fo. 141; cf. S. Doran, ed., *Henry VIII: Man and Monarch* (London, 2009), p. 119.
24. Starkey, *Six Wives*, p. 318.
25. *LP*, IV ii 4227; TNA, PRO SP1/47 fo. 216 (*LP* IV ii 4197).
26. TNA, PRO, SP1/48 fo. 199 (*LP*, IV ii 4408).
27. *LP*, V 11: Anne Boleyn was granted custody of William Carey's lands during the minority of Henry, son and heir, with wardship and marriage.
28. TNA, PRO, SP1/49 fos 95–95v (*State Papers*, i. no. clviii pp. 313–14; *LP*, IV ii 4488).
29. *LP*, IV ii 4477; Stemmler, *Liebesbriefe Heinrichs VIII*, pp. 124–5.
30. *LP*, IV ii 4477; Stemmler, *Liebesbriefe Heinrichs VIII*, pp. 124–5.
31. TNA, PRO, SP1/49 fos 95–95v (*State Papers*, i. no. clviii pp. 313–14; *LP*, IV ii 4488).
32. *LP*, IV ii 4507.
33. TNA, PRO, SP1/49 fo. 106 (*LP*, IV ii 4508).
34. *LP*, IV ii 4509.
35. TNA, PRO, SP1/51 fo. 35 (*LP*, IV ii 4950).
36. Gwyn, *King's Cardinal*, pp. 321–3.
37. Cavendish, *Life of Wolsey*, pp. 29, 35–6, 46, 43, 44.
38. Ibid., p. 137.
39. Starkey, *Six Wives*, p. 295.
40. *Cal. S.P., Spanish*, III pt. ii no. dcxx p. 887.
41. *LP*, IV ii 5210. Anne had in March 1528 already interceded for Sir Thomas Cheyney, a gentleman from Kent and a courtier, asking Wolsey to be good and gracious lord to him, assuring Wolsey that Cheyney was very sorry that he had displeased Wolsey (TNA, PRO SP1/47 fo. 111 [*LP*, IV ii 4081]).
42. TNA, PRO, SP1/52 fos 105–6 at 106 (*State Papers*, vii no. ccxxix, pp. 143–5; *LP*, IV iii 5152).
43. TNA, PRO, SP1/53 fos 210–11 (*State Papers*, vii no. ccxxxix, pp. 166–9; *LP*, IV iii 5481).
44. TNA, PRO, SP1/53 fo. 245v (*State Papers*, vii no. ccxxxix, p. 170; *LP*, IV iii 5519). Starkey thinks Bryan—son of Anne's mother's stepsister—was 'her eyes and ears as well as Henry's' (Starkey, *Six Wives*, p. 342), but Bryan's words do not bear that out.
45. TNA, PRO, SP1/54 fos 53–4 (*LP*, IV iii 5635); *La Correspondance du Cardinal Jean du Bellay*, ed. R. Scheurer (2 vols, Paris, 1969–73), i. no. 22, pp. 63–4 (*LP*, IV iii 5862); cf. Gwyn, *King's Cardinal*, 587, 590–1. Jean du Bellay seems at one point to have suggested that it was Anne Boleyn who was responsible for the despatch of Suffolk to

Francis I (*Correspondance du Jean du Bellay*, i. no. 17 p. 58 (but *LP*, IV iii 5742 says it was the duke of Norfolk, and Le Grand, *Histoire du divorce de Henry VIII*, iii. 333, leaves blanks); earlier, however, du Bellay wrote how Suffolk went to France 'de la part de son maistre' (*Correspondance du Jean du Bellay*, i. no. 8 p. 25 [*LP*, IV iii 5601]).

46. *LP*, IV iii 5523; BL, Cotton MS Vitellius B xi. fo. 169 (*LP*, IV iii 5703); *LP*, IV iii 5707; TNA, PRO, SP1/54 fos 96–7 at 96v (*LP*, IV iii 5711); BL, Cotton MS, Vitellius, B xi. fo. 166 (*LP*, IV iii 5715); BL, Cotton MS, Vitellius B xi. fo. 194 (*LP*, IV iii 5762); BL, Cotton MS, Vitellius, B xi. fo. 192 (*LP*, IV iii 5761); BL, Cotton MS, Vitellius B xi. fo. 203 (*LP*, IV iii 5780); PRO, SP1/55 fos 5–8 (in cipher; *LP*, IV, iii 5897; dating and authenticity discussed by Gwyn, *King's Cardinal*, pp. 527–8).

47. *LP*, IV iii 6076 (from Bodleian Library, Oxford, Jesus MS 74 c. fos 170ff.).

48. BL, Cotton App. L fo. 17 (*LP*, IV iii 6114; *State Papers*, i. 351).

49. *LP*, IV iii 6011 (Le Grand, *Histoire du divorce de Henry VIII*, iii. 375).

50. Vienna, Haus-, Hof- und Staatsarchiv, England, Karton 4, Korrespondenz, Berichte, 1530, fo. 286v (*Cal. S.P., Spanish*, IV i no. cclvii p. 450; *LP*, IV iii 6199).

51. Vienna, Haus-, Hof- und Staatsarchiv, England, Karton 4, Korrespondenz, Berichte, 1530, fos 356v–357 (*Cal. S.P., Spanish*, IV i no. dix, p. 819; *LP*, IV iii 6738).

52. *LP*, IV iii 6019 (Le Grand, *Histoire du divorce de Henry VIII*, iii. 377); cf. similar remarks by Chapuys, Vienna, Haus-, Hof- und Staatsarchiv, England, Karton 4, Korrespondenz, Berichte, 1529, fo. 212v.

53. 'Ce que en faict ladicte dame est tout par le commandement dudit seigneur roy': Le Grand, *Histoire du divorce de Henry VIII*, iii. 556–7 (*LP*, VI 1187).

54. Ives, *Anne Boleyn*, p. 302.

55. Starkey, *Six Wives*, pp. 285–6.

56. Foxe, *Acts and Monuments*, v. 137; Vienna, Haus-, Hof- und Staatsarchiv, England, Karton 7, Korrespondenz, Berichte, 1536, fo. 69v (*LP*, X 601).

57. Foxe, *Acts and Monuments*, iv. 656–8; cf. discussion by T.S. Freeman, 'Research, rumour and propaganda: Anne Boleyn in Foxe's "Book of Martyrs"', *Historical Journal*, xxxviii (1995), pp. 802–3, 805–6, 809–10.

58. J.G. Nichols, ed., *Narratives of the Days of the Reformation*, Camden Society, 1st ser., lxxvii (1857), pp. 52–6; J. Strype, *Ecclesiastical Memorials* (3 vols, in 6 parts, Oxford, 1822), I i. 171–2.

59. Vienna, Haus-, Hof- und Staatsarchiv, England, Karton 5, Korrespondenz, Berichte, 1531, fo. 19v (*Cal. S.P., Spanish*, IV ii (i) no. dcxli p. 71; *LP*, V 112).

60. Vienna, Haus-, Hof- und Staatsarchiv, England, Karton 5, Korrespondenz, Berichte, 1532, fo. 28v (*Cal. S.P., Spanish*, IV ii (i) no. dclxiv pp. 96–7; *LP*, V 148).

61. Vienna, Haus-, Hof- und Staatsarchiv, England, Karton 5, Korrespondenz, Berichte, 1532, fo. 19v (*Cal. S.P., Spanish*, IV ii (i) no. cmxv p. 405; *LP*, V 850).

62. Vienna, Haus-, Hof- und Staatsarchiv, England, Karton 5, Korrespondenz Berichte, 1531, fo. 19v (*Cal. S.P., Spanish*, IV ii (i) no. dcxli p. 71; *LP*, V 112).

63. Vienna, Haus-, Hof- und Staatsarchiv, England, Karton 5, Korrespondenz, Berichte, 1531, fo. 67 (*Cal. S.P., Spanish*, IV ii (i) no. dccv p. 261; *LP*, V 472).

64. TNA, PRO SP1/72 fo. 18v (*LP*, VI 1564); *LP*, VII 1717 is incorrect; pace Starkey, *Six Wives*, p. 468.

65. Vienna, Haus-, Hof- und Staatsarchiv, England, Karton 5, Korrespondenz, Berichte, 1531, fo. 64 (*Cal. S.P., Spanish*, IV ii (i) no. dccxcvi p. 248; *LP*, V 432).

66. Le Grand, *Histoire du divorce de Henry VIII*, iii. 231–2 (*LP*, IV ii 5016).

67. Le Grand, *Histoire du divorce de Henry VIII*, iii. 260 (*LP*, IV ii 5063).

68. Hall, *Chronicle*, pp. 754–5.

69. *LP*, IV iii 6026.

70. G. Mattingly, *Catherine of Aragon* (London, 1942), p. 223.

71. Ibid., pp. 223–4.

72. *LP*, IV iii 6411; BL, Lansdowne MS, 115 fo. 1.

73. Vienna, Haus-, Hof- und Staatsarchiv, England, Karton 5, Korrespondenz, Berichte, 1531, fo. 18v (*Cal. S.P., Spanish*, IV ii (i) no. dcxli p. 7; *LP*, V 112).

74. Vienna, Haus-, Hof- und Staatsarchiv, England, Karton 5, Korrespondenz, Berichte, 1531, fo. 24 (*Cal. S.P., Spanish*, IV ii (i) no. dcxlvi p. 78; *LP*, V 120).

75. Vienna, Haus-, Hof- und Staatsarchiv, England, Karton 5, Korrespondenz, Berichte, 1531, fos 53–54v (*Cal. S.P., Spanish*, IV ii (i) no. dccliii pp. 197–201; *LP*, V 308); Hall, *Chronicle*, p. 781 (Henry never saw her after 14 July).

76. Vienna, Haus-, Hof- und Staatsarchiv, England, Karton 5, Korrespondenz, Berichte, 1531, fo. 55v (*Cal. S.P., Spanish*, IV ii (i) no. dcclxv p. 212; *LP*, V 340).

77. *LP*, V 614.

78. Hall, *Chronicle*, p. 788.

79. Vienna, Haus-, Hof- und Staatsarchiv, England, Karton 5, Korrespondenz, Berichte, 1531, fos 41v–42 (*LP*, V 216).

80. Vienna, Haus-, Hof- und Staatsarchiv, England, Karton 5, Korrespondenz, Berichte, 1531, fos 73–73v (*Cal. S.P., Spanish*, IV ii (i) no. dcccxviii p. 278; *LP*, V 512).

81. Vienna, Haus-, Hof- und Staatsarchiv, England, Karton 5, Korrespondenz, Berichte, 1532, fo. 99v (*Cal. S.P., Spanish*, IV ii (i) no. miii p. 527; *LP*, V 1377).

82. Vienna, Haus-, Hof- und Staatsarchiv, England, Karton 5, Korrespondenz, Berichte, 1531, fo. 57v (*Cal. S.P., Spanish*, IV ii (i) no. dcclxxv pp. 223–4; *LP*, V 361).

83. BL, Additional MS, 20,030 (LP, V pp. 747ff.).

84. Ibid., fo. 2v.

85. Ibid., fo. 7v.

86. *LP*, IV iii app. 256.

87. Starkey, *Six Wives*, p. 413.

88. BL, Additional MS, 20,300 fos 115–115v.

89. Ibid., fos 26, 64v.

90. Vienna, Haus-, Hof- und Staatsarchiv, England, Karton 5, Korrespondenz, Berichte, 1532, fos 3–3v (*Cal. S.P., Spanish*, IV ii (i) no. dccclxxx p. 354; *LP*, V 696).

91. BL, Additional MS, 20,300 fo. 126v.

92. Ibid., fos 51v, 68v.

93. *LP*, V 594.

94. BL, Additional MS 6113 fo. 70 (*LP*, V 1274); *LP*, V 1370 (1–3); 1499.

95. *LP*, V 1292; cf. BL, Additional MS 6113 fo. 70 (LP, V 1274 (3)).

96. Hall, *Chronicle*, p. 793; *LP*, V 1485.

97. Cf. *LP*, V 1484, 1485.

98. 'La dame sestoit fort aydee a la promocion du cas et lauoit effectuee': Vienna, Haus-, Hof- und Staatsarchiv, England, Karton 5, Korrespondenz, Berichte, 1532, fo. 102 v (*Cal. S.P., Spanish*, IV ii (ii) no. mviii p. 534 ; *LP*, V 1429).

99. Vienna, Haus-, Hof- und Staatsarchiv, England, Karton 5, Korrespondenz, Berichte, 1533, fo. 20v (*Cal. S.P., Spanish*, IV ii (ii) no. mliii pp. 608–9; *LP*, VI 180).

100. Starkey, *Six Wives*, p. 461.

101. Vienna, Haus-, Hof- und Staatsarchiv, England, Karton 5, Korrespondenz, Berichte, 1532, fo. 90 (*Cal. S.P., Spanish*, IV ii (ii) no. cmlxxxvi p. 495; *LP*, V 1256).

102. TNA, PRO, SP1/71 fo. 19 (*LP*, V 1299).

103. Hall, *Chronicle*, p. 794.

104. Vienna, Haus-, Hof- und Staatsarchiv, England, Karton 5, Korrespondenz, Berichte, 1533, fo. 15v (*Cal. S.P., Spanish*, IV ii (ii) no. mxlvii p. 600; *LP*, VI 142).

105. Vienna, Haus-, Hof- und Staatsarchiv, England, Karton 5, Korrespondenz, Berichte, 1533, fo. 17 (*Cal. S.P., Spanish*, IV ii (ii) no. mxlviii p. 602; *LP*, VI 160).

106. Vienna, Haus-, Hof- und Staatsarchiv, England, Karton 5, Korrespondenz, Berichte, 1533, fo. 20 (*Cal. S.P., Spanish*, IV ii (ii) no. mliii p. 609; *LP*, VI 180).

107. *LP*, VI 661.

108. Vienna, Haus-, Hof- und Staatsarchiv, England, Karton 5, Korrespondenz, Berichte, 1533, fo. 23. This letter escaped the attention of the compilers of the calendars: it

was noted, not altogether accurately, by P. Friedmann, *Anne Boleyn* (2 vols, 1884), i. 189–90, on whom Starkey, *Six Wives*, pp. 477, 481, relies. 'Prunes' are plums, not apples.

109. Vienna, Haus-, Hof- und Staatsarchiv, England, Karton 5, Korrespondenz, Berichte, 1533, fo. 30v (*Cal. S.P., Spanish*, IV ii (ii) no. mlv p. 613; *LP*, VI 212).

110. Vienna, Haus-, Hof- und Staatsarchiv, England, Karton 5, Korrespondenz, Berichte, 1533, fo. 58v (*Cal. S.P., Spanish*, IV ii (ii) no. mlxi p. 643; *LP*, VI 351).

111. *LP*, VI 529, 528.

112. BL, Harleian MS, 41 fo. 1 (*LP*, VI 601).

113. Hall, *Chronicle*, p. 799.

114. *The noble tryumphaunt coronacyon of quene Anne wyfe unto the most noble kynge Henrye the viij* (1533) (RSTC 656), sig. A i v.

115. *LP*, VI 563; BL, Harleian MS, 41 fos 2–3 (*LP*, VI 601).

116. *LP*, VI 584.

117. BL, Harleian MS, 41 fo. 3v (*LP*, VI 601).

118. *LP*, VI 720.

119. Hall, *Chronicle*, p. 800.

120. *LP*, VI 583.

121. For a detailed analysis of the poetry of the pageants see A. Hunt, *The Drama of Coronation: Medieval Ceremony in Early Modern England* (Cambridge, 2008), pp. 64–76.

122. S. Foister, *Holbein and England* (London, 2004), pp. 128–30, for the latest discussion.

123. Hall, *Chronicle*, pp. 801–2; *LP*, VI 561; 584; 601. Hall seems aware of BL, Harleian MS, 41 fos 1–11v (*LP*, V 601).

124. BL, Royal MS, 18 A lxiv (F.J. Furnivall, ed., *Ballads from Manuscripts* [2 vols, 1868–72], i. 364–401).

125. Hunt, *The Drama of Coronation*, p. 52.

126. Hall, *Chronicle*, p. 803; BL, Harleian MS, 41 fo. 9v (*LP*, VI 601).

127. *LP*, VI 584; BL, Harleian MS, 41 fo. 10 (*LP*, VI 601).

128. BL, Harleian MS, 41 fo. 11 (*LP*, VI, 601) [fo. 12 is a sketch of the dining arrangements]; Hall, *Chronicle*, p. 804; *LP*, VI 562.

129. Hall, *Chronicle*, p. 805; De Carles, *Anne Boullant*, pp. 235–6.

130. *LP*, VI 585.

131. Vienna, Haus-, Hof- und Staatsarchiv, England, Karton 5, Korrespondenz, Berichte, 1533, fo. 87 (*Cal. S.P., Spanish*, IV ii (ii) no. mlxxxi p. 704; *LP*, VI 653).

132. Vienna, Haus-, Hof- und Staatsarchiv, England, Karton 5, Korrespondenz, Berichte, 1533, fos 94–94v (*Cal. S.P., Spanish*, IV ii (ii) no. mc p. 740; *LP*, VI 805).

Chapter 5: 'The most happy': King Henry and Queen Anne

1. Ives suggests 'storm followed sunshine, sunshine followed storm' (*Anne Boleyn*, p. 196), but his account minimises the storms.

2. Vienna, Haus-, Hof- und Staatsarchiv, England, Karton 5, Korrespondenz, Berichte, 1531, fos 41v–42 (*LP*, V 216).

3. Vienna, Haus-, Hof- und Staatsarchiv, England, Karton 5, Korrespondenz, Berichte, 1531, fo. 51 (*Cal. S.P., Spanish*, IV ii (i) no. dccxxxix p. 177; *LP*, V 287).

4. Vienna, Haus-, Hof- und Staatsarchiv, England, Karton 5, Korrespondenz, Berichte, 1533, fo. 9v (*Cal. S.P., Spanish*, IV ii (ii) no. mxlvii p. 594; *LP*, VI 142).

5. TNA, PRO, SP3/6 fo. 33 (*LP*, VI 879).

6. TNA, PRO, SP1/78 fo. 28 (*LP*, VI 891).

7. TNA, PRO, SP3/7 fo. 40 (*LP*, VI 948); cf. TNA, PRO, SP3/15 fo. 4 (*LP*, VI 963): the king and queen were in 'tres bonne sante'.

8. *LP*, VI 975.
9. Vienna, Haus-, Hof- und Staatsarchiv, England, Karton 5, Korrespondenz, Berichte, 1533, fo. 104v (*Cal. S.P., Spanish*, IV ii (ii) no. mcxvii p. 777; *LP*, VI 1018).
10. Vienna, Haus-, Hof- und Staatsarchiv, England, Karton 5, Korrespondenz, Berichte, 1533, fo. 108 (*Cal. S.P., Spanish LP*, IV ii (ii) no. mcxxiii p. 788; *LP*, VI 1069). Ives misdates this to 1534 (*Anne Boleyn*, p. 196).
11. Hall, *Chronicle*, pp. 805–6.
12. Vienna, Haus-, Hof- und Staatsarchiv, England, Karton 5, Korrespondenz, Berichte, 1533, fo. 126v (*Cal. S.P., Spanish*, IV ii (ii) no. mcxliv p. 842; *LP*, VI 1392).
13. There is no contemporary decipher: Vienna, Haus-, Hof- und Staatsarchiv, England, Karton 5, Korrespondenz, Berichte, 1533, fo. 148v. I have used the transcript in TNA, PRO, PRO31/18/2/1 fo. 1021v (*Cal. S.P., Spanish*, IV ii (ii), no. mclviii p. 878; *LP*, VI 1510).
14. TNA, PRO, SP3/13 fo. 47 (*LP*, VI 1293).
15. TNA, PRO, SP3/6 fo. 107 (*LP*, VII 126).
16. TNA, PRO, SP3/14 fo. 6 (*LP*, VII 556).
17. TNA, PRO, SP3/2 fo. 94 (*LP*, VII 682).
18. TNA, PRO, SP3/7 fo. 69 (*LP*, VII 823), TNA, PRO, SP3/7 fo. 62 (*LP*, VII 888).
19. Vienna, Haus-, Hof- und Staatsarchiv, England, Karton 5, Korrespondenz, Berichte, 1534, fo. 42v (*Cal. S.P., Spanish*, V i no. vii p. 21; *LP*, VII 114).
20. TNA, PRO, SP3/14 fo. 6 (*LP*, VII 556).
21. *LP*, VII 1668.
22. *LP*, VII, 958, 1013.
23. TNA, PRO, SP1/89 fo. 136 (*LP*, VIII 196).
24. Vienna, Haus-, Hof- und Staatsarchiv, England, Karton 5, Korrespondenz, Berichte, 1534, fo. 64v (*Cal. S.P., Spanish*, V i no. xc p. 264; *LP*, VII 1193).
25. J. Dewhurst, 'The alleged miscarriages of Catherine of Aragon and Anne Boleyn', *Medical History*, xxviii (1984), pp. 49–56.
26. Ives speculates that when Henry's intermittent impotence returned, 'the confidence and stimulation of the new marriage was shattered' (*Anne Boleyn*, p. 192).
27. Vienna, Haus-, Hof- und Staatsarchiv, England, Karton 5, Korrespondenz, Berichte, 1534, fo. 64v (*Cal. S.P., Spanish*, V i no. xc p. 264; *LP*, VII 1193).
28. *LP*, VII 1174, 1228.
29. Ives says she plotted with Anne to pick a quarrel with Henry's new fancy and force her to withdraw from court: Ives, *Anne Boleyn*, p. 194.
30. Vienna, Haus-, Hof- und Staatsarchiv, England, Karton 5, Korrespondenz, Berichte, 1534, fo. 66 (*Cal. S.P., Spanish*, V i no. xcvii p. 280; *LP*, VII 1257).
31. *LP*, VII 1279.
32. Vienna, Haus-, Hof- und Staatsarchiv, England, Karton 5, Korrespondenz, Berichte, 1534, fos 70v–71 (*Cal. S.P., Spanish*, V i no. cii p. 300; *LP*, VII 1297).
33. *LP*, VII 1369.
34. *LP*, VII 1397.
35. Vienna, Haus-, Hof- und Staatsarchiv, England, Karton 5, Korrespondenz, Berichte, 1534, fos 86–7 (*Cal. S.P., Spanish*, V i no. cxviii pp. 343–4; *LP*, VII, 1554). Ives casts doubt on what Carew says—a 'tainted source' (*Anne Boleyn*, p. 194).
36. *LP*, VII 1581.
37. Vienna, Haus-, Hof- und Staatsarchiv, England, Karton 7, Korrespondenz, Berichte, 1535, fo. 37 (*LP*, VIII 263). For a suggestion that Henry was pursuing Mary Shelton, see J.S. Block, 'Shelton family (1504–1558)', *Oxford Dictionary of National Biography* (Oxford, 2004): the difficulty with that identification is that 'Madge' is an abbreviation of Margaret not Mary.
38. Ives, *Anne Boleyn*, pp. 195–6.
39. Vienna, Haus-, Hof- und Staatsarchiv, England, Karton 7, Korrespondenz, Berichte, 1535, fos 2–2v (*Cal. S.P., Spanish*, V i no. clvi p. 454; *LP*, VIII 666).

40. Ives, *Anne Boleyn*, pp. 195–6.
41. *Cal. S.P., Venetian*, v. 1534–54, no. liv p. 27. Ives is sceptical of 'the conventional interpretation . . . that the marriage of Henry VIII and Anne Boleyn was breaking or had broken up'. That is because his overall interpretation has Anne in charge: but if Henry was having affairs, then Anne would manifestly not be in charge, and Henry would be capable of acting rather more independently than Ives generally allows (cf. Ives, *Anne Boleyn*, p. 195).
42. Vienna, Haus-, Hof- und Staatsarchiv, England, Karton 7, Korrespondenz, Berichte, 1535, fo. 32 v (*Cal. S.P., Spanish*, V i no. xlxxiv p. 493; *LP*, VIII 876).
43. G. Walker, *Plays of Persuasion* (Cambridge, 1991), p. 227, citing *LP*, VIII 949 (*Cal. S.P., Spanish*, V i no. clxxix p. 506).
44. TNA, PRO, SP1/96 fo. 101 (*LP*, IX 310); TNA, PRO, SP1/97 fo. 108 (*LP*, IX 555); *LP*, IX 571.

Chapter 6: She 'wore yellow for the mourning': Anne against Catherine

1. Starkey, *Six Wives*, p. 516.
2. Vienna, Haus-, Hof- und Staatsarchiv, England, Karton 5, Korrespondenz, Berichte, 1533, fo. 44v (*Cal. S.P., Spanish*, IV ii (ii) no. mlviii p. 630; *LP*, VI 324).
3. Vienna, Haus-, Hof- und Staatsarchiv, England, Karton 5, Korrespondenz, Berichte, 1533, fo. 58v (*Cal. S.P., Spanish*, IV ii (ii) no. mlxi pp. 642–3; *LP*, VI 351).
4. Vienna, Haus-, Hof- und Staatsarchiv, England, Karton 5, Korrespondenz, Berichte, 1533, fo. 74 (*Cal. S.P., Spanish*, IV ii (ii) no. mlxxiii p. 677; *LP*, VI 508).
5. Vienna, Haus-, Hof- und Staatsarchiv, England, Karton 5, Korrespondenz, Berichte, 1533, fo. 122v (*Cal. S.P., Spanish*, IV ii (ii) no. mcxxxiii p. 821; *LP*, VI 1249).
6. Vienna, Haus-, Hof- und Staatsarchiv, England, Karton 5, Korrespondenz, Berichte, 1533, fo. 128 (*Cal. S.P., Spanish*, IV ii (ii) no. mcxlix p. 855; *LP*, VI 1419).
7. Vienna, Haus-, Hof- und Staatsarchiv, England, Karton 5, Korrespondenz, Berichte, 1533, fo. 156v (*Cal. S.P., Spanish*, IV ii (ii) no. mclxiv p. 893; *LP*, VI 1558).
8. Vienna, Haus-, Hof- und Staatsarchiv, England, Karton 5, Korrespondenz, Berichte, 1534, fos 39v–40v (*Cal. S.P., Spanish*, V i no. iv pp. 11–13; *LP*, VII 83).
9. Vienna, Haus-, Hof- und Staatsarchiv, England, Karton 5, Korrespondenz, Berichte, 1534, fo. 45v (*Cal. S.P., Spanish*, V i no. viii p. 27; *LP*, VII 121).
10. There is no contemporary decipher. I have drawn on the transcript in TNA, PRO, PRO31/18/3/1 fos 31–2 (*Cal. S.P., Spanish*, V i no. x pp. 32–4; *LP*, VII 171).
11. There is no contemporary decipher. I have drawn on the transcript in TNA, PRO, PRO31/18/3/1 fos 42v–43 (*Cal. S.P., Spanish*, V i no. xvii p. 57; *LP*, VII 214).
12. Ives, *Anne Boleyn*, p. 198.
13. Vienna, Haus-, Hof- und Staatsarchiv, England, Karton 5, Korrespondenz, Berichte, 1534, fo. 74 (*Cal. S.P., Spanish*, V i no. xxii p. 72; *LP*, VII 296).
14. Vienna, Haus-, Hof- und Staatsarchiv, England, Karton 5, Korrespondenz, Berichte, 1534, fo. 85v (*Cal. S.P., Spanish*, V i no. xxxii p. 96; *LP*, VII 393).
15. Vienna, Haus-, Hof- und Staatsarchiv, England, Karton 5, Korrespondenz, Berichte, 1534, fo. 14 (*Cal. S.P., Spanish*, V i no. lviii p. 165; *LP*, VII 690).
16. Vienna, Haus-, Hof- und Staatsarchiv, England, Karton 5, Korrespondenz, Berichte, 1534, fos 21–21v (*Cal. S.P., Spanish*, V i no. lx p. 172; *LP*, VII 726). Cf. England, Karton 7, Korrespondenz, Berichte, 1536, fo. 113 (*Cal. S.P., Spanish*, V ii no. liv p. 122; *LP*, X 909) in which Chapuys recalls, after Anne's condemnation, how before the king married her she used to tell him that she knew well that there was a prophecy that at around this time a queen of England should be burned, but to please the king she said she did not care; after the marriage she would jest that some of what was in those prophecies had already come to pass, but she had not yet been

condemned. They might well have said to her, Chapuys drily observed, what was said to Caesar: the Ides have come—but not yet gone.

17. Vienna, Haus-, Hof- und Staatsarchiv, England, Karton 5, Korrespondenz, Berichte, 1534, fos 67–67v (*Cal. S.P., Spanish*, V i no. cii p. 294; *LP*, VII 1297).

18. Vienna, Haus-, Hof- und Staatsarchiv, England, Karton 5, Korrespondenz, Berichte, 1534, fo. 96 (*Cal. S.P., Spanish*, V i no. cxviii p. 343; *LP*, VII 1554).

19. Vienna, Haus-, Hof- und Staatsarchiv, England, Karton 5, Korrespondenz, Berichte, 1534, fo. 35–35v (*Cal. S.P., Spanish*, V i no. lxviii p. 198; *LP*, VII 871).

20. Vienna, Haus-, Hof- und Staatsarchiv, England, Karton 5, Korrespondenz, Berichte, 1534, fo. 14 (*Cal. S.P., Spanish*, V i no. lviii p. 165; *LP*, VII 690).

21. Vienna, Haus-, Hof- und Staatsarchiv, England, Karton 5, Korrespondenz, Berichte, 1534, fo. 97v (*Cal. S.P., Spanish*, V i cxviii p. 345; *LP*, VII 1554).

22. TNA, PRO, SP1/87 fos 54–7 (*State Papers*, vii. no. ccccxvii pp. 586–7; *LP*, VII 1483); cf. *LP*, VII 1554.

23. There is no contemporary decipher. I have drawn on the transcript in TNA, PRO 31/18/3/1 (1534), fos 158–9 (*Cal. S.P., Spanish*, V i no. cxii pp. 330–3; *LP*, VII 1482).

24. There is no contemporary decipher. I have drawn on the transcript in TNA, PRO 31/18/3/1 (1535), fo. 181 (*Cal. S.P., Spanish*, V i no. cxxvii p. 376; *LP*, VIII 48).

25. J. Le Laboureur, ed., *Mémoires de Michel de Castelnau* (2 vols, Brussels, 1731), i. 405–8 (*LP*, VIII 174).

26. *Mémoires de Castelnau*, i. 412 (*LP*, VIII 174).

27. Vienna, Haus-, Hof- und Staatsarchiv, England, Karton 5, Korrespondenz, Berichte, 1534, fos 86–7 (*Cal. S.P., Spanish*, V i no. cxviii pp. 343–4; *LP*, VII, 1554).

28. Vienna, Haus-, Hof- und Staatsarchiv, England, Karton 7, Korrespondenz, Berichte, 1535, fo. 65 (*Cal. S.P., Spanish*, V i no. cxlii p. 423; *LP*, VIII 431).

29. Vienna, Haus-, Hof- und Staatsarchiv, England, Karton 5, Korrespondenz, Berichte, 1533, fos 2–2v (*Cal. S.P., Spanish*, IV ii (ii) no. clvi p. 454; *LP*, VI 666).

30. Vienna, Haus-, Hof- und Staatsarchiv, England, Karton 7, Korrespondenz, Berichte, 1535, fo. 44v (*Cal. S.P., Spanish*, V i no. clxxxiii pp. 518–19; *LP*, VIII 1105).

31. Vienna, Haus-, Hof- und Staatsarchiv, England, Karton 7, Korrespondenz, Berichte, 1535, fo. 8 (*LP*, IX 777).

32. Vienna, Haus-, Hof- und Staatsarchiv, England, Karton 7, Korrespondenz, Berichte, 1535, fo. 83v (*Cal. S.P., Spanish*, V i no. ccxxix pp. 570–1; *LP*, IX 861); cf. *LP*, IX, 862 to Granvelle stressed how Cromwell 'stands above every one but the Lady'.

33. Hall, *Chronicle*, p. 818.

34. Vienna, Haus-, Hof- und Staatsarchiv, England, Karton 7, Korrespondenz, Berichte, 1536, fo. 13v (*Cal. S.P., Spanish*, V ii no. ix p. 19; *LP*, X 141).

35. Vienna, Haus-, Hof- und Staatsarchiv, England, Karton 7, Korrespondenz, Berichte, 1536, fo. 3v (*Cal. S.P., Spanish*, V ii no. iii p. 6; *LP*, X 59).

36. Vienna, Haus-, Hof- und Staatsarchiv, England, Karton 7, Korrespondenz, Berichte, 1536, fo. 13 (*Cal. S.P., Spanish*, V ii no. ix p. 18; *LP*, X 141).

37. Vienna, Haus-, Hof- und Staatsarchiv, England, Karton 7, Korrespondenz, Berichte, 1536, fo. 5v (*Cal. S.P., Spanish*, V ii no. ix p. 11; *LP*, X 141).

38. Vienna, Haus-, Hof- und Staatsarchiv, England, Karton 7, Korrespondenz, Berichte, 1536, fo. 13 (*Cal. S.P., Spanish*, V ii no. ix p. 19; V *LP*, X 141).

39. Vienna, Haus-, Hof- und Staatsarchiv, England, Karton 7, Korrespondenz, Berichte, 1536, fo. 7 (*Cal. S.P., Spanish*, V ii no. ix p. 12; *LP*, X 141).

40. Vienna, Haus-, Hof- und Staatsarchiv, England, Karton 7, Korrespondenz, Berichte, 1536, fo. 22v (*Cal. S.P., Spanish*, V ii no. xiii p. 27; *LP*, X 199).

41. Vienna, Haus-, Hof- und Staatsarchiv, England, Karton 7, Korrespondenz, Berichte, 1536, fo. 40 (*LP*, X 307 (ii)).

42. Vienna, Haus-, Hof- und Staatsarchiv, England, Karton 7, Korrespondenz, Berichte, 1536, fo. 38 (*Cal. S.P., Spanish*, V ii no. xxi p. 44; *LP*, X 307); cf. J. Gairdner, 'Preface', *LP*, X, pp. x–xi.
43. Ives, *Anne Boleyn*, p. 197.
44. Ibid., p. 198.

Chapter 7: 'I have done many good deeds in my life': Anne Boleyn's religion

1. Ives, *Anne Boleyn*, pp. 260–1.
2. M. Dowling, 'Anne Boleyn and reform', *Journal of Ecclesiastical History*, xxxv (1984), pp. 30–46.
3. Dowling, M. ed, 'William Latymer's Cronickille of Anne Bulleyne', *Camden Miscellany*, xxx, Camden Society, 4th ser., xxxix (1990), pp. 27–44, an edition of Bodleian Library, Oxford, MS Don c. 42.
4. Bodleian Library, MS Don c. 42 fos 28v–30 (Dowling, 'Latymer's Cronickille', pp. 56–60).
5. Ibid., fo. 23 (Dowling, 'Latymer's Cronickille', p. 49).
6. Ibid., fo. 23v (Dowling, 'Latymer's Cronickille', p. 49).
7. Ibid., fos 24–24v (Dowling, 'Latymer's Cronickille', p. 50).
8. Ibid., fos 24v, 25 (Dowling, 'Latymer's Cronickille', pp. 51–2).
9. Ibid., fos 27, 26 (Dowling, 'Latymer's Cronickille', pp. 54, 53).
10. Foxe, *Acts and Monuments*, v. 175.
11. Quoted Freeman, 'Research, rumour and propaganda', p. 799.
12. Foxe, *Acts and Monuments*, v. 60, 137, 260.
13. P. Collinson, 'Truth and legend: the veracity of John Foxe's Book of Martyrs', in A.C. Duke and C.A. Tamse, eds, *Clio's Mirror: Historiography in Britain and the Netherlands, Britain and the Netherlands*, viii (1985), pp. 31–54, esp. 36–7, 39, 42–3.
14. S.J. Smart, 'John Foxe and "The Story of Richard Hun, Martyr"', *Journal of Ecclesiastical History*, xxxvii (1986), pp. 1–14; S.J. Smart, '"Favourers of God's Word": John Foxe's Henrician martyrs', Univ. of Southampton M. Phil. thesis, 1988.
15. Dowling, 'Latymer's Cronickille', p. 43. Dowling does not build on that insight.
16. Ives, *Anne Boleyn*, p. 279.
17. Vienna, Haus-, Hof- und Staatsarchiv, England, Karton 7, Korrespondenz, Berichte, 1536, fo. 97 (*Cal. S.P., Spanish*, V ii no. xlvii pp. 106–7; *LP*, X 752).
18. There is no contemporary decipher. I have drawn on the transcript in TNA, PRO, PRO 31/18/3/1 fo. 44v (*Cal. S.P., Spanish*, V i no. xix pp. 59–60; *LP*, VII 232).
19. D. Starkey, *The Reign of Henry VIII: Personalities and Politics* (London, 1985), p. 91; Ives, *Anne Boleyn*, p. 313; R.M. Warnicke, *The Rise and Fall of Anne Boleyn* (Cambridge, 1990), pp. 25, 27, 109, 153.
20. James P. Carley, *The Books of King Henry VIII and his Wives* (London, 2004), p. 124.
21. Ives, *Anne Boleyn*, p. 269, citing BL, Sloane MS 1207 ff. iv, 3.
22. A.G. Dickens, *The English Reformation* (2nd edn, London, 1989), p. 152, followed by Ives, *Anne Boleyn*, p. 270.
23. Ives, *Anne Boleyn*, p. 270.
24. Ibid., p. 313; M. Deansley, *The Lollard Bible* (1920), pp. 6–7, 336, 339–40; M.B. Tait, 'The Brigittine monastery of Syon (Middlesex) with special reference to its monastic usages', Univ. of Oxford D. Phil. thesis, 1975, pp. 74–5, 217–19; R.N. Swanson, *Church and Society in Late Medieval England* (Oxford, 1989), p. 25; J.H. Blunt, ed., *The myroure of our ladye* (RSTC 17542), Early English Text

Society, extra ser., xix (1873), xl–xliv; A.J. Collins, ed., *The Bridgettine Breviary at Syon Abbey*, Henry Bradshaw Society (1969 for 1963), pp. xxxi–xl.

25. BL, Cotton MS, Cleopatra E v fo. 350v (*LP*, VII 664).
26. Carley, *Books of Henry VIII*, p. 129. Carley's main interest lies less in the theology revealed in these books or in the precise degree of religious commitment of Anne and her brother than in their place in the larger history of the book.
27. I am grateful to Edward Wilson for sharing his thoughts on this. Starkey, referring to 'the evidence of Anne Boleyn's own books', remarks that 'these demonstrate, beyond argument, that she was a convinced Evangelical, even (as the Imperial ambassador, Chapuys, insisted) a Lutheran' (D. Starkey, 'Preface', in Carley, *Books of Henry VIII*, p. 28), but nothing in Carley's work sustains Starkey's claims for Anne as Lutheran.
28. Carley, *Books of Henry VIII*, p. 128.
29. BL, Additional MS, 20,030, fos 75, 81, 98, 101v, 109v, 117, 135v.
30. BL, Harleian MS 6561, fos 2–2v.
31. Ibid., fos 165, 146, 57v.
32. Ibid., fos 74, 93v, 94.
33. Ibid. fo. 17.
34. Ibid., fos 122, 123–123v.
35. Ibid., fo. 149.
36. Ibid., fo. 129v.
37. Ibid., fo. 114v.
38. Ibid., fo. 91v.
39. Ives, *Anne Boleyn*, p. 279.
40. Ibid., p. 272.
41. Carley, *Books of Henry VIII*, p. 129; lecture, Oxford, 30 Jan. 2006.
42. Ives, *Anne Boleyn*, p. 274.
43. Carley, *Books of Henry VIII*, p. 125.
44. BL, Cotton MS, Otho C x. fo. 224v (*LP*, X 797). This manuscript, with many others in the Cotton collection, was badly damaged by fire in 1731. Here and in later quotations from this volume, missing words have been supplied from the transcripts made before the fire by John Strype: Strype, *Ecclesiastical Memorials*, I i. 434.
45. Ives, *Anne Boleyn*, p. 280.
46. Vienna, Haus-, Hof- und Staatsarchiv, England, Karton 5, Korrespondenz, Berichte, 1533, fo. 23. This letter has not been calendared. Friedmann, *Anne Boleyn*, i. 189–90, followed by Starkey, *Six Wives*, p. 477, has Anne resolving to go on pilgrimage if she was *not* pregnant.
47. BL, Cotton MS, Otho C x. fo. 225 (*LP*, X 793); BL, Cotton MS, Otho C x fo. 224v (*LP*, X 797).
48. *LP*, X 371; M. Dowling, 'The gospel and the court: reformation under Henry VIII', in M. Dowling and P. Lake, eds, *Protestantism and the National Church in Sixteenth Century England* (London, 1987), pp. 36–77 at p. 47.
49. Vienna, Haus-, Hof- und Staatsarchiv, England, Karton 5, Korrespondenz, Berichte, 1535, fo. 65 (*Cal. S.P., Spanish*, V i no. cxliv p. 433; *LP*, VIII 431).
50. Vienna, Haus-, Hof- und Staatsarchiv, England, Karton 5, Korrespondenz, Berichte, 1534, fos 21–21v (*Cal. S.P., Spanish*, V i no. lx p. 172; *LP*, VII 726). Cf. England, Karton 7, Korrespondenz, Berichte, 1536, fo. 113 (*Cal. S.P., Spanish*, V ii no. liv p. 122; *LP*, X 909) and p. 210 n.16 above.
51. Hunt, *The Drama of Coronation*, pp. 42, 61.
52. Ives, *Anne Boleyn*, p. 240.
53. Froissart, *Chroniques*, c.1390, and J.W. Hassell, *Middle French Proverbs, Sentences and Proverbial Phrases, Subsidia Medievalia*, xii (Toronto, 1982), p. 85/C325, cited

and characterised by Edward Wilson, *The Times*, 27 Oct. 1997 and in personal correspondence.

54. BL, Cotton MS, Otho C x fos 226–226v (*LP*, X 792).
55. Ives, *Anne Boleyn*, p. 284.
56. Vienna, Haus-, Hof- und Staatsarchiv, England, Karton 5, Korrespondenz, Berichte, 1534, fo. 92 (*Cal. S.P., Spanish*, V i no. xl p. 118; *LP*, VII 469).
57. Vienna, Haus-, Hof- und Staatsarchiv, England, Karton 5, Korrespondenz, Berichte, 1533, fo. 20 (*Cal. S.P., Spanish*, IV ii (ii) no. mliii pp. 608–10; *LP*, VI 180).
58. BL, Cotton MS, Cleopatra, E v fos 110–10v; H.A. Kelly, *The Matrimonial Trials of Henry VIII* (Stanford, CA, 1976; new edn 2004).
59. BL, Cotton MS, Otho C x fo. 226v (*LP*, X 792).
60. *LP*, IV iii 6247; V 327.
61. *LP*, VI 437, 451, 491, 493.
62. *LP*, IV iii 6247; V 1320, 1660.
63. *LP*, IV iii 3913, 4167, 4251, 6505; V 238, 251, 340, 368, 393, 427; VII 1602 (3).
64. *LP*, VII 939, 1169.
65. *LP*, VI 333, 981, 1011, 1014, 1226, 1385; IV app. 724; VI 1067.
66. *LP*, VII 1528–30; VIII 412, IX 1091; X 527, 730.
67. Foxe, *Acts and Monuments*, v. 135; vi app; vii. 459–61, 473–7; *LP*, VI 246–7, 317, 411–12, 433 (i–iii), 573, 796, 1214, 1249; VII 29–30, 32, 228, 578; G.R. Elton, *Policy and Police* (Cambridge, 1972), p. 117.
68. *LP*, IX 203, 252, 272; X 1257 (ix); XI 117 (7).
69. *LP*, VII 589 [8].
70. BL, Cotton MS, Otho C x fo. 224v (*LP*, X 797).
71. Foxe, *Acts and Monuments*, v. 60; viii. 71–2; *LP*, VII 14, 19–21; Bodleian Library, Oxford, MS Don c. 42 fo. 30.
72. TNA, PRO, SP1/92 fo. 139 (*LP*, VIII 710).
73. Bodleian Library, Oxford, MS Don c. 42 fos 28–28v (Dowling, 'Latymer's Cronickille', p. 56).
74. BL, Harleian MS 6148 fo. 79 (*LP*, VII 693).
75. BL, Cotton MS, Cleopatra E iv. fo. 31 (ink) (*LP*, VI 115); and cf. BL, Cotton MS, Cleopatra E iv. fo. 35 (pencil) (*LP*, VI 116).
76. BL Cotton MS Cleopatra E iv. fo. 29 (ink) (*LP*, V 1525).
77. TNA, PRO, SP1/76 fo. 69 (*LP*, VI 512); cf. TNA, PRO, SP1/79 fo. 164 (*LP*, VI 1264).
78. BL, Cotton MS, Cleopatra E iv. fo. 31 (ink)(*LP*, VI 115).
79. TNA, PRO, SP1/76 fo. 69 (*LP*, VI 512).
80. *LP*, VII 29. *Writings and Letters of Thomas Cranmer*, ed. J. E. Cox, Parker Society (Cambridge, 1846), p. 308.
81. Ives, *Anne Boleyn*, p. 283.
82. TNA, PRO, SP6/1 fos 7–10v (LP, X 615 [4]), partially quoted by S.E. Lehmberg, *The Reformation Parliament 1529–1536* (Cambridge, 1970), pp. 244–5; TNA, PRO SP6/2 fos 1–3 for interrogatories.
83. E.W. Ives, 'Anne Boleyn and the early Reformation in England: the contemporary evidence', *Historical Journal*, xxxvii (1994), pp. 397–400.
84. TNA, PRO, SP6/1 fos 8v–9. My emphasis.
85. Vienna, Haus-, Hof- und Staatsarchiv, England, Karton 7, Korrespondenz, Berichte, 1536, fo. 33 (*Cal. S.P., Spanish*, V ii no. xxi p. 41: *LP*, X 282).
86. TNA, PRO, SP6/1 fos 9–9v; SP1/103 fo. 79.
87. Ives, *Anne Boleyn*, p. 320.
88. TNA, PRO, SP6/1 fo. 9v. Skip drew freely on Demosthenes, *Against Timocrates*.
89. TNA, PRO, SP1/103 fos 79v–80v.
90. TNA, PRO, SP6/1 fos 9v–10.
91. TNA, PRO, SP1/103 fos 80v–81.

92. BL, Cotton MS, Otho C x fo. 224v (*LP*, X 797), supplemented from Strype, *Ecclesiastical Memorials*.
93. BL, Cotton MS, Otho C x fo. 225 (*LP*, X 793).
94. BL, Cotton MS, Otho C x fo. 224v (*LP*, X 797).
95. Ibid.
96. Vienna, Haus-, Hof- und Staatsarchiv, England, Karton 5, Korrespondenz, Berichte, 1533, fo. 99v (*Cal. S.P., Spanish*, IV ii (ii) no. mcvii p. 756; *LP*, VI 918).
97. Aymot, 'Constantyne', p. 65.
98. Hall, *Chronicle*, p. 819; John Spelman, *The Reports of Sir John Spelman*, ed. L.H. Baker, Selden Society, xciii, xciv (1977), i. 59; *Wriothesley's Chronicle*, p. 42.
99. Foxe, *Acts and Monuments*, v. 135.
100. De Carles, *Anne Boullant*, p. 270, lines 1219–50, esp. 1229–32.

Chapter 8: Anne's miscarriage

1. *LP*, X 450.
2. *LP*, X 528.
3. *LP*, X 575.
4. Vienna, Haus-, Hof- und Staatsarchiv, England, Karton 7, Korrespondenz, Berichte, 1536, fo. 13v (*Cal. S.P., Spanish*, V ii no. ix p. 19; *LP*, X 141).
5. Vienna, Haus-, Hof- und Staatsarchiv, England, Karton 7, Korrespondenz, Berichte, 1536, fos 23–23v (*Cal. S.P., Spanish*, V ii no. xiii p. 28; *LP*, X 199); cf. R.M. Warnicke, 'Sexual heresy at the court of Henry VIII', *Historical Journal*, xxx (1987), pp. 257–8 for redating.
6. TNA, PRO, 31/18/2/1 fo. 1025 (*LP*, VI 1528).
7. Vienna, Haus-, Hof- und Staatsarchiv, England, Karton 7, Korrespondenz, Berichte, 1536, fo. 51 (*Cal. S.P., Spanish*, V ii no. xxix p. 59; *LP*, X 351).
8. Vienna, Haus-, Hof- und Staatsarchiv, England, Karton 7, Korrespondenz, Berichte, 1536, fo. 53 (*LP*, X 352).
9. Warnicke, *Anne Boleyn*, pp. 191–234, 3–4.
10. Vienna, Haus-, Hof- und Staatsarchiv, England, Karton 7, Korrespondenz, Berichte, 1536, fo. 31 (*Cal. S.P., Spanish*, V ii no. xxi p. 39; *LP*, X 282).
11. *Wriothesley's Chronicle*, p. 33
12. 'Son ventre plain et son fruit advanca/ Et enfanta ung beau filz avant terme,/ Qui nasquit mort dont versa mainte lerme': De Carles, *Anne Boullant*, p. 242, lines 324–6.
13. Cf. Warnicke, *Anne Boleyn*, pp. 203, 214, 226, 231, 235, 241.
14. Nicholas Remy, *Demonolatry by Nicholas Remy*, trans. E.A. Ashwin, ed. M. Summers (London 1930), pp. 93–103, esp. 94–5.
15. *Malleus Maleficarum of Heinrich Kramer*, ed. M. Summers (London, 1927), pp. 55, 87–9.
16. L.M. Sinistrari, *Demoniality*, ed. M. Summers (London, 1927), p. 21; E. Fenton, *Certaine secrete wonders of nature* (1569), p. 17.
17. Vienna, Haus-, Hof- und Staatsarchiv, England, Karton 7, Korrespondenz, Berichte, 1536, fos 23–23v (*Cal. S.P., Spanish*, V ii no. xiii p. 28; *LP*, X 199).
18. Cf. Warnicke, *Anne Boleyn*, pp. 203, 214, 226, 231, 235, 241.
19. Ibid., p. 195; cf. G.R. Elton, *Thomas Cromwell* (Bangor, 1990), p. 37 n. 48.
20. Warnicke, *Anne Boleyn*, p. 202; Warnicke, 'Sexual heresy', p. 255.
21. Warnicke, *Anne Boleyn*, p. 235.
22. Vienna, Haus-, Hof- und Staatsarchiv, England, Karton 7, Korrespondenz, Berichte, 1536, fo. 109 (*Cal. S.P., Spanish*, V ii no. lv p. 129; *LP*, X 908).
23. Foxe, *Acts and Monuments*, v. 135.

24. BL, Additional MS, 25114 fo. 175 (*LP*, XI 29).
25. Vienna, Haus-, Hof- und Staatsarchiv, England, Karton 7, Korrespondenz, Berichte, 1536, fos 107v–108 (*Cal. S.P., Spanish*, V ii no. lv p. 127; *LP*, X 908).
26. Vienna, Haus-, Hof- und Staatsarchiv, England, Karton 7, Korrespondenz, Berichte, 1536, fo. 31v (*Cal. S.P., Spanish*, V ii no. xxi pp. 39–40; *LP*, X 282).
27. Vienna, Haus-, Hof- und Staatsarchiv, England, Karton 7, Korrespondenz, Berichte, 1536, fo. 69 (*Cal. S.P., Spanish*, V ii no. xliii pp. 84–5; *LP*, X 601).
28. Vienna, Haus-, Hof- und Staatsarchiv, England, Karton 7, Korrespondenz, Berichte, 1536, fo. 56v (*LP*, X 495).
29. Vienna, Haus-, Hof- und Staatsarchiv, England, Karton 7, Korrespondenz, Berichte, 1536, fo. 69 (*Cal. S.P., Spanish*, V ii no. xliii pp. 85; *LP*, X 601); Ives, *Anne Boleyn*, p. 348.
30. Henry 'fut encores inclines a festoyer et server dames' ; but 'voudroit il vivre honestment en chastement continuant en son mariage': Vienna, Haus-, Hof- und Staatsarchiv, England, Karton 4, Korrespondenz, Berichte, 1536, fos 66–7 (*Cal. S.P., Spanish*, V ii no. xliii p. 82; *LP*, X 601)
31. Kelly, *Matrimonial Trials of Henry VIII*, ch. 14.
32. J.J. Scarisbrick, *Henry VIII* (London, 1968), p. 350.
33. Vienna, Haus-, Hof- und Staatsarchiv, England, Karton 7, Korrespondenz, Berichte, 1536, fos 100–101v (*Cal. S.P., Spanish*, V ii no. xlviii p. 107; *LP*, X 782).
34. Vienna, Haus-, Hof- und Staatsarchiv, England, Karton 7, Korrespondenz, Berichte, 1536, fo. 38v (*Cal. S.P., Spanish*, V ii no. xxi p. 44).
35. 'Et venant le roy a lofferande il y eust grand concours de gens, et vne partie pour veoir quelles mynes la concubine et moy nous tiendrons, elle en vsast assy cortissement car comme jestoye derrier la porte par ou elle entroit, elle se retournast du tout pour me faire la reuerance conforme a celle que luy fiz': Vienna, Haus-, Hof- und Staatsarchiv, England, Karton 7, Korrespondenz, Berichte, 1536, fos 80v–83, esp. 82 (*Cal. S.P., Spanish*, V ii no. xliii (a) pp. 91–4; *LP*, X 699).
36. *State Papers*, vii. 683–8 (*LP*, X 726).
37. G. Walker, 'Rethinking the fall of Anne Boleyn', *Historical Journal*, xlv (2002), pp. 13–14.

Chapter 9: Conspiracy?

1. Ives, *Anne Boleyn*, p. 301: cf. *LP*, VIII 1106.
2. D. Starkey, *The Reign of Henry VIII: personalities and politics* (1985), p. 110.
3. Vienna, Haus-, Hof- und Staatsarchiv, England, Karton 7, Korrespondenz, Berichte, 1536, fo. 69v (*Cal. S.P., Spanish*, V ii no. xliii p. 85; *LP*, X 601).
4. Vienna, Haus-, Hof- und Staatsarchiv, England, Karton 7, Korrespondenz, Berichte, 1536, fos 94–95v (*Cal. S.P., Spanish*, V ii no. xlvii p. 106; *LP*, X 752).
5. S.R. Johnson, 'Nicholas Carew', in S.T. Bindoff, ed., *The History of Parliament: The House of Commons 1509–1558* (3 vols, London, 1982), i. 576.
6. 'Il ne tiendra au dit escuies [Carew] que ladite concubine ne soit desarconnee et ne cesse de conseiler maistress Semel [Jane Seymour] ains autres conspirateurs pour lui faire vne venue': Vienna, Haus-, Hof- und Staatsarchiv, England, Karton 7, Korrespondenz, Berichte, 1536, fos 94–95v (*Cal. S.P., Spanish*, V ii no. xlvii p. 106; *LP*, X 752).
7. Vienna, Haus-, Hof- und Staatsarchiv, England, Karton 7, Korrespondenz, Berichte, 1536, fos 96–97v (*LP*, X 753).
8. *LP*, X 1134 (4).
9. Vienna, Haus-, Hof- und Staatsarchiv, England, Karton 7, Korrespondenz, Berichte, 1536, fo. 108v (*Cal. S.P., Spanish*, V ii no. lv p. 124; *LP*, X 908).

10. R.M. Warnicke, 'The fall of Anne Boleyn: a reassessment', *History*, lxx (1985), pp. 1–5.
11. Foxe, *Acts and Monuments*, v. 136–7.
12. Starkey, *Reign of Henry VIII*, pp. 111–12.
13. Vienna, Haus-, Hof- und Staatsarchiv, England, Karton 7, Korrespondenz, Berichte, 1536, fo. 95 (*Cal. S.P., Spanish*, V ii no. xlvii p. 106; *LP*, X 752).
14. Vienna, Haus-, Hof- und Staatsarchiv, England, Karton 7, Korrespondenz, Berichte, 1536, fos 96–97v (*LP*, X 753).
15. Ives, *Anne Boleyn*, p. 412 n. 7 from *LP* VI 555, 707, VIII 174.
16. Ives, *Anne Boleyn*, p. 419.
17. Starkey, *Reign of Henry VIII*, p. 110.
18. Ives, *Anne Boleyn*, p. 317.
19. Ibid., p. 315.
20. Cf. Vienna, Haus-, Hof- und Staatsarchiv, England, Karton 5, Korrespondenz, Berichte, 1533, fo. 78 (*Cal. S.P., Spanish*, IV ii no. 1076 p. 687; *LP*, VI 541): Charles had warned Chapuys not to embitter matters, not to threaten anything like war or diminution of friendship.
21. Vienna, Haus-, Hof- und Staatsarchiv, England, Karton 5, Korrespondenz, Berichte, 1535, fo. 24 (*Cal. S.P., Spanish*, V i no. clxx p. 484; *LP*, VIII 826).
22. Vienna, Haus-, Hof- und Staatsarchiv, England, Karton 7, Korrespondenz, Berichte, 1536, fos 65–66v *Cal. S.P., Spanish*, V ii no. xliii p. 81; *LP*, X 601).
23. Vienna, Haus-, Hof- und Staatsarchiv, England, Karton 5, Korrespondenz, Berichte, 1534, fos 67v–68, 70 (*Cal. S.P., Spanish*, V i no. cii pp. 294–300; *LP*, VII 1297).
24. Vienna, Haus-, Hof- und Staatsarchiv, England, Karton 7, Korrespondenz, Berichte, 1536, fos 80v–83 (*Cal. S.P., Spanish*, V ii no. xliii (a) pp. 93–9; *LP*, X 699).
25. Ives has now conceded that 'if his only problem had been the disagreement over foreign affairs, the minister could, perhaps, have remained sanguine': Ives, *Anne Boleyn*, p. 315.
26. Ibid., p. 316.
27. Cf. *Lisle Letters*, ed. M. St C. Byrne (6 vols, Chicago, 1981), iii. 235.
28. Jonathan Hughes vaguely asserts that 'he had links with opponents of Thomas Cromwell, who was probably glad of an excuse to strike at him', but without offering any evidence: J. Hughes, 'Weston, Sir Francis (1511–1536)', *ODNB*.
29. BL, Additional MS, 20,030 fos 20ᵛ, 45, 96, 134ᵛ, 189; *LP*, V pp. 749, 752, 757, 760, 761.
30. P. Roberts, review of G. Williams, *Recovery, Reorientation and Reformation. Wales c.1415–1642* (Oxford, 1987), in *TLS*, 18 March 1988, p. 309.
31. E.W. Ives, ed., *Letters and Accounts of William Brereton of Malpas*, Record Society of Lancashire and Cheshire, cxvi (1976), pp. 34, 2, 36; Ives, 'Court and county palatine in the reign of Henry VIII: the career of William Brereton of Malpas', *Transactions of the Historic Society of Lancashire and Cheshire*, cxxiii (1972), p. 30.
32. *LP*, V 506 [25], IX 1063 [11].
33. Ives, 'Palatine', pp. 4–5, 28–9, 18–19. My emphasis.
34. T. Thornton, 'The integration of Cheshire into the Tudor nation state in the early sixteenth century', *Northern History*, xxix (1993), pp. 51, 48.
35. Vienna, Haus-, Hof- und Staatsarchiv, England, Karton 7, Korrespondenz, Berichte, 1536, fo. 1v (*Cal. S.P., Spanish*, V ii no. lxi p. 137; *LP*, X 1069). Ives translates that as '"think up and plan" the coup against Anne' without making it clear that these words were spoken in June (*Anne Boleyn*, p. 318).
36. Vienna, Haus-, Hof- und Staatsarchiv, England, Karton 7, Korrespondenz, Berichte, 1536, fo. 108 (*Cal. S.P., Spanish*, V ii no. lv p. 127; *LP*, X 908).

Chapter 10: 'A much higher fault': the countess of Worcester's charge against Anne

1. De Carles, *Anne Boullant*, p. 240.
2. TNA, PRO, SP3/12 fo. 57 (*LP*, X 964).
3. TNA, PRO, SP3/12 fo. 37 (*LP*, X 953). It is possible that when Sir John Spelman, the judge, wrote that 'this matter was disclosed by a woman called the lady Wingfield, who had been a servant to the said queen and of the same qualities', he intended to write 'the Lady Worcester': Spelman, *Reports* i. 71. A 'scandalous account of Henry 8th' in French (BL Lansdowne 105 fos 18–19v [Pocock, *Records of the Reformation*, ii. no. ccclix, p. 573]), after describing how Henry married Anne 'plus belle que chaste', and how Anne, not satisfied by a gentleman called Brereton nor by Norris, committed incest with her brother, and then with 'un joueur d'instruments homme de basse condition' who 'accordoit sa harpe sur le corps de la royne', declared that 'toutes ses folles pratiques furent descouvertes par un autre des concubines du roy, soeur de un medecin nomme Antoine Brun'. Anthony Browne was not a doctor, and nowhere else is there any suggestion that Browne's sister was one of Henry's concubines, but nonetheless the identification of Browne as the informant of the king is interesting. Cf. Friedmann, *Anne Boleyn*, ii. 346.
4. BL, Cotton MS, Otho C x. fo. 225 (*LP*, X 793).
5. W.R.B. Robinson, 'The lands of Henry, earl of Worcester in the 1530s. Part 3: Central Monmouthshire and Herefordshire', *Bulletin of the Board of Celtic Studies*, xxv (iv), (1974), pp. 460, 492.
6. *LP*, V p. 748.
7. BL, Harleian MS, 41 fo. 10 (*LP*, VI 601).
8. TNA, PRO, SP1/129 fo. 174 (*LP*, XIII i 450). In 1533 she had appealed to Cromwell from Greenwich in her husband's absence over violent disputes in Glamorgan in which her husband's deputy had been set upon and one of his servants murdered: *LP*, VI 662 (but wrongly calendared under 1532), V 298; cf. W.R.B. Robinson, 'Patronage and hospitality in early Tudor Wales: the role of Henry, earl of Worcester, 1526–49', *Bulletin of the Institute of Historical Research*, li (1978), p. 30 nn. 62–3.
9. De Carles, *Anne Boullant*, p. 240.
10. Hume, ed., *Chronicle of King Henry VIII*, pp. 56–8, 66.
11. Vienna, Haus-, Hof- und Staatsarchiv, England, Karton 7, Korrespondenz, Berichte, 1536, fos 108v–109 (*Cal. S.P., Spanish*, V ii no. lv p. 128; *LP*, X 908).
12. BL, Additional MS, 25,114 fo. 160 (*LP*, X 873).
13. Contrast the first edition of Ives, *Anne Boleyn* (Oxford, 1986), p. 376, and the second edition, p. 60. Ives on the one hand sees de Carles as simply Cromwell in verse but on the other hand dismisses de Carles's poem as 'popular gossip and speculation' rather than the official line
14. BL, Additional MS, 25,114 fo. 267 (*LP*, XII ii 78).
15. Cf. Ascoli, *La Grande-Bretagne*, pp. 66–7.

Chapter 11: 'You would look to have me': Anne's lovers?

1. BL, Cotton MS, Otho C x fo. 225 (*LP*, X 793).
2. BL, Cotton MS, Otho C x fo. 224v (*LP*, X 797).
3. De Carles, *Anne Boullant*, p. 191.
4. *Wriothesley's Chronicle*, p. 36.
5. BL, Cotton MS, Otho C x fo. 224v (*LP*, X 797). The document is damaged: the missing words are suggested in square brackets.
6. BL, Cotton MS, Otho C x fo. 222 (*LP*, X 798). 'Marvelled' is supplied from Strype's transcripts: *Ecclesiastical Memorials*, I i. 435.

7. BL, Cotton MS, Otho x. fo. 225 (*LP*, X 793): some words have been supplied from Strype's transcript: *Ecclesiastical Memorials*, I i. 432.

8. BL, Cotton MS, Otho C x fo. 224v (*LP* X 797): some words have been supplied from Strype's transcript: *Ecclesiastical Memorials*, I i. 434.

9. BL, Cotton MS, Otho C x. fo. 225 (*LP*, X 793): some words have been supplied from Strype's transcript: *Ecclesiastical Memorials*, I i. 432.

10. BL, Cotton MS, Otho C x. fo. 225 (*LP*, X 793).

11. BL, Cotton MS, Otho C x fo. 222v (*LP*, X 798).

12. BL, Cotton MS, Otho C x fo. 225 (*LP*, X 793): some phrases have been supplemented from Strype, *Ecclesiastical Memorials*, I i. 432.

13. Starkey, *Six Wives*, p. 566: 'Anne's words are unutterably foolish'.

14. BL, Cotton MS, Otho C x fo. 209v (*LP*, X 799).

15. BL, Cotton MS, Otho C x fo. 225v (*LP*, X 793): words in square brackets supplied from Strype, *Ecclesiastical Memorials*, I i. 432.

16. *LP*, X 876 (7–8); TNA, PRO, KB 8/9–11.

17. Ives, *Anne Boleyn*, p. 344; cf. *Lisle Letters*, iii. 238–9.

18. Vienna, Haus-, Hof- und Staatsarchiv, England, Karton 7, Korrespondenz, Berichte, 1536, fo. 106v (*Cal. S.P., Spanish*, V ii no. lv pp. 125–6; *LP*, X 908); cf. Ives, *Anne Boleyn*, p. 420 n. 22.

19. De Carles, *Anne Boullant*, p. 201.

20. *Wriothesley's Chronicle*, pp. 37–8.

21. Vienna, Haus-, Hof- und Staatsarchiv, England, Karton 7, Korrespondenz, Berichte, 1536, fo. 106v (*Cal. S.P., Spanish*, V ii no. lv p. 126; *LP*, X 908). The odds are wrongly translated as 'two to one' in *Cal. S.P., Spanish*, V ii no. lv p. 126.

22. *Wriothesley's Chronicle*, p. 39.

23. Vienna, Haus-, Hof- und Staatsarchiv, England, Karton 7, Korrespondenz, Berichte, 1536, fo. 106v (*Cal. S.P., Spanish*, V ii no. lv p. 126; *LP*, X 908). Ives thinks this had been no more than a joke—'with his problems, it's hard to see how the king ever produced Elizabeth'—that had gone dangerously wrong: Ives, *Anne Boleyn*, p. 349.

24. Kelly, *Matrimonial Trials of Henry VIII*, p. 243.

25. Vienna, Haus-, Hof- und Staatsarchiv, England, Karton 5, Korrespondenz, Berichte, 1533, fo. 57 (*LP*, VI 351).

26. Vienna, Haus-, Hof- und Staatsarchiv, England, Karton 7, Korrespondenz, Berichte, 1536, fo. 106v (*Cal. S.P., Spanish*, V ii no. lv p. 125; *LP*, X 908).

27. Vienna, Haus-, Hof- und Staatsarchiv, England, Karton 7, Korrespondenz, Berichte, 1536, fo. 109 (*LP*, X 908)

28. Starkey, *Six Wives*, p. 580.

29. Spelman, *Reports*, ii. 71.

30. De Carles, *Anne Boullant*, pp. 261–4, 253, 257–60.

31. BL, Additional MS, 25114 fos 176–176v (*LP*, XI 29).

32. *LP*, X 876 (7–8); TNA, PRO, KB 8/9–11.

33. Vienna, Haus-, Hof- und Staatsarchiv, England, Karton 7, Korrespondenz, Berichte, 1536, fo. 106v (*Cal. S.P., Spanish*, V ii no. lv p. 125; *LP*, X 908).

34. Aymot, 'Constantyne', p. 64.

35. J.A. Froude, *History of England from the Fall of Wolsey to the Defeat of the Spanish Armada* (12 vols, 1858–70), ii. 383–4, 388.

36. Spelman, *Reports*, i. 71.

37. BL, Cotton MS, Otho C x fos 226–226v (*LP*, X 792); R. Williams, 'Sermon on the 450th anniversary of the martyrdom of Thomas Cranmer', http://www.archbishopofcanterbury.org/sermons_speeches/060321.htm

38. BL, Cotton MS, Otho C x fo. 260 (*LP*, X 942).

39. De Carles, *Anne Boullant*, pp. 262–3.

40. Vienna, Haus-, Hof- und Staatsarchiv, England, Karton 7, Korrespondenz, Berichte, 1536, fo. 104 (*Cal. S.P., Spanish*, V ii no. lv p. 127; *LP*, X 908).
41. Vienna, Haus-, Hof- und Staatsarchiv, England, Karton 7, Korrespondenz, Berichte, 1536, fo. 110v (*Cal. S.P., Spanish*, V ii no. lv p. 131; *LP*, X 908).
42. BL, Cotton MS, Otho C x fo. 223 (*LP*, X 910).
43. E.W. Ives, 'The fall of Anne Boleyn reconsidered', *English Historical Review*, cvii (1992), p. 653.
44. BL, Harleian MS 283 fo. 134 (*LP*, X 890).
45. *LP*, X 1070. I have been unable to locate the original letter in Vienna: nor have I been able to find a transcript in the National Archives.
46. BL, Cotton MS, Otho C x fo. 228–28v (*LP*, X 808). I have also disregarded the fanciful account by the Scottish reformer Alexander Ales (Alesius) presented to Queen Elizabeth on her accession (TNA, PRO, SP70/7 fos 1–11; *Calendar of State Papers, Foreign, 1559–1560*, no. 1303, pp. 524–34), a farrago of improbabilities and chronological impossibilities.
47. Froude, *History of England*, ii. 372–5.
48. De Carles, *Anne Boullant*, p. 214.
49. Aymot, 'Constantyne', pp. 65–6. According to notes made by Sir John Spelman, she knelt, saying 'to Christ I commend my soul': Spelman, *Reports,* i. 59.
50. *Wriothesley's Chronicle*, pp. 41–2.
51. Hall, *Chronicle*, p. 819.
52. TNA, PRO, SP1/103 fo. 275 (*LP*, X 855).
53. BL, Cotton MS, Cleopatra E ii fo. 110 (*LP*, XIII i 981 [2]).
54. Vienna, Haus-, Hof- und Staatsarchiv, England, Karton 7, Korrespondenz, Berichte, 1536, fo. 145v (*Cal. S.P., Spanish*, V ii no. lv p. 129; *LP*, X 908).
55. Wyatt was briefly mentioned in BL, Cotton MS, Otho C x fo. 222 (*LP*, X 798) and in letters by Lord Lisle's agent John Hussee (TNA, PRO, SP1/103 fo. 275 [*LP*, X 855], TNA, PRO, SP1/103 fo. 278 [*LP*, X 865]); for Cromwell, see Sir Henry Wyatt's letter, TNA, PRO, SP1/103 fo. 266 (*LP*, X 840); cf. De Carles, *Anne Boullant*, p. 249 line 560.
56. *LP*, XIII ii 270.
57. De Carles, *Anne Boullant*, p. 246 line 478; Aymot, 'Constantyne', p. 64.
58. Warnicke, *Anne Boleyn*, pp. 218–20.
59. Wyatt, *Complete Poems*, no. cxcvii p. 256 lines 49–50.
60. De Carles, *Anne Boullant*, p. 267.
61. BL, Cotton MS, Otho C x. fo. 225 (*LP*, X 793).
62. De Carles, *Anne Boullant*, p. 191.
63. Carley, *Books of Henry VIII*, p. 129.
64. A.S.G. Edwards, ed., *Metrical Visions by George Cavendish* (Columbia, SC, 1980), p. 39.
65. Wyatt, *Complete Poems*, no. cxcvii p. 255 lines 21–2.
66. Cf. C.B. Herrup, *The Common Peace: Participation and the Criminal Law in Seventeenth Century England* (Cambridge, 1987), pp. 148–9, 158, 198; E. Powell, *Kingship, Law and Society: Criminal Justice in the Reign of Henry V* (Oxford, 1989), p. 80.
67. E.W. Ives, 'The fall of Anne Boleyn reconsidered', *English Historical Review*, cvii (1992), p. 651.
68. Thornton, 'Integration of Cheshire', pp. 48–9.
69. Hughes, 'Weston, Sir Francis', *ODNB*.
70. TNA, PRO, SP1/103 fo. 280v (*LP*, X 869).
71. Cavendish, *Life of Wolsey*, p. 30.
72. Ives, *Anne Boleyn*, p. 392.
73. Aymot, 'Constantyne', p. 64. Starkey suggests that Norris's refusal to confess, even when pressed by the king personally, made Henry think that Norris valued the king's wife above the king: *Reign of Henry VIII*, p. 119.

74. Vienna, Haus-, Hof- und Staatsarchiv, England, Karton 7, Korrespondenz, Berichte, 1536, fo. 112v (*Cal. S.P., Spanish*, V ii no. liv p. 121; *LP*, X 909): cf. Vienna, Haus-, Hof- und Staatsarchiv, England, Karton 7, Korrespondenz, Berichte, 1536, fo. 59v (*Cal. S.P., Spanish*, V ii no. lxxii p. 198; *LP*, XI 41).
75. *LP*, XI 41.
76. Wyatt, *Complete Poems*, no. cxcvii, p. 255, lines 26–7.

Chapter 12: 'Incontinent living so rank and common': was Anne guilty?

1. TNA, PRO, SP1/69 fo. 203v (*LP*, V 907).
2. TNA, PRO, SP6/7 fo. 10 (*LP*, VI 733); cf. Elton, *Policy and Police*, p. 347, who dates this to 1534 since 22 June last is described as a Monday.
3. TNA, PRO, SP1/78 fo. 102 (*LP*, VI 964).
4. TNA, PRO, SP1/79 fo. 63 (*LP*, VI 1254).
5. TNA, PRO, SP1/84 fo. 178 (*LP*, VII, 840 [2]).
6. TNA, PRO, SP1/88 fo. 21 (*LP*, VII, 1609), SP1/93 fo. 42 (*LP*, VIII 844); cf. Elton, *Policy and Police*, p. 11.
7. TNA, PRO, SP1/99 fo. 58 (*LP*, IX 846); cf. Elton, *Policy and Police*, p. 24.
8. TNA, PRO, SP1/89 fo. 136 (*LP*, VIII 196).
9. TNA, PRO, SP1/84 fo. 178 (*LP*, VII, 840 [2]).
10. BL, Cotton MS, Cleopatra E iv fo. 99v (pencil) (*LP*, VI 923).
11. Vienna, Haus-, Hof- und Staatsarchiv, England, Karton 7, Korrespondenz, Berichte, 1535, fo. 3v (*Cal. S.P., Spanish*, V i no. cxxii p. 355; *LP*, VIII 1).
12. TNA, PRO, SP1/79 fo. 3v (*LP*, VI 1065).
13. Vienna, Haus-, Hof- und Staatsarchiv, England, Karton 5, Korrespondenz, Berichte, 1533, fo. 108 (*Cal. S.P., Spanish*, IV ii (ii) no. mcxxiii p. 788; *LP*, VI 1069).
14. TNA, PRO, SP1/82 fo. 19v (*LP*, VII 21); BL, Cotton MS, Vitellius, B xiv. 68 (*LP*, VII 148). This repeats the wording of instructions to Gardiner and Foxe when they were sent off to the pope in February 1528 (*LP*, IV ii 3913): see above, pp. 37–8.
15. *LP*, VIII 985.
16. *LP*, VII 9. The table fountain was most likely designed by Hans Holbein: see the drawing in the Kunstmuseum, Basel (Foister, *Holbein and England*, pp. 138, 199). Ives questions whether what Anne gave Henry was the table fountain depicted by Holbein; but the description seems to match rather well, even if it does not mention the satyrs. However that may be, Ives cites two further sketches in Holbein's distinctive hand, one of a nude spraying milk from her right breast, and one of a fountain with three semi-naked women at the foot, which, he suggests, may well both have been sketches for the fountain that Anne gave Henry in 1534 (Ives, 'The queen and the painters: Anne Boleyn, Holbein and Tudor royal portraits', *Apollo*, cxl (1994), pp. 37–8; S. Foister, *Holbein in England* (2006), p. 86).
17. Vienna, Haus-, Hof- und Staatsarchiv, England, Karton 5, Korrespondenz, Berichte, 1533, fo. 23.
18. TNA, PRO, SP1/76 fo. 195 (*LP*, VI 613).
19. Ives, *Anne Boleyn*, p. 349.
20. Foxe, *Acts and Monuments*, v. 60–1.
21. BL, King's MS 9, fos 231v, 66v.
22. Carley, *Books of Henry VIII*, pp. 124, 131.
23. I am grateful to Edward Wilson for this especially clear formulation.
24. 'Et que souvent je n'ai prins fantasie/Encontre luy de quelque jalousie': De Carles, *Anne Boullant*, p. 263, lines 1007–8; Vienna, Haus-, Hof- und Staatsarchiv, England, Karton 5, Korrespondenz, Berichte, 1533, fo. 108 (*Cal. S.P., Spanish*, IV ii (ii) no. mcxxiii p. 788; *LP*, VI 1069).

25. Vienna, Haus-, Hof- und Staatsarchiv, Egland, Karton 7, Korrespondenz, Berichte, 1536, fo. 112 (*Cal. S.P., Spanish*, V ii no. lv pp. 121–2; *LP*, X 909).
26. Cf. D. Cohen, 'Law, society and homosexuality in classical Athens', *Past and Present*, cxvii (1987), pp. 3–21.
27. K.V. Thomas, 'The double standard', *Journal of the History of Ideas*, xx (1959), pp. 195–216.
28. Vienna, Haus-, Hof- und Staatsarchiv, England, Karton 5, Korrespondenz, Berichte, 1534, fo. 87 (*Cal. S.P., Spanish*, V i no. cxviii p. 344; *LP*, VII 1554).
29. *LP*, VII, 1655.
30. Vienna, Haus-, Hof- und Staatsarchiv, England, Karton 7, Korrespondenz, Berichte, 1536, fo. 112 (*Cal. S.P., Spanish*, V ii no. liv p. 121; *LP*, X 909).
31. TNA, PRO, KB8/9 11 (*LP*, X 876).
32. Walker, 'Rethinking the fall of Anne Boleyn', pp. 26, 29.
33. BL, Cotton MS, Otho C x fo. 222 (*LP*, X 798).
34. Walker, 'Rethinking the fall of Anne Boleyn', pp. 1–29.

Epilogue

1. Ives, *Anne Boleyn*, p. 196.
2. TNA, PRO, SP1/84 fo. 94v (*LP*, VII 754).

Appendix: the portraits of Anne Boleyn

1. B. Dolman, 'Tudor regal portraiture: identity, uncertainty and interpretation', paper read at the conference on 'Henry VIII and the Tudor Court 1509–2009', Hampton Court Palace, 15 July 2009. I am very grateful to Brett Dolman for most generous guidance and many references. For a survey of all these images, including Holbein's *Ambassadors*, see Ives, 'The queen and the painters,' pp. 36–45. Further surveys include Ives, *Life and Death of Anne Boleyn*, pp. 40–4; Foister, *Holbein and England*, p. 199; Foister, *Holbein in England*, p. 58. For David Starkey's identification of Anne with both the Buccleuch miniature and the Windsor drawing, see *The Independent*, 23 April 1991, *The Times*, 14 March 2007, and J. Rowlands and D. Starkey, 'An old tradition reasserted: Holbein's portrait of Queen Anne Boleyn', *Burlington Magazine*, cxv (1985), pp. 88–92. For Horenbout see R. Hui, 'A reassessment of Queen Anne's portraiture' http://www.geocities.com/rolandhui_2000/abportraiture.htm) (I owe this reference to Brett Dolman). For the sweeping challenge to all the panel portraits of Anne Boleyn see S.E. James, *The Feminine Dynamic in English Art 1485–1603: Women as Consumers, Patrons and Painters* (Aldershot, 2009), pp. 125, 128, 38. For the Holbein drawing see M. Hayward, *Dress at the Court of King Henry VIII* (Leeds, 2007), p. 169. For information about the National Portrait Gallery *Making Art in Tudor Britain* project and guidance about the dating of panel portraits, I am grateful to Tarnya Cooper and Catherine Daunt.

BIBLIOGRAPHY

PRIMARY SOURCES: MANUSCRIPT

British Library, London
Cotton MS,   Cleopatra E ii, iv, v, xiv; Galba vii; Otho C x; Titus B i; Vespasian
   F iii, xiii; Vitellius B iii, xi, xiii, xiv, xix; App L
Harleian MS, 41, 283, 419, 6561
Landsowne MS, 105, 115
Royal MS, 18 A
Additional MS 6113, 20,030, 25,114

Public Record Office, London
SP1
SP3
SP6
PRO31/18
E36
KB8/9

Bodleian Library, Oxford
MS Don C. 42.
Jesus College MS C. 74

Bibliothèque Nationale, Paris
Fonds français, nos 1742, 2370, 12795

Haus-, Hof- und Staatsarchiv, Vienna
England, Karton 4, Korrespondenz, Berichte, 1529–30

England, Karton 5, Korrespondenz, Berichte, 1531–34
England, Karton 7, Korrespondenz, Berichte, 1535–36

PRIMARY SOURCES: PRINTED

Ascoli, G., *La Grande Bretagne devant l'opinion française depuis la guerre de cent ans jusqu'à la fin du XVIe siècle* (Paris, 1927).

La Correspondance du cardinal Jean du Bellay, ed. R. Scheurer (2 vols, Paris, 1969–73).

Blunt, J.H., ed., *Myroure of oure Ladye* (STC 17542), Early English Text Society, extra ser., xix (1873).

Brewer, J.S., Gairdner, J. and Brodie, R.H., eds, *Letters and Papers, Foreign and Domestic, of the Reign of Henry VIII* (21 vols in 36, 1862–1932).

Calendar of State Papers, Spanish, ed. G.A. Bergenroth, P. de Gayangos and M.A.S. Hume (1862–54).

Calendar of State Papers, Venetian, ed. R. Brown et al. (1864–1947).

Camusat, Nicolas, *Meslanges historiques* (Troyes, 1619).

de Carles, Lancelot, *Anne Boullant, Epistre contenant le process criminel faict a l'encontre de la royne Anne Bovllant d'Angleterre* (Lyons, 1545); reprinted in G. Ascoli, *La Grande Bretagne*.

de Carles, Lancelot, *Anne Boullant, Epistre contenant le process criminel faict a l'encontre de la royne Anne Bovllant d'Angleterre*.

Mémoires de Michel de Castelnau, ed. J. Le Laboureur (2 vols, Brussels, 1731).

Cavendish, George, *The Life and Death of Cardinal Wolsey*, ed. R.S. Sylvester, Early English Text Society, ccxliii (1959).

Cavendish, George, *The Life of Cardinal Wolsey*, ed. S.W. Singer (2 vols, 1825).

Edwards, A.S.G., ed., *Metrical Visions by George Cavendish* (Columbia, SC, 1980).

Collins, A.J., ed., *The Bridgettine Breviary at Syon Abbey*, Henry Bradshaw Society (1969 for 1963).

Writings and Letters of Thomas Cranmer, ed. J.E. Cox, Parker Society (Cambridge, 1846).

Life and Letters of Thomas Cromwell, ed. R.B. Merriman (2 vols, 1904).

Dowling, M., ed., 'William Latymer's Cronickille of Anne Bulleyne', *Camden Miscellany*, xxx, Camden Society, 4th ser., xxxix (1990), pp. 27–44.

Ellis, H., *Original letters illustrative of English History* (11 vols in 3 ser., 1824).

Fenton, E., *Certaine secrete wonders of nature* (1569).

Foxe, John, *Acts and Monuments*, ed. J. Pratt (8 vols, 1877).

Furnivall, F.J., *Ballads from Manuscripts* (2 vols, 1868–72).

Le Grand, *Histoire du divorce de Henry VIII* (3 vols, Paris, 1688).

Hall, Edward, *Chronicle* (1809 edn).

Nicholas Harpsfield's Life and Death of Sir Thomas More, ed. E.V. Hitchcock and R.W. Chambers, Early English Text Society, clxxxvi (1932).

Harpsfield, Nicholas, *The Pretended Divorce between Henry VIII and Catherine of Aragon*, ed. N. Pocock, Camden Society, 2nd ser., xxi (1878).

Herbert of Cherbury, Lord, *Life of Henry VIII* (1649).

Hume, M.A.S., ed., *Chronicle of King Henry VIII of England* (1889).

Malleus Maleficarum of Heinrich Kramer, ed. M. Summers (1927).

Latimer, Hugh, *Sermons*, Parker Society (1844).

Lisle Letters ed., M. St C. Byrne (6 vols, Chicago, 1981).

Lords Journals, 1513–1800, vol. i.

Correspondance de l'Empereur Maximilien Ier et de Marguerite d'Autriche, ed. A.J.G. Le Glay (2 vols, Paris, 1839).

Correspondence of Thomas More, ed. E. Rogers (Princeton, NJ; 1947).

The Lyfe of Sir Thomas Moore Knight by William Roper, ed. E.V. Hitchcock, Early English Text Society, cxcvii (1935).

Nichols, J.G., ed., *Narratives of the Days of the Reformation*, Camden Society, 1st ser., lxxvii (1857).

Correspondence of Matthew Parker, ed. J. Bruce and T.T. Perowe, Parker Society (1853).

The noble tryumphaunt coronacyon of quene Anne wyfe unto the most noble kynge Henrye the viij (1533) (RSTC 656).

Pocock, N., ed., *Records of the Reformation* (2 vols, Oxford, 1870–71).

Pollard, A.W., Redgrave, G.R., Jackson, W.A., Ferguson F.S. and Pantzer, K.F., *A Short-Title Catalogue of Books Printed in England, Scotland and Ireland, 1475–1640* (revised edn, 1986).

Reginald Pole's Defense of the Unity of the Church, ed. J.G. Dwyer (Westminster, MD, 1965).

Remy, Nicholas, *Demonolatry by Nicholas Remy*, trans. E.A. Ashwin, ed. M. Summers (1930).

Rymer, T., *Foedera* (1739–45 edn).

Sander, Nicholas, *Rise and Growth of the Anglican Schism*, trans. and ed. D. Lewis (1877).

L.M. Sinistrari, *Demoniality*, ed. M. Summers (1927).

Spelman, John, *The Reports of Sir John Spelman*, ed. J.H. Baker, Selden Society, xciii, xciv (1977).

State Papers of Henry VIII (11 vols, 1830–52).

Statutes of the Realm (12 vols, 1810–28).

Stemmler, T., *Die Liebesbriefe Heinrichs VIII an Anna Boleyn* (Zurich, 1988).

Strype, J., *Ecclesiastical Memorials* (3 vols in 6 parts, Oxford, 1822).

The Anglica Historia of Polydore Vergil, ed. D. Hay, Camden Society, lxxiv (1950).

Wilkins, D., *Concilia Magnae Britanniae* (4 vols, 1737).

Wriothesley's Chronicle, ed., W.D. Hamilton, Camden Society, 2nd series, xi (1875).

The Life and Letters of Sir Thomas Wyatt, ed. K. Muir (Liverpool, 1963).

Wyatt, Thomas, *Sir Thomas Wyatt: Complete Poems* ed., R.A. Rebholz (1978).

The Papers of George Wyatt, ed. D.M. Loades, Camden Society, 4th ser., v (1968).

SECONDARY SOURCES

Aymot, T., 'A memorial from George Constantyne to Thomas Lord Cromwell', *Archaeologia*, xxiii (1831), pp. 50–78.

Beckett, N., 'Sheen Charterhouse from its foundation to its dissolution', Univ. of Oxford D. Phil. thesis (1992).

Bedouelle, G. and Le Gal, P., eds, *Le Divorce du Roi Henry VIII* (Geneva, 1987).

Bernard, G.W., 'The fall of Anne Boleyn', *English Historical Review*, cvi (1991), pp. 584–610, reprinted in G.W. Bernard, *Power and Politics in Tudor England* (Aldershot, 2000), pp. 80–107.

Bernard, G.W., 'The fall of Anne Boleyn: a rejoinder', *English Historical Review*, cvii (1992), pp. 665–74.

Bernard, G.W., 'Anne Boleyn's religion', *Historical Journal*, xxxvi (1993), pp. 1–20.

Bernard, G.W., 'The making of religious policy, 1533–1546: Henry VIII and the search for the middle way', *Historical Journal*, xli (1998), pp. 321–49.

Bernard, G.W., 'The piety of Henry VIII', in S.N. Amos and H. van Nierop, eds, *The Education of a Christian Society: Humanism and the Reformation in Britain and the Netherlands* (1999), pp. 62–88.

Bernard, G.W., 'Elton's Cromwell', *History*, lxxxiii (1998), pp. 587–607, reprinted in G.W. Bernard, *Power and Politics in Tudor England* (Aldershot, 2000), pp. 108–28.

Bernard, G.W., *Power and Politics in Tudor England* (Aldershot, 2000).

Bernard, G.W., 'The tyranny of Henry VIII', in G.W. Bernard and S.J. Gunn, eds, *Authority and Consent in Tudor England* (Aldershot, 2002), pp. 113–30.

Bernard, G.W., *The King's Reformation: Henry VIII and the Remaking of the English Church* (2005).

Bindoff, S.T., *The History of Parliament: the House of Commons 1509–1558* (3 vols, 1982).

Brigden, S., *London and the Reformation* (Oxford, 1989).

Burnet, G., *History of the Reformation of the Church of England* (3 vols in 6, 1820).

Carley, J.P., ed., *The Libraries of Henry VIII* (2000).

Carley, J.P., *The Books of King Henry VIII and his Wives* (2004).

Chester, A.F., *Hugh Latimer: Apostle to the English* (Philadelphia, 1954).

Cohen, D., 'Law, society and homosexuality in classical Athens', *Past and Present*, cxvii (1987), pp. 3–21.

Collinson, P., 'Truth and legend: the veracity of John Foxe's Book of Martyrs', in A.C. Duke and C.A. Tamse, eds, *Clio's Mirror: Historiography in Britain and the Netherlands, Britain and the Netherlands*, viii (1985), pp. 31–54.

Deansley, M., *The Lollard Bible* (1920).

Dewhurst, J., 'The alleged miscarriages of Catherine of Aragon and Anne Boleyn', *Medical History*, xxviii (1984), pp. 49–56.

Dickens, A.G., *The English Reformation* (1st edn, 1964; 2nd edn, 1989).

Doran, S., ed., *Henry VIII: Man and Monarch* (2009).

Dowling, M., 'Anne Boleyn and Reform', *Journal of Ecclesiastical History*, xxxv (1984), pp. 30–46.

Dowling, M., 'The gospel and the court: reformation under Henry VIII', in M. Dowling and P. Lake, eds, *Protestantism and the National Church in Sixteenth Century England* (1987), pp. 36–77.

Duffy, E., *The Stripping of the Altars* (1992).

Elton, G.R., *Policy and Police* (Cambridge, 1972).

Elton, G.R., *Thomas Cromwell* (Bangor, 1990).

Fenlon, D., *Heresy and Obedience in Tridentine Italy: Cardinal Pole and the Counter-Reformation* (Cambridge, 1972).

Foister, S., *Holbein and England* (2004).

Foister, S., *Holbein in England* (2006).

Freeman, T.S., 'Research, rumour and propaganda: Anne Boleyn in Foxe's "Book of Martyrs"', *Historical Journal*, xxxviii (1995), pp. 797–819.

Friedmann, P., *Anne Boleyn* (2 vols, 1884).

Froude, J.A., *History of England from the Fall of Wolsey to the Defeat of the Spanish Armada* (12 vols, 1858–70).

Gairdner, J., 'The age of Anne Boleyn', *English Historical Review*, x (1895), p. 104.

Gunn, S.J., *Charles Brandon, Duke of Suffolk 1484–1545* (Oxford, 1988).

Guy, J., 'Henry VIII and the *praemunire* manoeuvres of 1530–31', *English Historical Review*, xcvii (1982), pp. 481–503.

Gwyn, P., *The King's Cardinal: The Rise and Fall of Thomas Wolsey* (1990).

Hardy, T.D., *Report upon the Documents in the Archives and Public Libraries of Vienna* (1886).

Herrup, C.B., *The Common Peace: Participation and the Criminal Law in Seventeenth Century England* (Cambridge, 1987).

Hoskins, A., 'Mary Boleyn's Carey children: offspring of Henry VIII', *Genealogists' Magazine* (Mar. 1997).

Hughes, P., *The Reformation in England* (3 vols, 1954).

Hunt, A., *The Drama of Coronation: Medieval Ceremony in Early Medieval England* (Cambridge, 2008).

Ives, E.W., 'Faction at the court of Henry VIII: the fall of Anne Boleyn', *History*, lvii (1972), pp. 169–88.

Ives, E.W., 'Court and county palatine in the reign of Henry VIII: the career of William Brereton of Malpas', *Transactions of the Historic Society of Lancashire and Cheshire*, cxxiii (1972), pp. 1–38.

Ives, E.W., ed., *Letters and Accounts of William Brereton of Malpas, Record Society of Lancashire and Cheshire*, cxvi (1976).

Ives, E.W., *Anne Boleyn* (Oxford, 1986), reissued with revisions as *The Life and Death of Anne Boleyn* (Oxford, 2004).

Ives, E.W., 'Henry VIII's will: a forensic conundrum', *Historical Journal*, xxxv (1992), pp. 779–804.

Ives, E.W., 'The fall of Anne Boleyn reconsidered', *English Historical Review*, cvii (1992), pp. 651–64.

Ives, E.W., 'Anne Boleyn and the early reformation in England: the contemporary evidence', *Historical Journal*, xxxvii (1994), pp. 389–400.

Ives, E.W., 'Henry VIII: the political perspective', in D. MacCulloch, ed., *The Reign of Henry VIII: Politics, Policy and Piety* (Basingstoke, 1995), pp. 13–34.

Kelly, H.A., *The Matrimonial Trials of Henry VIII* (Stanford, CA, 1976, new edn 2004).

Kelly, M.J., 'Canterbury jurisdiction and influence during the episcopate of William Warham, 1503–1532', Univ. of Cambridge Ph.D. thesis, 1965.

Kelly, M.J., 'The submission of the clergy', *Transactions of the Royal Historical Society*, 5th ser., xv (1965), pp. 97–119.

Lehmberg, S.E., *The Reformation Parliament 1529–1536* (Cambridge, 1970).

Lehmberg, S.E., *The Later Parliaments of Henry VIII 1536–1547* (Cambridge, 1977).

MacCulloch, D., 'Two dons in politics: Thomas Cranmer and Stephen Gardiner, 1503–1533', *Historical Journal*, xxxvii (1994), pp. 1–22.

MacCulloch, D., 'Henry VIII and the reform of the church', in D. MacCulloch, ed., *The Reign of Henry VIII: Politics, Policy and Piety* (Basingstoke, 1995), pp. 159–80.

MacCulloch, D., *Thomas Cranmer* (1996).

Mattingly, G., *Catherine of Aragon* (1942).

Moreau, J.-P., *Rome ou l'Angleterre? Les réactions politiques des catholiques anglais au moment du schisme (1529–1553)* (Paris, 1984).

Murphy, V., 'The debate over Henry VIII's first divorce: an analysis of the contemporary treatises', Univ. of Cambridge Ph.D. thesis, 1994.

Murphy, V., 'The literature and propaganda of Henry VIII's first divorce', in D. MacCulloch, ed., *The Reign of Henry VIII: Politics, Policy and Piety* (Basingstoke, 1995), pp. 135–58.

Paget, H., 'The youth of Anne Boleyn', *Bulletin of the Institute of Historical Research*, liv (1984), pp. 162–70.

Parker, T.M., *The English Reformation to 1558* (2nd edn, Oxford, 1966).

Paul, J.E., *Catherine of Aragon and her Friends* (1966).

Powell, E., *Kingship, Law and Society: Criminal Justice in the Reign of Henry V* (Oxford, 1989).

Powicke, F.M., *The Reformation in England* (Oxford, 1941).

Rex, R., *Henry VIII and the English Reformation* (2nd edn, Basingstoke, 1993).

Robinson, W.R.B., 'The lands of Henry, earl of Worcester in the 1530s. Part 3: Central Monmouthshire and Herefordshire', *Bulletin of the Board of Celtic Studies*, xxv (iv), (1974), pp. 454–500.

Robinson, W.R.B., 'Patronage and hospitality in early Tudor Wales; the role of Henry, earl of Worcester, 1526–49', *Bulletin of the Institute of Historical Research*, li (1978), pp. 20–36.

Scarisbrick, J.J., *Henry VIII* (1968).

Schenk, W., *Reginald Pole: Cardinal of England* (1950).

Smart, S.J., 'John Foxe and "The Story of Richard Hun, Martyr"', *Journal of Ecclesiastical History*, xxxvii (1986), pp. 1–14.

Smart, S.J., '"Favourers of God's Word": John Foxe's Henrician Martyrs', Univ. of Southampton M. Phil. thesis, 1988.

Starkey, D., *The Reign of Henry VIII: Personalities and Politics* (1985)

Starkey, D., *Six Wives: the Queens of Henry VIII* (2003).

Swanson, R.N., *Church and Society in Late Medieval England* (Oxford, 1989).

Tait, M.D., 'The Brigittine monastery of Syon (Middlesex), with special reference to its monastic usages', Univ. of Oxford D.Phil. thesis, 1975.

Thomas, K.V., 'The double standard', *Journal of the History of Ideas*, xx (1959), pp. 195–216.

Thornton, T., 'The integration of Cheshire into the Tudor nation state in the early sixteenth century', *Northern History*, xxix (1993), pp. 40–63.

Walker, G., *Plays of Persuasion: Drama and Politics at the Court of Henry VIII* (Cambridge, 1991).

Walker, G., 'Rethinking the fall of Anne Boleyn', *Historical Journal*, xlv (2002), pp. 1–29.

Warnicke, R.M., 'The fall of Anne Boleyn: a reassessmemt', *History*, lxx (1985), pp. 1–15.

Warnicke, R.M., 'Sexual heresy at the court of Henry VIII', *Historical Journal*, xxx (1987), pp. 247–68.

Warnicke, R.M., *The Rise and Fall of Anne Boleyn* (Cambridge, 1990).

Warnicke, R.M., 'The fall of Anne Boleyn revisited', *English Historical Review*, cviii (1993), pp. 653–65.

Williams, R., 'Sermon on the 450th anniversary of the martyrdom of Thomas Cranmer', http://www.archbishopofcanterbury.org/sermons_speeches/060321.htm

Wooding, L.E.C., *Rethinking Catholicism in Reformation England* (Oxford, 2000).

INDEX

My lord after my most humble recommendacions this shall be to give unto yo grace
of I am most bound my humble thankes for the gret payn and travell that yo
grace doth take in studyeng by yo wysdome and gret dylygens howe to brynge
to pas honerably the gretyst welth that is possible to cowd to any creatur lyvyng
and in especyall remembryng howe wretchyd and unwrthy I am in ordyng answeryng
to his hyghnes and for you I do knowe my self never to have desseyvd by my desert
that you shuld take this gret payn for me yet dayly of yo goodnes I do prove
by all my ffrendes and thoughe that I have nott knowlege by them the dewe
profe of yo deds doth declare yo words and wrytyng toward me to be
trewe notwstandyng my lord yo dyscressyon may consyder as yet howe lyttle it
is in my power to recompence you but all onely wt my good wyl the whiche
I assewer you that after this matter is brought to pas you shall fynd me
as I am bownd in the meane tyme to owe you my servys and then looke
what thyng in this worlde I can ymagen to do you plesure in you
shall fynd me the gladdyst woman in the worlde to do yt and next
unto the kynges grace of one thyng I make you full promes to be assewred
to have yt and that is my harty love unfaynydly duryng my lyf
and beyng fully determynd wt godds grace never to chaunge thys
purpos I make an ende of thys my rude and trewe menynd letter
prayeng othe lord to send you muche increse of honer wt long lyfe
wrytten wt the hand of her that besechyth yo grace to acceptt this letter
as procedyng from on that is most bound to be

From Mrs Anne Bullen befor hir Mariag to the king

yo humble and
obedyent servaunt
Anne Boleyn